CU01514318

THE GATE C

Leaves from the autobiography
of Fredric Winterleigh,
A soul in Paradise

Originally recorded & published
for the Author in 1931
By
Robert James Lees

Volume Three

Also in this series, Vol 1 "Through the Mists"
and Vol 2 "The Life Elysian"

This paperback edition published 2009
By

Sanders & Co UK Ltd
5 Artizan Road, Northampton NN1 4HU
England

THE GATE OF HEAVEN

CONTENTS

RECORDER'S FOREWORD

It is with feelings of deepest gratitude that I am now able to give to the world this third series of Leaves from the Autobiography of Aphraar. It is now over thirty years since Through the Mists went forth upon its mission—a mission which is far more popular to-day than when it first commenced. Seven years later.

The Life Elysian followed; and now I have been called upon to record his arrival at THE GATE OF HEAVEN.

In passing the present volume on to my publisher, I am deeply and gratefully conscious of the fulfilment of an assurance given by the Master, when He said, "Every scribe which is instructed unto the kingdom of heaven is like unto a man that is a householder which bringeth forth out of his treasure, things new and old." In the present pages the reader will find himself invited to visit old scenes in the pilgrimage of Aphraar, but he will do so with new and larger powers of vision, deeper revelation; far clearer comprehension. Aphraar, in passing forward, meets with new teachers, who expound to him the old truths in the fuller light of new interpretations, not inconsistent with, but rather with a wider amplification than he has so far been able to grasp, so that he begins to understand the relationship of part to part in the expanding scheme of existence, and comprehend the use, meaning, and purpose of details which had hitherto proved to be mysterious stumbling blocks in the path. Let me point out an illustrative suggestion of what I mean. His new teachers, Omra and Rael, carry Aphraar into the theatre of Allegory, where he is permitted to watch the progress of the great drama of life. In the shadowless light in which he is now watching the true unfolding, he is able to trace the exact point at which theological emendators have made excisions or introduced such confusions as make the existence of a priestly cult necessary to the subjection of humanity, and the perversion of the truth as it is in Jesus.

The first part of this drama of existence, according to the teaching of the Christ, is shown to Aphraar to consist of three acts, beyond which he has as yet no power to penetrate its mystery:

ACT I.

The Mortal or Infancy Stage of Being. The child not yet able to discriminate between the evil and the good, is in itself sinless—"Of such is the kingdom of heaven." It is, however, presently able to understand "Do this," or "Don't do that," and is so far responsible for disobedience, and consequently becomes liable to chastisement and correction. The falling of the curtain, called Death, is not the end, but simply a change of scene introducing:

ACT II.

The Scholastic Period or the Youth of Existence. (This is the great region of theological fog, controversy, and confusion, variously called the Intermediate State, Purgatory, or the Seven Spheres). It is in reality the Schoolroom in which the soul is educated and prepared to take its position in life as a Son of God. In another Allegory of the Master it is represented as the harvest field, where the soul is made to reap the harvest of its infantile actions; or in a third, it is audit time where the soul is made to report and balance its account for the use of its opportunities in obedience or otherwise, and be subject to such commendation or penalty as the balance shows. But in the dispensation of justice, an infallible and all-loving Father "who will have all men to be saved," makes the award.

ACT III.

The Manhood of the Soul. The necessary educational stage past, and the soul having been purified from the infirmities of the flesh, it enters upon its inheritance as a Son of God—a condition so markedly different from what has gone before that it is shadowed forth in two strangely varied allegories: "Ye must be born again," and "an espousal to the Christ," or yet again the Master pictures it as the reaching home of the Prodigal Son, and the bestowal of the ring, the robe, the kiss, and great rejoicing. In interweaving this allegorical teaching into the actuality of Aphraar's experience the greater part of this volume is devoted, and the consistent figure adopted is that of the second birth as presented to Nicodemus. Here I venture to suggest that whether Rael or Omra takes up the parable to instruct their pupil, the reader will find each of them to be both interesting and consistent in following in the steps of the Master in whose service they are working. Of course, I am prepared for some of my readers shrinking with something like horror at the thought of Aphraar's second birth taking place more than forty years after he has thrown off the mortal body, but this is not the first breath of theological heresy that has been wafted across our records from the plains of heaven, nor is it anywhere demanded in the Bible that the transition must be obtained during the terrestrial stage of being, and yet Paul was authorized to declare that "As in Adam all die, even so in Christ shall all be made alive." It is therefore obvious that if the regeneration necessary is not received here, it must be acquired there. Having been privileged to write the following records under Aphraar's direction, and thereby knowing something of the difficulties he encountered in taking the step, it would be an easy matter for me here to say what his advice would be to each and all of his readers concerning it, but I will not anticipate. It is best for him to unfold his own story, and in his own way show how impregnable are the defences that ensure the kingdom so that "there shall in no wise enter into it anything that defileth, neither whatsoever worketh abomination, or maketh a lie."

Robert James Lees

THE HEAVEN and EARTH

Genesis i - 1 & 8

SECTIONAL DIAGRAM

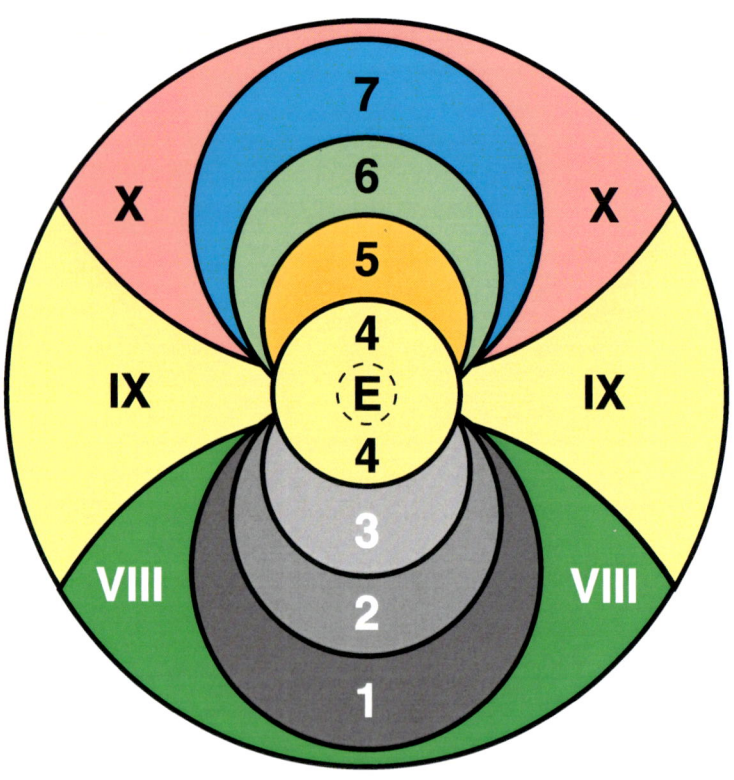

EXPLANATION OF THE DIAGRAM

The outer circle indicates the position of the Psychic Sphere.

The 'firmament' or heaven of (Gen. i, 8). This, as described in the following pages, embraces every provision for the reception and maturing of the newly-born soul until it reaches the Spiritual condition of a son of God.

E - The Earth. Its position in the Physical indicated by the dotted circle.

1-7 - The Seven Spheres, or Intermediate State. The Schoolroom where the youth of the soul is passed in Spiritual preparation.

VIII - The location of the uncultured, or "nations that forget God," in which they are suitably instructed and prepared.

IX - The Sleep State, where the sleep-life is spent by all mankind in communion with the departed. (Job xxxiii, 14-18)

X - The Great Nursery, where children who pass away prior to birth, or before they "know to refuse the evil, and choose the good" (Isa. vii, 16), are developed and educated.

All these states are Psychic or Intermediary between the Physical and Spiritual, as the twilight divides the light from the darkness in the natural world. The first Spiritual Sphere lies beyond this circle and is attained by "the Second Birth" (John iii, 3) as set forth in the following pages.

THE GATE OF HEAVEN

CHAPTER 1

AN AWAKENING

Again I am asking my Recorder to take up his pen in order that I may once more speak to my brethren in the flesh out of the fullness of my soul's desire.

In his instant response, he calls my notice to a mass of correspondence containing questions to which I am asked to reply, but, for the present I must confine my attention to one point which particularly presses upon me, in the consideration of which I shall, incidentally, be enabled to deal with many of the problems raised, while I shall try to unfold one of the deep mysteries of spiritual experience as I have encountered it which gives it a greater significance and places it in a new light to that in which theology has, certainly in these later days, been in the habit of regarding it.

I am speaking of that cryptic utterance of the Christ to Nicodemus where He said, "Verily, verily, I say unto thee, except a man be born again, he cannot see the kingdom of God." The master in Israel failed to understand Him; the schoolmen of the intervening ages have been little, if indeed any more successful, and blind leading the blind, both prophet and people have stumbled into the ditch of doubt, because the light that was in them was darkness.

Once I was blind-blind as anyone whose foot slipped over the line dividing the mortal from the immortal, but by the grace of God a guiding hand has led me into the light by which I see, and, standing in that light, my soul yearns more than ever to tell what has been revealed to me. I want others to see and to learn the unspeakable beauties of the light of truth. I want every soul that crosses the stage of earth to know, as I have come to know, something of the irresistible fascination of the heavenly music sounding in that declaration of the Master, "God so loved the world, that He gave His only begotten Son, that whosoever believeth in Him should not perish, but have everlasting life." (John iii, 16)

That is why I cannot linger to answer all these queries now. Whatever comes in the direct path I have to tread will be fully dealt with, but all else must stand aside as being of secondary importance to the one great problem. "How can a man be born when he is old? Can he enter a second time into his mother's womb, and be born?" (John iii, 4)

There is, however, one of these enquiries to which I must refer briefly, before I proceed. "Do the records made show the full course of instruction to which a soul akin to Aphraar is subjected on entering the other life, or are they just outline indications of some more elaborate plan?"

They are indicative jottings, without any reference to consecutive arrangement, of incidents spread over an experience of nearly thirty years' extent. I make this calculation of the period covered, in the hope of its being helpfully suggestive. Further, in the treatment of an individual soul, there is no technical hard and fast curriculum or mechanical procedure in God's great university. Each soul enters, having its own special features, needs, environment, and requirements.

Every contributory cause to its present condition is taken into analytical account. Sins which are due to the father are carried to the father's account, and receive a corresponding consideration in relation to the child. Not a stain or taint is found upon the soul, but is scrupulously traced back to its source in fulfilment of the law that, "Whatsoever a man soweth that shall he also reap," and when the righteous result is ascertained, then the soul is dealt with, with a view to securing its ultimate atonement with God.

It is in such an adaptive arrangement as this that the Psalmist discovers that "The law of the Lord is perfect, converting the soul." (Ps. xix, 7) We, who are not yet perfected, are not in a position to know all that this implies, but this I do know-this one thing I have seen and spoken of more than once already, and I earnestly commend it to the notice of every soul who reads these records. 'In the judgment passed on the soul as it steps into the immortal, the righteousness of God stands prominent as a surprising leniency; we discover Justice to be a compassionate divinity and not an avenging fury.'

If there is one fact more deeply engraved on my consciousness than another by the revelations of this higher life, it is this; that God has in His mind but one purpose concerning the whole family of man-to love him with an everlasting love, and with loving-kindness to draw him back again to the inheritance he has forsaken through the machinations of sin. Can there be a more pathetic and yearning declaration of this, than is heard in the invitation of the Christ, who speaks as the voice of the Father, "Come unto me, all ye that labour and are heavy laden and I will give you rest!" (Matt. xi, 28)

From what a babel of confusion the world would escape; what a clearer conception of God would dawn, if, setting aside the theological dogmas and unauthorized interpretations, the wandering soul would accept the simple invitation of the God-appointed mediator, and learning of Him who is meek and lowly in heart, find the needed rest! "The wayfaring men, though fools, shall not err therein." (Isa. xxxv, 8)

I know whereof I speak when I make this suggestion. How often have I yearned for the opportunity to draw aside, that I might meditate upon the ever increasing surprises I encounter, as I watch this law of God in working operation around me here.

I have, at length, reached this one goal of my desire- have tasted of the sweet waters I may draw from the well of meditation-have opened my eyes to behold the vistas of revelation which lie unrolled before me, while He affords me the promised rest; have found therein a door of opportunity opening into an unsuspected ministry I had not dreamed of-a service I might render to the Master, which He has been pleased to call me to; a service of sowing, for which I had not long to wait before I reaped a rich harvest of more than a hundred-fold increase.

I had repaired to a hallowed spot, sacred by the memory of previous meditations, and had again lost myself in the azure realm, when a tender hand rested on my shoulder. Vaone stood behind me. "Aphraar, I hope I have not disturbed you, but I so wish you would answer me one question," she said apologetically.

"Not one, but a hundred, dear, if you wish to ask so many. What is it you desire to know?"

"Have you found heaven to be all that you expected?"

There was a suspicion of anxious indecision in her nervous enquiry, and the nature of it seemed so extraordinary, coming upon me so suddenly at such a time, that, for the moment, I hesitated what or how to reply.

"Heaven-all I expected?" I repeated. "What do you mean?"

"Forgive me if I have expressed myself vaguely," she replied, as she took a seat beside me, "but the idea has only just crossed my mind how very different this life is from what we were taught it would be. And as I realized the contrast, I saw you, and came to ask if you also had found it to be so?"

The confusion the question occasioned in my mind was not so much to do with its form, as the discovery that Vaone had been sufficiently aroused as to institute a comparison. I had not known her in the flesh, but I knew that her record was one of loyal and unquestioned orthodoxy. My experience of discarnate influences had shown me that they had a tendency towards a fixity of ideas rather than otherwise, and I had found Vaone almost indolently inclined, so far, to be content to accept everything as she found it. Now she had actually felt the spur of a new idea and under its unwonted stimulus was asking for information.

For the moment I was at a loss how best to answer her. How I wished that I was gifted with Myhanene's tact and skill in dealing with such a case. I could feel how much hung upon the issue, and for the first time I realized what a tremendous responsibility rests upon the shoulders of any man who attempts to fill the role of teacher, but when that office is held in connection with spiritual things, the added responsibility is, or should be seen to be, so much greater as to make one seriously pause before assuming it.

"Behold, a sower went forth to sow." That is the sketch Christ made of a teacher going to his work. "Whatsoever a man soweth that shall he also reap." After many days. "Some thirty, some sixty, and some a hundredfold," whether it be of wheat or tares. What would the harvest be if I ventured to answer Vaone's enquiry without Myhanene, or one of the others being present to correct any errors I might make?

It was at this juncture that I first saw the wisdom of Myhanene not allowing me to make use of my Recorder except in the presence of some responsible member of his band.

How we fret and worry ourselves as we impatiently wait for the coming of some desired opportunity, but should it present itself dressed in an unsuspected guise, we fail to recognize it, and allow it to pass unnoticed.

I am speaking from experience now. How often had I yearned to be able to tell all the good things my teachers had made known to me? I am almost afraid that at such times I had been too much enamoured of the position of the teacher to realize the weight of responsibility attaching to it.

When the latter was revealed to me, I shrank and called for Myhanene to come and reply to Vaone.

"This is your opportunity," he replied. "Tell her, in your own way, what you have seen and heard."

There was no escape. It was my first real call to duty. Vaone was waiting-wondering at my delay.

Just at that juncture, a strange and curious experience befell me. A ray of illumination darted across my consciousness, vivid and brief as a lightning flash, but in its passing it distinctly left behind three differently disconnected revelations; the heartless system of domination-social and spiritual-under which Vaone had passed her earth life; the real nature of the enfranchisement secured by the ministry of the Magnetic Chorale, but by far the most impressive was the discovery of some new faculty in myself, which seemed to break down all limitations by which I had hitherto been bound, and impart a power of comprehension under the influence of which I boldly faced the duty to which I was called.

"Yes, it is different-strangely, incomparably different from anything, everything I had conceived it would be," I answered, wondering where my newly-found inspiration would lead me. "But the difference, as I see it, appears to lie in the opposite direction to that which you have discovered.

"If I understand aright the tone in which you make your enquiry, this life comes short of your anticipations; to me it taxes every power I have at my command to express by how far it exceeds my greatest expectations. Let me explain as best I am able, wherein this difference lies."

"Yes, help me, Aphraar."

"Of course I will help you, though I am afraid I shall be but a poor and uncertain support for you to lean upon. But I will do my best, according to what I myself have learned."

"I will trust you," she replied, perhaps with more confidence than my authority warranted.

Then I must begin by explaining something I am surprised that you have not known before."

"And that is...?"

"That neither you nor I are in a position to express any opinion respecting heaven at present."

"What do you mean? Why are we not able to speak of heaven? Do you wish me to think that this life in which so much of our soul's desires have been granted to us is nothing better than a long drawn-out dream, from which we shall presently awake; I to take up again the cross of my slavery to the tyranny of another, and you to resume the heartache from which this sacred sleep has temporarily relieved you? Is it true you would have me anticipate the revelation you are so frequently saying is yet to be made to us? May God preserve me from such a blasphemy of death!"

Vaone had sprung to her feet under the first impulse of her

protestation. The resentment it aroused was so opposed to her usually complaisant disposition as to astonish herself. I, no less astonished at the unexpected ebullition, was at first inclined to smile, but seeing how deeply the idea had moved her, I at once set myself to reassure her.

"No! You may at once dismiss any such a possibility from your mind.

"However much we might, under given circumstances, desire it, sleep is powerless to carry us back again into the yesterday of life; it always bears us forward into the to-morrow. We cannot wake again into the limitations and servitude of the flesh; the sleep of death has no power or alternative but to carry us forward into the daybreak of the spirit. There is no occasion for any alarm. Had I taken more time to consider my reply to your enquiry, I should have framed it less abruptly, and so avoided the misconception I created. Let me try to put what I mean in another form."

"Do you mean that we have not yet reached heaven, but are in an intermediate state?"

"That is exactly what I wish to say."

"But I don't believe..."

"My dear Vaone, the altitude of our belief by no means affects the validity of a fact. The wise men of the ancients asserted that the earth was flat, with four corners, but all the beliefs of philosophers, scientists, and churchmen in that respect was wrong. Beliefs are always subject to revision on the discovery of facts, and we are now standing face to face with a fact which proves to us, that modern ecclesiastics are not more infallible than their predecessors.

"The difficulty confronting you is not that the life upon which you have now entered is wrong, but rather that the conception you formed of it-under the direction of those who knew no more of its realities than yourself-is wrong. But you yourself have lost nothing in the discovery. If you have not entered into the immediate rewards they foretold and promised in return for your belief, neither have you been visited by the punishments with which they threatened unbelief. Apart from this, is there any other disappointment this life has occasioned you?" She hesitated before venturing her reply.

"N-no-perhaps not. But suppose they had been right and I had not believed them?"

"That just represents the position I occupied. I honestly could not accept the pretensions the church made, and accepting the standard of the golden rule as the law of my life, I made an endeavour-a very imperfect one, but still an effort of a kind -to follow it. What is the result? Do I find myself in any way penalized in comparison with yourself? Is it not you rather that comes to me expressing a disappointment, while I am constrained to admit that, so far, this life is a more glorious revelation of the loving-kindness and tender mercy of God than ever entered into my mind to conceive? Of course, we do miss the theatrical accessories the Church so wonderfully employs to render its stage temptingly ornate.

"We find no 'Heigh! Presto, change!' transformations, by means of which a leprous soul is transferred to the front rank of saints by the receiving of a so-called "extreme unction"; or a prayer that is scarcely finished before the flesh is discarded. On the other hand, we do find law, order, beauty, forethought and an adapted ministry suitable to every possible demand which the ravages of sin and rebellion have created. In all the wide realm of possibility, no bane can be found for the correction of which an antidote has not been provided here, beyond the reach and influence of the enemy; but each and all of these blessed provisions of God operate in accordance with established law, and never in response to any erratic command.

"This being so, do you not see-especially with the great advantage we now possess of having the circumstantial evidence of the higher life to guide us in our conclusions-that it is exactly as impossible for any soul to pass at a single step from the state of sin to righteousness, as it would be for an infant to reach manhood's estate by a similar process.

Between infancy and manhood lie the intermediate stages of childhood and youth which are absolutely necessary to secure physical and mental vigour, and by parity of reasoning, it is equally essential for a similar interval of transformation to be allowed for the conversion of a sinner into a saint.

"If anything further were needed to prove the necessity of an intermediate state, I could easily furnish it by asking whether you ever thought of holding a reception without providing a cloak-room for the convenience of your visitors. To suggest that such a contretemps should ever come within the region of possibility is almost unpardonable, but if this is so in ordinary social life, why should it be considered such an outrage to assert that a corresponding provision exists, where travel-stained pilgrims may make a suitable preparation for being ushered into the presence of the King of Kings?"

"Therefore there is no reason for you to feel discouraged or disappointed, any more than I have cause to be overjoyed at the position in which we find ourselves at present. You have not yet reached the height of your great ideal, while I, in many respects, have transcended my most sanguine expectations; but we are not yet in heaven.

"Our eyes have not yet beheld the vision of the pearly gate and the golden street which was granted to John in Patmos, but we have cast off the burden of the flesh, and in the vestibule of heaven we are resting our wearied feet, taking refreshment, and being instructed in reference to what will be required when we may be called into the holy of holies. The unexpected existence of this-what we may call a robing room adjoining the audience chamber, need occasion no alarm. It is simply the result of relying on unauthorised directions and promises; it does not jeopardize, but only temporarily delays realization, so far as you are concerned-for myself, I have been far more than satisfied to find what I have already attained to, and am hopefully looking forward, as I would advise you to do, to that which has yet to be revealed."

Vaone listened with a nervously intent patience to all I had to say; the smile of hope and the shade of doubt alternating visibly on her face. Presently I discovered a suspicion of animation gaining an ascendancy over her usual composure, and I wondered at the success I could see my ministry was achieving. And yet it was not I. It was something beyond outside myself. Something that had been left behind and evolved from that mysterious ray of illumination I received at the outset of her enquiry-a guiding impulse that had carried me forward, furnishing me with all I said, and using me to speak of things I had never considered nor dreamed of before, with an assurance as foreign to myself as was the role of teacher I had been constrained to assume.

"Have you quite finished?" she asked, after a moment's pause.

"I think I have said all that is necessary for the time, unless there is anything more you would like to ask me," I replied.

"I am just beginning to feel how much there is that I do not know, and the sense of it confuses me. I feel it, but have no knowledge how to give expression to it. When I came to you it hung in front of me, like a restless uncertainty I could only speak of as a sense of disappointment that contravened all my ideas of heaven. That is why I came. While you were speaking, it all seemed to change-the disappointment changed into mystery which fills everywhere-everything. Past, present, future-all is mystery, and I want you to go on talking about it. Tell me what it is."

"I can tell you that in a single word," I replied, more thankful at her confession than I can express, since it opened my eyes clearly to what was really taking place in her. "It is your own awakening to Life. Life is mystery-a mystery so deep, so profound, so vast, so glorious, that it is a problem whether any eye, save that of Deity, will ever be capable of penetrating it. For ourselves, we have to await its revelation. Its brilliant dawning beam is just beginning to touch your soul, Vaone. You must feel it, see it, know it for yourself. No one can tell you what it is, whence it proceeds, or wither it goes, save God. Rouse yourself to know Him.

"With all your heart, soul, mind, and strength reach out after and finding, follow Him who alone is able to lead you into the true light of Life." She did not answer me again, but turned and walked away, as I had more than once turned from Myhanene when he had brought me face to face with one of his great revelations.

I made no attempt to follow her. I knew that all was well, and just then, I had enough to do in making acquaintance with my newly-found self.

* * *

CHAPTER 2

THE EYE OF FAITH

My newly found self" significantly expresses my condition and outlook at the time when Vaone left me. In the revelation which Jesus Christ made to John in Patmos, He that sat upon the throne and is heard to declare "Behold; I make all things new" (xxi, 5); and Paul, writing to the Corinthians, assures us that, "if any man be in Christ he is of new creature" (2 Cor. v, 17); but the nebulous uncertainty which exists as to when the realization of this condition is to be reached, together with an intimate knowledge of my own imperfections, prevents me venturing to hope that such a culmination had so far been even approximately attained in my own case. And yet that curious ray of illumination that darted through my consciousness while Vaone was trying to explain herself, had left me markedly other than it had found me.

The genial breath of spring had, as it were, touched the barrenness of winter, and Nature, responsive to the wooing, had leapt forward, offering her countless blushing buds in answer to the call of love. Or, dropping all figures of speech, may I not say that the mysterious influences and operations I have been subjected to since crossing the mystical Jordan, have secretly worked in the evolving of new faculties, capacities and powers, which are carrying me forward into such new conditions of being, that I am already scarcely able to recognize my old self.

Don't misunderstand me. I am in the presence of a problem that has never yet been solved, and I wish to deal with it reverently. The most unique production the earth contains is Man-a congeries of apparently insoluble mysteries. A creature formed of clay, but bearing the image of the invisible God. A curious compound of animal and angel, with one foot on either side the line dividing the two dimensions of space, the physical part operating in the third, and the spiritual working in the fourth. In the daytime he is employed in subduing and replenishing the earth, and in the sleep of his nights he is called to study and graduate in the university of heaven.

In this qualification and adaptation to occupy a position of citizenship in two worlds, we can see at once the sublimity and dignity of manhood, as designed and provided for by the matchless wisdom of the Creator. In this great achievement, consciousness, through the agency of the sleep-life communion, bears witness that we are sons of God, and interblends us with heaven, as warp and woof of a fabric are woven together in one.

I have already spoken of a revelation I received from the archives of this same channel, when, in company with Cushna, I touched "the point of recollection"1 and stood amazed at the mysteries it then cleared up. The second ray of illumination had carried that revelation a stage forward, unfolding more and more surprises in my past experience, until I have been constrained to say that, "I am scarcely able to recognize myself." But I need not be afraid; the woof of consciousness abides as the guarantor of my identity.

In the past I did my dreaming, but now I am awake, and find available all the dream treasures I collected in those transient visits from the other side. It was God's plan that they should have been available for service in the lower life, and thus prepare us for a better entrance into this. But such assistance would have destroyed any pretence for a priestly cult, and so "the superstition" of the validity of dreams had to go. Such was the reason that led to this corridor of communion being closed "by authority," and few there be that find it in the present age. It does still exist, however, for "whatsoever the Lord doeth it shall be forever," and they who by patient searching find it, discover a treasure of incomparable value. How differently should I have been placed, had I been thus fortunate, and yet it lay nigh to my hand, but in my blindness I missed it, passing by on the other side.

Thus it was that Vaone's approach had interrupted my meditations and opened the door of opportunity to a most unexpected ministry. It had done more than this. As I quietly reviewed the incident, I began anxiously to examine myself as to the manner in which I had discharged the unexpected duty that had been demanded of me. Had I risen to the occasion, and considerately sown such seed on the prepared soil as would bring forth the needed harvest, or had I been taken at a disadvantage-been found asleep at my post, or away from my watch, and thus failed to do that which I ought to have done? The result of the enquiry was not so reassuring as I could have wished. I had done something, but my more mature reflection showed me how much I might have said that did not occur to me at the time.

How differently I might have replied to her enquiry had I paused to consider before following the impulse of that ray of illumination. Was I acting wisely in taking the course I did? Would it have helped her better had I told her the story of my own experience from the time I woke, to find myself lying on the slopes where Helen came to my assistance? Had I done so, I should have told that this new life had not only been free from any shade of doubt or regret, but beyond that negative result it had been far beyond all I had ever dared to dream or pictured possible it could ever be, because I had refused to believe in the illogical ideas the Churches propounded.

My refusal to conform to the customary religious observances was not that I lacked any sense of reverence, or did not concern myself with any consideration of a possible hereafter. I was kept at a distance by the too certain absence in practice, within the pale of the elect, of fundamental virtues the Church demanded in precept. That is why I stood aloof and ventured to follow the dictates of my own heart in marking out a law of life. In the result, I discovered that I had not wandered very far astray in my decision.

In my heart I had an unconquerable yearning to find a love I had never known, though I felt sure it existed somewhere; I sought, but could not find it. Experience told me that I was not singular in my quest, nor was I alone in the failure to attain my end. Then, feeling that touch of nature that makes all men kin, I attempted to relieve my own sense of loss by stretching out a helping hand to such as I might find who were even more pitiably situated. It was in the search for such a field of ministry that I discovered the little Bethel in Whitechapel, where I found what of heart's ease the world had to offer me in the practice of the golden rule.

As a recompense, I received the brand of a heretic from the Church; an estrangement from my scrupulously orthodox family; a communion of sympathy and affection with the helpless; and when I had passed beyond the reach of theologies and orthodoxies, I found a welcome awaiting me which was more than a recompense for all I had experienced.

This is an outline of an alternative recital I might have given to Vaone had I not followed the impulse born of that illuminating ray; then I could have finished by the declaration with which I first answered her; "and yet I am not in a position to speak of heaven."

How is it possible for one to speak with authority of that which he has not seen-how can he tell of that which he does not know? So far, I had only been entertained in the ante-room, where my senses had been so bewildered with its abundance of treasures that I failed to grasp its beauties-how could I possibly describe the audience chamber of the throne room?

I came to the conclusion that I had taken the better course in following the leading of that ray of illumination. It may have been-probably was-that I failed to rise to all that was demanded of me on the occasion; that I came short of doing all that the revelation was intended to accomplish.

Still, though I had not scored a victory, I could comfort myself with the thought that I had not closed my eyes to the vision, nor resisted the call that had been made upon me. With this I had to be content. How blindly had I been led onward since my arrival, and yet it was turning out all right. My eyes had, to a very great extent, been holden, but I was beginning to see that I had been the gainer by the guidance I had submitted to. Was it not Solomon who said, "Man's goings are of the Lord; how can a man then understand his town way? " (Prov. xx, 24)

Intellect may resent and rebel against the requirement of the spirit to "walk by faith, not by sight." But intellect is not supreme in the realm of spirit, any more than the laws of a democracy would be valid in an autocratic empire. When God, breathing into man, made him to be a living soul, the Intellect was subordinated to Morality, and the fidelity of morality is tested by obedience, not by reason.

I shall return to this at length later on; in the meantime allow me to assert that, in the direction in which we are moving, faith secures a benediction intellect never could acquire. Reason may outreach its hand, its finger-tips may even be able to touch the silken fringe, it can do no more; but Faith will grasp the spirit robe, and claim the life-giving blessing which is only bestowed upon obedience.

I speak of that I know-of acquirements I have secured in the school of experience. I had already reached Vaone before the first foreshadow of this great truth began to break upon my true comprehension. Since then the revelation has continued until I am able to discern that the outward appearances are always transient, while those that are hidden-those at present unseen-are the truly substantial and eternal.

Looking back from the light in which I was then standing, I could see that, from the time that Helen discovered me lying in vague uncertainty on the slopes, I had been-while outwardly engaged with Myhanene, Cushna, or some other of their ministering companions-in some mysterious and unrealized sense, communing with an invisible and unknown stranger, as we trod another roadway leading from Jerusalem to Emmaus, with occasional glimpses of His much-loved Galilee, as He made my heart to burn within me.

How completely did He succeed in hiding himself under the semblance of Helen, Arvez, Siamedes, Cushna, Myhanene, or

Eilele, until the moment for Him to reveal Himself arrived. My heart had been stirred to its depths with the declaration of Helen, as she exclaimed:

"Why, God is love, Fred." The throb of hope she caused by that inspiring utterance never left me again, but each succeeding conductor or experience fanned, fed, and encouraged it to increase, and yet I continued the communion without suspecting who my real Instructor had been.

I cannot believe that the eternal ages will suffice to dim the vivid details of that kaleidoscopic vision of faith in my memory.

What is faith?

It may help us if we anticipate a little at this point in order to get a clearer idea of this great faculty of the soul. I shall deal with the subject more at length later on, but a suggestion here will assist us in grasping an idea.

The soul, as I have already indicated, always works in the fourth dimension-from the physical towards the spiritual, from the visible to the invisible. Faith is what may be called a tele-microscopic faculty, the soul discovers in the depth of being, which, pressed into service, penetrates and illuminates the interior darkness and enables the soul to live in the future as if that future were already present.

If once this inherently penetrating power of the soul can be clearly conceived and grasped, there will no longer be the slightest foundation for any doubt that "faith is the substance of things hoped for, the evidence of things not seen." (Heb. xi, 1) The transformation which the relevation of it wrought in me will be the measure of the effect it will produce in you, my reader; then you will begin to understand something of what is meant by a second birth.

Under the inexpressible charm of its restfulness and satisfaction, I did not wish to disturb the solitude of the communion it evoked. I felt, as dear old Dr. Watts must have felt, when he sang:

My willing soul would stay
In such a frame as this,
And sit and sing herself away
To everlasting bliss.

And yet that scarcely conveys what I wish to express, for had I not already reached that everlasting bliss? It seemed to me as if the rapture of that heavenly employment had already been attained, and all I further needed was to be left undisturbed to revel in and feed upon the many hidden unfoldings that were buried beneath the surface of every individual scene and incident I had witnessed since my arrival.

Shall I briefly indicate what I mean?

I had just awakened from my-sleep? on the slopes. My little, almost unrecognized protégé was revelling in the fairy-like transformation which had taken place. In my wonderment I caught the sound of Helen's voice. Then everything changed; I was lying on the side of another mountain, listening to the music of a Great Teacher, who spake as never man spake before, in the rehearsal of a series of beatitudes which seemed to hold his vast audience spellbound. He struck one chord that woke a harmony from somewhere beyond all the eternities and only seemed to find a feeble echo in the heaven from which he spake, as he said, "Blessed are they that hunger and thirst after righteousness, for they shall be filled." It was only a brief sentence-one low, sweet chord, but it contained and rang with a melody which introduced a change of scene.

It was the banquet of a Wedding feast beside the river- and beneath the branches of the tree of life. The whilom Preacher was no longer enunciating the laws of a kingdom He was endeavouring to establish, but in bridal attire He was welcoming His guests to His nuptials in the kingdom to which He had succeeded, where His every promise would be fully redeemed, and concluded with the assurance that, "they shall hunger no more, neither thirst any more; neither shall the sun light on them, nor any heat; for the

Lamb which is in the midst of the throne shall feed them, and shall lead them unto living fountains of waters; and God shall wipe away all tears from their eyes." (Rev. vii, 16-17)

The vision fades away, and I am once more listening to the soul-stirring anthem of the Magnetic Chorale, while Siamedes is using the contributed life currents of the multitude to bathe the souls of the oppressed into a restoration to freedom and beauty, anticipatory of Myhanene coming to bestow the kiss of compensation, which will arouse the sleepers into a real newness of life. As I watch the holy ministry, faith carries me away again, and I am standing with the heroic and fearless Elijah as, single-handed, he defies and challenges the whole cult of Baal, to demonstrate which god is God.

One man opposed to eight hundred and fifty and the full patronage of such a king and queen thrown in. One man, alone; and the jury of a prejudiced nation to give the verdict. What a test of faith! What a perfect lens Elijah had discovered! How faultlessly pure; how beautifully he had it focussed! No wonder the chariots and horses of heaven were attendant on him! Oh, the irony of the sarcasm with which he taunts and encourages the priests! But Elijah already knew that he, who stands alone with God against a world, stands with the true Majority. So he won his verdict, even as Siamedes secured his victory.

As I watched, waiting for the fire to fall and burn up Elijah's sacrifice, I lifted my eyes and beheld the sombre robe that clothed, and the lightning strokes that were smiting Sinai, beyond the Wilderness of Sin.

"There were thunders and lightnings, and a thick cloud upon the mount, and the voice of the trumpet exceeding loud; so that all the people that were in the camp trembled." (Ex. xix, 16) No wonder that "when the people saw it they removed, and stood afar off." (xx, 18) I, too, trembled as I beheld the vision, and recalled the warning, "It is a fearful thing to fall into the hands of the living God." (Heb. x, 31) But out of the blackness, above the terror of the thunder, came to me the soft strains, as it were of a harp, and I heard the sweet voice of a singer proclaiming, "The Lord is merciful and gracious, slow to anger, and plenteous in mercy." (Ps. ciii, 8) In the soothing cadence of that evangel I lost the mount, and was once more in the company of that mountain-side Preacher, who invited me to revisit the region in which Ladas conducts his ministry. A shadow swept across the face of my conductor as he read Dante's pessimistic legend written over the portal, "Abandon hope all ye who enter here." He knit his brows in disapprobation as he read, but never spake a word. With one sweep of his hand he wiped away such a libel on the everlasting-the unchangeable love.

"Who is this that darkeneth counsel by words without knowledge?" (Job xxxviii, 2), he asked sorrowfully. "Is it not written, 'If I make my bed in hell, behold, thou art there?'" (Ps. cxxxix, 8) And blazing in letters of living fire, set deep in the bosom of that dark domain, he effaced the dogma and inscribed the song, that even they who wandered into the region of "the uttermost" might catch the echo of the invitation. "Come now, and let us reason together, saith the Lord; though your sins be as scarlet, they shall be as white as snow; though they be red like crimson, they shall be as wool." (Isa. i, 18)

Such a gospel in such a place needed no additional preaching to proclaim the everlasting love of such a God, as alone outlined it. It transfigures the soul as it drinks in its restoring appeal. It arouses the prodigal into consciousness of what he has lost and constrains him to say, "I will arise, and go to my Father."

The vision lingered-unfolded-carried me away. I was listening to my Guide in other scenes surrounded by publicans, sinners, scribes and Pharisees, as he told that graphic story of the erring lad.

Had I not hungered with him for a parent's love? Was not the yearning sympathy, the tender forbearance, the winsome solicitude, and the redeeming pity of the speaker too irresistible to be refused? No man had given unto me, but his voice, his look, his attitude; his hand offered the one cup for which I thirsted. I ate; I drank; I was refreshed, strengthened, redeemed! Of course the lad came home. Such a story, so told, would empty hell. It was this story, more briefly told, that he had written in a single sentence over that gloomy portal where Ladas ministers. What would its harvest be? might go on, and step by step traverse the whole of my experience as it rose before me, as faith revealed it in my meditation, and as each incident passed by I might have pictured to Vaone its manifest and hidden aspects, as the vision bore me hither and thither, that she might have seen how the requirements of every soul are carefully discerned and ministered to in preparation for its better advancement.

I am content, however, to think I acted wisely in the course I took. Had my experience been better than the illustrations I used, it would have been meted out to her from the beginning. With that I made myself hopeful that my imperfect ministry might be in some measure used to Vaone's benefit. And in recording the two courses that were open to me, I trust I have said enough to assure my readers that, in dealing with souls in

the beyond, there is a surprising consideration shown to individual requirement prescribed by a Father whose attitude to one and all is, "I have loved thee with an everlasting love; therefore with loving-kindness have I drawn thee." (Jer. xxxi. 3)

* * *

CHAPTER 3

I SIGHT THE GATE

Let me here draw attention to one of the pleasing contrasts which the spiritual life affords to the physical. The probability of failure which overshadows even the noblest effort in the lower life considerably increases the burden of existence. On the contrary, in the higher life, nobility of aim and purpose invariably commands success. It is a fundamental law of the kingdom, declared by the Christ, that "every one that asketh, receiveth; and he that seeketh, findeth; and to him that knocketh it shall be opened." (Matt. vii, 8) Why, if this-one of the least attractions it has to offer-were the only inducement heaven held out, should it not be enough to gather in every crushed, bruised, disappointed and defeated soul? Can one wonder at the tormented Hamlet pondering:

To die,-to sleep;-
No more; and, by a sleep, to say we end.
The heart-ache, and the thousand natural shocks
That flesh is heir to-'tis a consummation
Devoutly to be wished.

but it is not the totality of heaven's bestowal upon the "weary and heavy-laden" who respond to the invitation to "Come in and rest." 'Tis but the fragmental earnest of the good things that are yet to come, which are given to all liberally-"good measure, pressed down, and running over."

It is this superabundant outpouring of rest, joy, peace, sympathy, compassion, and love that makes heaven to be the supreme attraction of every oppressed and lonely soul. I was but just beginning to feel the fascination of it at the time of which I speak. I had heard of love-had been possessed of a yearning I did not understand, but I had not tasted of its sweetness-was ignorant of the real food for which I hungered.

Then Vaone became the angel of my resurrection, calling me into a newness of life by her question, that mysterious ray opened my eyes to behold that vision which brought the invisible into view and made me see the God inherent in the creature working out the grand enigma of redemption.

Looking back from the light that was afterwards revealed and to the comprehension of which I wish to confine myself entirely to the end of this volume-even then I shall but vaguely have indicated all that my soul would declare. Looking back, I say, from the clearer vision of the shadowless morning, I can see that when Vaone came to me with her enquiry, the immediate result to be attained concerned myself far more than I anticipated. She would benefit, but the seed of the ministry I was called upon to perform had to be sown, germinate, take root, grow and ripen before the harvest could be reaped. In myself, another harvest had been maturing almost unconsciously, while my active interests had been more energetically engaged in other directions. Or, should I not say that my eyes had been riveted on the things which were more superficial to the neglect of the hidden things which were "working out a far more exceeding and eternal weight of glory." It proved to be even so. The moment for Vaone's query to be propounded, the precise form in which it had been framed, and the nicety of detail with which it was balanced, made it successful in its twofold purpose, leaving the immediate advantage very unexpectedly to myself.

Fortunately, she had left me, and I was free again to pursue my desired meditation, to which the interruption-had it served no other purpose-had certainly the advantage of turning it in a definite direction. It promised to provide me with meat and drink, for which I had hungered without being able to discover the source of its supply. So, in order to escape any further hindrance to my desire, I left my retreat and wandered off with no other object than feasting on the meditation to which I had been so auspiciously directed.

It was most unusual for me to covet a brown study when taking exercise; it was equally a novelty to find myself forsaking the law and assuming the office of critic and expounder of the gospel; but, by far the most amazing thing was to find my sober, judicial mind straying into the fields of romance, in its eager determination to reach the goal of a nebulous ideal. Yet it was so.

I was like one who had awakened from a restless evading dream before daybreak. I had been searching through the darkness for a robe I yearned to possess. Again and again my nervous, outstretched fingers had touched its silken fringe, but I failed to seize the prize. In my disappointment I awoke- confused. Through the darkness a mystic fore-gleam of the morning quivered, and for an instant I beheld the object of my quest. Thank God it was not a phantom of my dreams. It had reality. The morning was breaking. I would go forth and find it, trusting to the voice within which I heard crying, "This is the way," to lead me to my goal.

Perhaps, to paraphrase a thought from one of Eilele's poems I have already quoted:

When mine eyes can bear the glory
Which my victory revealed-

when the burst of exultation has subsided, and I am in a position to review the experience, as I am now enabled to recall my previous progress up to the close of my previous volume- I shall know the way I took, and what of adventure I encountered in reaching the place where I next found myself.

I was standing before what I believe to be the most surprising botanical phenomenon I ever had, and probably ever shall behold. It was at once a grove of giant trees, and a vast, exquisitely proportioned cathedral nave, with an aisle on either side which contributed in no small degree to the completeness of the architectural design. Its length might be three hundred yards or more, with which its breadth and height most proportionately corresponded. There were twelve trees on either side, standing in well-dressed lines and equi-distant-not simple, rounded stems like crude Norman columns, or gnarled deformities to introduce discordance into the scheme, but their massive trunks had, in growth, been moulded into stalwart and shapely piers from which arch and groining sprang to carry out its stately Gothic plan.

The ends were free and open; the sides were walled by the dense foliage of some giant flowering shrub; the roof being perfectly provided for by the luxuriant leafage of the trees. The floor was carpeted with a thick, short velvety sward into which the feet nestled as into the embrace of the most alluring pile.

At the base of each tree a most inviting lounge had been arranged, thickly covered with aromatic mosses, soft as down, while other conveniences for repose or converse were placed here and there both in the nave and aisles.

The central feature of the around plan was a slightly sunken fountain, lying in an artistic basin of pink coral, which, when rising above the grass, was worked into most delicate tracery through which the slender tendrils of the aquatic plants crept with most charming effects, while the slender threads of dancing water added a suggestion of fairyland to the whole scene.

At the further side of the fountain from where I stood, the floor took a very slight, almost imperceptible rise, just enough to break the idea of a dead level, a feature which was continued for some little distance beyond the end of the court. It was in following the extent of this triviality, that I made a discovery which surprised me with wonder that I had not noticed it before.

Standing just over the rising ground, but directly confronting me, were two round, open towers connected by a delicate bridge of material and construction en suite with the basin of the fountain, and clothed with an equally attractive creeper. Beneath the bridge, from either tower, opened twin gates, which seemed to me to be of opal or mother-of-pearl, so beautiful they looked in the soft, sympathetic light.

Looking from the gate to the fountain, then back again to the gate and its surroundings, I asked myself whether there was not some close connection between the two, and, if so, what was its nature and import?

It was vain to ask. I was not in a position to furnish the reply.

This brought me back again to the consciousness of my own inability to stand alone. How, then, could I hope to find my way through the thousand problems by which I felt myself surrounded, without the assistance of a guiding hand? Oh, for another illuminating ray or a voice to whisper, "This is the way."

For the first time since my arrival I had a sense of being overshadowed-enveloped in a cloud of loneliness and indecision. Alone with an invisible and undefinable presence, which awed and was slowly but surely gaining a stronger control over me. I was wavering on the balance of some portentous crisis, as one poised on the moment of suspense preceding a false sentence. "I looked, and there was none to help, and I wondered that there was none to uphold." (Isaiah I xiii, 5)

Under the pressure of the situation, I turned my eyes to see if, among the groups occupying the Court, I could discern one to whom I might appeal for some assistance and relief-for, although I have not mentioned the fact, the court was not by any means deserted. The effort was successful in reducing the tension. It proved to be the trifle that arrests the attention and distracts the mind at the fateful instant. The suspense was eased, and I began to notice how many varied and hitherto unknown colours were to be found among the robes worn by different members of the various groups. My curiosity excited interest, and I soon found myself attempting to find names for, and classifying all the novelties in colour which were before me.

While thus occupied with an impossible task, my attention was arrested by someone approaching from the opposite side of the Court. My interest in him was aroused in that, with the exception of myself, he was the only solitary person to be seen, and the number was small in comparison with the area occupied.

From the instant that I saw him, I was confident his coming was to give me the help and guidance I so anxiously sought. That he had already identified me was equally certain from the first, since he came the whole length of the Court directly towards me, merely making a sign of recognition as he passed one or another, but never stopping on his way.

He came forward with that calm leisureliness which becomes so natural to this higher life, giving me ample opportunity to observe and feel assured that I should find in him such another friend as Myhanene had already proved to be.

"I am Rael, a friend both of Omra and Myhanene, "he said as he drew near, "on whose behalf I come to lend you whatever assistance I am able to give."

With this he made a gesture towards a seat.

"I know Myhanene well, and have come to look upon him almost as a brother," I replied, as I took the proffered seat, "but I am almost a stranger to Omra and at present stand somewhat in awe of him."

"That is not difficult for me to understand, since I know the circumstances under which you saw him. You would have the same feeling when you first saw Myhanene, yet you have learned to love him now, and I am equally certain that you will so esteem Omra when you know him better. As to you being a stranger, that is a strong commendation with me," he went on, with a touch of Myhanene's sparkling pleasantries twinkling in his eyes. "We have an exhortation in regard to this, which we regard as an imperative royal command, which says, 'Be not forgetful to entertain strangers; for thereby some have entertained angels unawares.' (Hebrews xiii, 2)

"I am afraid you will not experience such a discovery in connection with myself," I replied, already captivated by the fraternal spirit he manifested. "But how did Omra know of my presence-I just stumbled on this place, while I was lost in the labyrinth of a reverie?"

"Have you travelled so far across the border without making the discovery that we have many means of communication that are unknown to the earth? " "No! I should have been blind indeed had I not made acquaintance with at least one or two of these wonderful methods. Still, I do not know of any by which Omra could learn of my coming. I had told no one-in fact, as I say, I was lost in a reverie, and had no idea of anything outside until I woke to the admiration of the beauties of this court."

"Then you have still one or two further discoveries to make concerning us. I am hoping to be of some assistance to you in this direction. But, returning to our other reference-angels are not infrequent visitors here, and Omra is always watchful to be advised of all who pass."

"I hope his reward is greater than I am afraid he will find in the present instance."

"Why so?" he asked laconically, in a tone suggesting a possible difference of opinion.

"Because-well, simply because I am one of the very last who could lay claim to any such title."

"That may or may not be so," he replied; "I should like to read you a little better before venturing any opinion concerning it."

"But I think I may lay claim to that better knowledge in this case," I ventured.

"Yes, that is possible; and yet, even on that point I should need a better acquaintance before I commit myself to an opinion. Earth limitations and view-points frequently suggest erroneous and unjust conclusions, and it is more than possible that you may not be, at present, quite so far from them as to do justice even to yourself."

"Are you so charitable as to imagine that I should let them influence me to my own undoing?"

"If you insist on drawing inferences," he answered with an indulgent smile, "suppose we agree to leave it so for a while."

"Your reference to the earth limitations, and the probable mistakes that may arise from them, prompts me to ask a question that was exercising me at the time of your arrival, if I may."

"I am here for the purpose of assisting you, and am entirely at your disposal to give what help and guidance I can," he replied.

"I scarcely know how to explain myself," I began apologetically, but he considerately came to my relief at once.

"We will waive all explanations," he suggested, "and come at once to the question. The explanation may be reached more naturally and easier later."

"I don't see how."

"Perhaps not. It would surprise me if you did," he interjected with a kindly and reassuring smile. "I think I understand this situation more clearly than you anticipate. Experience has made me quite familiar with the confusion you are feeling, and I want you to let me take my own way in dealing with it. Like the Israelites when crossing the Jordan into Canaan, you need to be reminded that you 'have not passed this way heretofore,' and you stand in need of a directing voice and a guiding hand-how absolutely necessary this is you will soon discover. I have been asked to accompany you, because I have been considered the best adapted to your particular requirements, and am hoping to see you pass the gate triumphantly."

"Only so far as the gate? Are we to part company there?" I asked, surprised at his suggestion.

"Only so far as the gate," he repeated with a quiet significance. "But suppose it should prove to be a more lengthy journey than the distance appears to indicate? What if it turns out to be a case of 'so near, and yet so far?' Have you not already discovered how full this life is of surprises?"

"Indeed I have, but there cannot be much of surprise hiding in that which is so obviously transparent," I ventured to suggest.

"One would scarcely think it to be possible," he replied, as though quietly debating the proposition. Then, with more of confident animation, "Let me suggest that it would be more interesting to keep that idea prominently before your mind as we proceed. It may be that we should like to refer to it again later on, but just now you have other questions which are of more immediate importance."

"I have, certainly, but I am in such a confused state of mind that I positively don't know how to frame them."

"I understand and fully sympathize with you. Shall I state them for you, omitting the preamble?"

"You would do me a great service if you would."

"I will, and in doing so I shall follow the advice I gave you, and omit unnecessary explanations. If there is anything regarding your past I am not at present acquainted with-that is another surprise you were unprepared for," he facetiously threw in-"it is easily accessible when needed, so we can come at once to your two simple questions, 'Where am I,' and 'How did I come here'?"

"Yes, that is what I wished to ask; but how did you know?"

"By the exercise of a faculty that is enjoyed by every soul who reaches our estate-a faculty you had a prevision of when Vaone put to you the question as to whether heaven had proved to be all you anticipated. Ah, you start again! You will come to accept these surprises as matters of course presently. They are the commonplace experiences of a condition of being where we all 'know as we are known'-a condition across the frontier of which you are about to pass. This Court of Voices is an antechamber or vestibule to the gate, the passing of which is the most momentous step in the soul's great pilgrimage-I am speaking of that mystical second birth which the Christ discussed with Nicodemus. It is a change of far greater magnitude than the throwing off of the flesh, and was intended to be- but very rarely is-reached before the body is discarded.

"All your experiences, and the teaching you have received since your coming here, have had the one object of preparing you for this, and the underlying motive of all you have passed through has been to encourage and unfold the mysterious faculties and powers which you are just beginning to notice and employ with such astonishment. You are in the position of a child struggling in the birth-throes-all the energies you possess are being exerted to free yourself from your present limitations and gain the boundless freedom of immortality which intuitively impels the soul."

"Do you suggest, then, that I am bound to go forward, have no choice, no free will in the matter?"

"Free will, like all other terrestrial conditions, has its natural bounds and limitations. It would scarcely be thought of in the throes of a climax, such as I mention-Nature would simply assert itself and carry the process through. But, wishing to avoid a digression by discoursing free will and its limitations, let me reply to your enquiry by saying-I will not go so far as to say that you must go forward, but I do say that you will do so."

"Are you sure of it? I am not asking this captiously, but because I would like to hear your assurance."

"I understand you perfectly," he answered, "and have much pleasure in granting your desire. If you were now free to make your choice as to remaining here or going back to earth, which would you choose?"

I laughed at the ease with which he had so successfully captured me.

"Can there be the slightest doubt about it?"

"Let me make it doubly sure," he went on. Now, in your second choice, would you rather remain here where we are resting, or go forward as far as the gate?"

"Why, go on to the gate, of course," I replied, as I rose in readiness to do so.

"Not too hurriedly," he gently admonished me. "I knew what your choice would be, because with us the attractions on before are always greater than those we have already passed. That is why I am sure you will go forward. The attractive force of the future is irresistible, it is very beautifully expressed by Isaiah, where he puts these words into the mouth of God, "I have loved thee with an everlasting love, therefore with loving-kindness have I drawn thee." Who would break away from everlasting and omnipotent love after once feeling its sweet influences?

"Come, let us go now to meet Omra," he said, rising. "Perhaps he may have something to say that will help you towards true liberty." With this we went forward towards the gate.

CHAPTER 4

OMRA EXPLAINS MY POSITION

Rael was already proving himself to be a provokingly fascinating teacher. He had the rare skill of creating a thirst for knowledge by sketching bare outlines of subjects drawn in attractive forms and colours that excited interest, expectation, and desire; then quietly turning aside, for a time, without satisfying the appetite he had created.

In this, lay the great beauty and fertility of his design. A coveted treasure, discovered, out of reach, lost, sought for, and finally found, is far more precious than if it had been a plaything of our nursery.

I had been told that I was approaching the most momentous step in the soul's pilgrimage. How calmly, even cursorily, Rael had seemed to deal with it. Just a passing reference, then he turned abruptly to another subject equally engrossing, which he dismissed with similar brevity, then the door of opportunity was closed, and I had to stifle the flood of questions that rose to my lips and wait for some more convenient season-if I might meet with one-at Rael's suggestion that we should go forward to meet Omra.

Such was my introduction to the method my newly-found instructor intended to pursue.

My companion seemed disinclined for further conversation as we leisurely passed along the Court, nor had I any regret to find him so. He had already said enough to give me food for thought, and my active mind was not slow to accept the opportunity of digesting it. I could not hope clearly and definitely to solve the mysterious problem of the second birth which had been so cryptically referred to, but in trying to review Rael's declaration in the light of my previous experiences and attainments, might I not prepare myself in some measure to anticipate something that was in process of revelation?

The whole environment was suggestive of contemplation. The atmosphere was fragrant with peace; the silence musical with rest; the soft light liquid with a sense of communion too deep to find expression in language. Why disturb it by any attempt to continue our conversation?

My mind again reverted to the condition in which I found and now had left Vaone-the languor and listlessness experienced by such as her as they reach that Valley of Content after battling and struggling through the earth conditions, and the desire they feel to rest their over-wearied souls. For some reason I could not explain, in the mercy and by the grace of God, I had escaped this retaining influence, to all appearance, and when reaching what I have spoken of as the still water between life's ebb and flow, some benign current had carried me across the stagnancy into the rising flow of the eternal stream. I hesitated, almost trembled, as I found myself arriving at such a conclusion, which appeared to be the only logical interpretation of my condition in the light of what Rael had said. Had he been more explicit about the second birth, I might have had more confidence; but did not his reference to its momentous nature warrant my surmise? Was I not conscious of an unfolding within me of new faculties, capacities and powers which appeared to be carrying me into some enchanted land of being which already thrilled me with a hyper-susceptibility to which I had been hitherto absolutely oblivious?

How I wished I were alone.

Rael caught my thought almost before I was conscious of it myself.

"It may be," he said with soothing impressiveness, "that in your pilgrimage through the ages, you will not find another spot that will make such an ineffaceable impression on you as this hallowed Court of the Voices. It would be useless for me now to attempt to explain all that I mean by this-you are not yet in a position to understand what I tell you. Look, for instance, at the variation in the colouring and the decoration of the robes worn by those around us. When you are able to understand the meaning and significance of this variety, you will be able to appreciate the far-reaching attraction which will take root in your own soul in your present passing. It will never be lost- never lose the freshness of its first charm. It is your unconscious outreach after this benediction that makes you wish to be alone, and now I must leave you for a while, that you may experience its sacred baptism, that you may hear the voices in which this sanctuary will speak with you through every avenue of your being, that the eyes of your understanding may be opened to catch some glimpses of the infinity into which you are about to enter; that you may take your first plunge into the rapture of life's great and unspeakable glory. I will come back again presently, but while you listen to the first strains of this eternal music-while you breathe the first breath of its fragrant spiritual atmosphere, I will go to meet Omra."

As he finished he turned away, and I had my wish.

It was a master-stroke on his part, to select the obvious lesson of the styles and colouring of the robes around us, as an illustration of the inability to understand the development I was experiencing. It was one of the first explanations I had heard after my arrival that each colour bears its own significance, in their simplicity the darker denoting the lower and the lighter the higher conditions, but I had not yet been initiated into the meaning of the combinations and multiple variations which were represented around me. These denoted mysteries beyond my skill to fathom; they spoke of ranks and conditions of being, of which my comprehension had not at present heard, nor the heart of my imagination dreamed. They were suggestions of worlds of revelation lying deep within still unsuspected worlds to me, the beauties and glories of which would have blinded my vision with their radiance, had not mine eyes been mercifully held that their light might fall as darkness on my virgin ignorance.

But though my untrained faculties were not able to appreciate all the subtleties of the majestic music that rolled around me, I was permitted to partake thereof to a rich overflowing of my soul's content. I was conscious of sweet and strengthening influences playing around me; in the calm depths of my being were echoes of music-if not actual voices-rhythmical and captivating sounds I hungered to hear more fully; from hidden depths within me, shadowy angelic forms arose, crowned with an aureole of promise, beckoned me to follow, and I was saturated with a sense of life to which I was unable to find any satisfactory analogy.

How I longed to grasp and understand every detail and item of the overpowering experience to master each separate feature in a lingering analysis until had I made the whole part of my very self. Vain, covetous desire! As well might I have attempted to single out a solitary voice in that grand chorus of the Magnetic Chorale and balance its effect. The parts were so beautifully adjusted and interblended with the whole, that it became an absolute unit, before which I bowed my head in reverent adoration, while the silence breathed its benediction of peace.

After the silence "a still small voice" came to me-an echo from the distant past-carrying me back again to that little Zion Mission Room, where I met Helen and other over-burdened souls. It caused me to turn my eyes towards the gate, and I listened once more to the pathetic enquiry of one of their favourite hymns:

When my final farewell to the world I have said,
And gladly lie down to my rest;
When softly the watchers shall say; "He is dead,"
And fold my pale hands o'er my breast;

And when, with my glorified vision, at last
The Walls of "That City" I see,
Will anyone then, at the beautiful gate,
Be waiting and watching for me?

I could see no city-no wall-but the gate stood only a little distance away, and my feet were moving towards it. Were the influences and harmonies that were enthralling, enwrapping me, part of the accessories of the 'Welcome Home' those outcasts so confidently believed would await us there? Would their anticipation be realized after all? The possibility did not seem to be so incongruous now as once it appeared to be. Shall I find anyone there "watching and waiting for me?" What a question to ask. How could I expect it? I had been met, or rather found, on the slopes by Helen, but my mother was not there; and, in turn, I had come away and left her somewhere behind me, and probably should not know when she would reach the gate, and it was possible that I might not come to meet her. What had I done at any time-anywhere-to secure any such recognition? And yet had not Rael told me that even a greater than Myhanene-Omra-was even now on his way to meet me? Had not Rael gone away in order to meet him?

I should not only find someone waiting for me at the gate- it was evident they were not content to abide my coming till I arrived at the portal, but others than those I had known in the flesh were already on their way to give me welcome! There might be a readjustment in some details of the perspective-I had not found the gate to be standing on the margin of the river, as I had been promised, but it was evident that I had lost nothing in the rearrangement. How many times had I already discovered that God only delays in order to increase His blessings?

Just then I noticed Rael and Omra approaching, not from the direction of the gate, but from the opposite side of the Court. I took a step in my desire to meet them, when a musical whisper counselled me:

"Wait patiently for him."

I stood still. "Who was it spoke to me?" From above me came another silvern chime:

O life! how blessed! how divine;
High life, the earnest of a higher!

Surely this must be a vibration from the storehouse of my

memory. But I failed to trace it. Then I recalled the name by which Rael had spoken of the place, and, awestruck, marvelled at the thought of what might be before me.

Neither Rael nor Omra betrayed the slightest indication that they had as yet seen me, as they came in leisurely communion across the Court. I was somewhat relieved to find it so, since it gave me an opportunity of preparing to meet with one of whom, as I had told Rael, I felt a certain sense of awe, having only seen him in his official capacity at that baptism in the Sanctuary of Silence. My disquietude, however, proved to be groundless, as Rael had foretold me. Omra was another instance of the condescension in which greatness is lost in service. I only had to see him to desire his closer friendship-to recognize another Myhanene in him, at whose feet I would only be too happy to sit. In his figure and movement he was wonderfully like my better-known friend, but his simple pink robe spoke of another condition, as his light bronze complexion proclaimed another nationality.

They were drawing near, and still there was no visible sign of their knowledge of my presence, while I was wishing that more time had been at my disposal in which to study one to whom I was feeling an additional attraction at every step he took towards me, but that opportunity had now passed by.

Recalling the only occasion on which I had seen Omra, and coupling therewith what Rael had said of the importance of the step I was about to take, I had naturally associated the idea of our present meeting with some kind of formality. I think it was such an idea that had nervously disturbed my anticipation. What a mistake. There was not even the formality of introduction as we met. Rael held his friend's attention by some explanation he was making, in which Omra was deeply interested, as they came to a stand, then the laughing, liquid eyes were turned on me, a friendly hand gripped my shoulder and I was greeted with:

"Ah, my brother Aphraar, let me offer you a thousand welcomes on reaching such a stage in your journey!"

"I thank you for the generosity of your welcome," I replied. "I can readily understand and appreciate that, but I am afraid my ignorance as to where I am just now prevents my understanding the remainder of your greeting."

"We can easily excuse you in that respect. Let it satisfy you to know that we do not expect-even when the presence of genius is assured-to find scientific accuracy in the infant during its birth-throes." Omra playfully returned with mystic reference to the second birth Rael had already spoken of.

"Your veiled simile piques my curiosity," I replied, "but since I am able to detect the mystical nature of your allusion, should I be out of place in asking for some clearer explanation?"

"Not at all. It is one of the most natural requests you could make at this point. It is the anticipated response we hope the occasion will produce.

It is the declaration of your readiness to go forward. All that you ask in elucidation of this mystery-for such it is, even beyond your expectation-shall be granted you, as in the case of every other gift of God. But let me assure you, you will find it to be a subject of deeper import, greater complexity, and wider study than you have yet been given to understand, and it will be placed before you in its varied aspects and stages, by demonstrative illustration confirming what will be verbally explained."

Here Omra came to a deliberate pause upon which I was about to question him further, when he resumed, as if under the influence of an afterthought.

"Man, the climax and crown of creation, as far as his physical nature is concerned, is a member of the animal kingdom. 'The Lord God formed (him) of the dust of the ground' (Gen. ii, 7), as a potter fashioneth his vessel from the clay, and of this physical part God afterwards declared, "dust thou art and unto dust shalt thou return." (Gen. iii, 19) But our continued existence after our dust has returned to that, from which it was taken, forms an object lesson as to the incapacity of the physical to adjudicate in the domain of the spirit. It is when the potter has formed his vessel that he employs it as a receptacle. So God, having formed man, said,

'Let us make him the receptacle of our own image,' and 'breathed into his nostrils the breath of life; and man became a living soul.' (Gen. ii, 7) Thenceforward man is a physical vessel filled with a spiritual content-'there is a natural body and there is a spiritual body.' Now, while the foundation of the vessel is dust, which has to be wrought into shape by the hand and artifice of the potter before it is available for service, the germ of the soul is breath-invisible and intangible-which is enshrined in the secret place of the physical, to germinate and to be brought to the birth in the fulness of the appointed time.

"The physical carrier, possessing none of the attributes of the contents it has temporarily protected, breaks and returns to the dust as the soul bursts its prison-house and enters upon its great enfranchisement. 'Flesh and blood cannot inherit the kingdom of God,' which is spirit, a fact the Christ proclaimed when he said, 'Except a man be born again he cannot see the Kingdom of God.' To give this illustration a personal application, the pitcher has been broken-or perhaps better still, the chrysalis has escaped from the cocoon, and, bewildered at its newly-discovered self, instinctively proceeds to adapting itself to its new environment, faculties and duties which are but in process of unfolding.

"You have been subject to this adaptation since your discarnation, being prepared for and are now about to shake off the last trace of the dust of the physical and enter upon the active spiritual life."

"Of course, I am not unfamiliar with the idea of a second birth, but it has never been more to me than a verbal assent to it as to any other theological dogma," I replied, hoping to draw a yet further exposition.

"You are in no way peculiar in that respect," Omra responded. "Well spake the Master when He said, 'The kingdom of heaven is like unto treasure hidden in a field.' It is the same figure as I have spoken of-the spiritual treasure in the earthen vessel, and all the artifice and acumen of the earth is directed to uphold the authority of the flesh as being the teacher, rather than the servant, of the spirit. This necessitates the whole system of correction which you have seen established here, since it is an immutable law of the kingdom that 'there shall in no wise enter into it anything that defileth, neither whatsoever worketh abomination, or maketh a lie; but they which are written in the Lamb's Book of Life.' (Rev. xxi, 27)

"Will you pardon my persistence," I asked with some degree of hesitation, as I realized the deliberate emphasis with which he uttered this rejoinder. "I am not enquiring from any captious motive, but how is the question of elegibility determined?"

"Absolutely and entirely by the fact whether a man has experienced the second birth." He delivered this with even an added emphasis. Then paused before he said, "These are the words of the Master upon the point, 'Except a man be born of water and of the Spirit, he cannot enter into the kingdom of God. That which is born of the flesh is flesh, and that which is born of the Spirit is spirit.' (John iii, 5, 6) In other words, the physical is a procreation by the animal man; the spiritual is a germination from the breath of God. They are as distinct from each other as the water is from the pitcher. You are already aware of this in several ways, but the full beauty and extent of it you cannot appreciate until the change you are now experiencing has been completed. The soul is unable to sit down and feast upon the fruits of Paradise before it has passed the gate."

I had to be content to allow the mysticism of his concluding remarks to pass, and it was some time before I could trace therein an instance of the patient freedom they are willing to allow in the acceptance of an unapprehended truth. Omra was breaking new ground for me, and the force with which he accomplished it brought to my mind Paul's words:

"The word of God is quick, and powerful, and sharper than any two-edged sword, piercing even to the dividing asunder of soul and spirit;" (Heb. iv, 12) and like Moses on the mount, when he saw the lightning and heard the thunder and the trumpets, I said, "I exceedingly fear and quake." (Heb. xii, 21)

"How am I to know that I shall attain to such a consummation?" I presently enquired.

"You need have no fear on that point," he instantly replied. "You have the assurance of that in your presence here. God does not bring His children to the birth and then withhold the strength for delivery."

"And may I go on to know and understand this wonderful mystery?" I asked with returning confidence.

"It is not so much a question now of 'may' as 'must,' and that, not because your free will is interfered with, but time and circumstance have brought you into the clearer knowledge of God, whose everlasting and unchanging love has gained such an irresistible hold upon you that you must yield to its influences and follow where it leads. Your spiritual eyes are opening to see the beauty of the true light, the darkness caused by the glamour of reason is being superseded by the glory of revelation, which will shine more and more unto the perfect day, where your feet shall neither stumble nor turn aside. By the aid of that light you will be guided into all truth, all mysteries shall be made known to you, until you know even as you are known. The voices of this Court invite you to enter upon this course here and now, and we place ourselves at your disposal to lend you what assistance you may require in that direction."

I had been so engrossed with Omra's conversation that I had not noticed that Rael had left us, until Omra indicated his wish for us to take a seat, and we threw ourselves on one of the fragrant divans near at hand.

* * *

CHAPTER 5

A VISION AND ITS SEQUEL

The subtle distinctions of individuality make a wonderfully interesting study. I have already said that as Omra first approached me I saw in him another Myhanene. I had not to know much of him before I discovered that he was all I anticipated in that respect, with a variation in a direction that was very welcome in the circumstances in which I stood at the moment. Myhanene is a teacher indefatigable in imparting the riches of his treasures; Omra on the other hand, is essentially a student.

He sows ideas rather than verbal definitions, then leaves them to unfold as they may, according to the peculiarly fructifying ability of the soul in which the seed has fallen. Hence, having pointed out the fact that there is a certain incomparable treasure hidden in earthen vessels, he satisfies himself by adding one or two mystical sentences as to certain qualities which the treasure may be possessed of, and then is satisfied to allow the searcher to make what discovery he may for himself.

How often had I wished for Omra's invitation to meditation when Myhanene and others had been speaking to me; how I wished for Myhanene's lucid explanations now that Omra suggested reflection. Yet each in his time and place was equally desirous of giving me of his best. Wherein, then, lay the difference of treatment? Did it lie in that "subtle distinction of individuality," or was it to be found as an adaptation to some gradual and therefore unrecognized change that was taking place in myself?

In the dénouement, it proved to be a combination of the two. The experience which was unfolding was to be an illustration of the peculiar care the spiritual life exercises in the adaptation of the minutest detail to the exigencies of the circumstance and occasion, to produce the richest effect in the individual. Nothing could be more carefully arranged to demonstrate the fact of how far the ways of God are separated from the ways of men. Myhanene and Omra each stood in his divinely appointed place and the guiding hand of Providence brought me into touch of each exactly at the appointed time.

* * *

I had scarcely measured myself upon the luxurious couch to which Omra had invited me, before I felt myself sinking into the embrace of-how shall I describe it? It was a kind of semi-somnolence in which every faculty and power I possessed were quickened to a degree of sensitiveness that made me gasp. As in a dream, my whole surroundings were changed, and the vision which I beheld was far more ecstatic than the scenes through which I had recently been passing, but-did I hear, or was it only my memory that recalled the voice of Prospero declaring:

These our actors,
As I foretold you, were all spirits, and
Are melted into air, into thin air;
And, like the baseless fabric of this vision,
The cloud-capp'd towers, the gorgeous palaces,
The solemn temples, the great globe itself,
Yea, all which it inherit, shall dissolve,
And, like this insubstantial pageant faded,
Leave not a rack behind.

What did it mean? Had I been dreaming, and should I presently awake to find that this glorious after-life in which I had been so transcendently happy-where I had discovered and been attracted to follow after a love that was above all other loves the mind had heretofore conceived-where I had beheld the reign of a God that was greater and more perfect than the tongue of prophet had ever dared to declare-that the ideal heaven was only the figment of a midnight slumber, and with the morning I had to shoulder my weary cross again to continue the weary round of loneliness-heartache and sorrow?

It was a wonderful spasm of experience, but, fortunately, it was brief as it was sharp, and thus the baseless fabric of the vision faded as a hand reached forth to lead me from this into an inner vision.

* * *

I passed into a deeper, more intensely dreamlike scene, a veritable fairyland of ideal beauty-an open-air theatre, the outlines of which were defined by ornate columns of some semi-transparent material around which fragrantly flowering creepers wreathed themselves, then intertwined and interlaced to form walls of indescribable beauty. It was a spacious bower carpeted with a soft, luxuriant emerald sward in which the delicate tracery of infinitesimal flowers produced a novel and charming effect.

The auditorium was of limited extent, being provided with but a single seat in which I found myself already located-the solitary occupant of the secluded shrine. A short distance in front of me, three steps running across the entire width of the enclosure, led to a platform occupying at least two-thirds of the available space. There were no furnishings of any description save three low pedestals, standing as if to suggest an arc rather beyond the middle distance of the platform, and behind these stood a fourth of rather larger dimensions, as if built for the reception of a more important figure.

The light was not brighter than that of the vision I had left behind me, but it was potent with a clearness and power of revealing, which struck me with singular force as I entered, and yet, while I looked and wondered at what was about to happen, film after film of invisible veils appeared to be withdrawn, intensifying the clarity of vision until it seemed that the invisible itself had been brought into sight.

But while my vision grew clearer, my perplexity deepened. To what mystery was this singular prelude about to introduce me? I looked around, but there was no one to help, no guiding hand to lead, no welcome voice to counsel or explain. I was wrong. There was a voice from some invisible speaker, soft and musical, with kindly encouragement inviting me to:

"Behold and see."

That voice had the effect of the baton tap of a conductor calling his orchestra to attention. The vision was instantly a scene of animation.

Above the larger pedestal a luminous cloud about the size of a human fist appeared, expanded; then the cloud was rent and vanished, leaving an infant, just able to balance himself, standing upon the shaft, and on the plinth at his feet, in letters of light, was inscribed the legend:

SO GOD CREATED MAN IN HIS OWN IMAGE;
IN THE IMAGE OF GOD CREATED HE HIM.

It needed no interpreter to explain to me the meaning and significance of the presentment; it was all too patent, with the irresistible force of a revelation, that I was looking upon the true standard of humanity as it came from the hand of God in the beginning. As I gazed upon it with an adoring admiration, that voice spake again from out of the silence saying:

"In him dwells all the bodily fulness of the Godhead."

What an unrealized declaration! It marks the stupendous-almost incredible height on which the newly-created feet of man first rested. Think of it-"in the image of God created He him." Are your eyes able to bear and your mind to realize the dignity, the glory, the sublimity of the situation? If not, study it patiently. Wait! You will not be losing anything, but saving time, labour, and the agony of remorse, by refusing to move another step upon life's pilgrimage before your eyes are opened to behold, and your mind intelligently to realize the actual spot on which God placed the feet of man at his creation.

Then, having learned this solemn fact-beseeching Him to hold your hand-draw near and search the depths of the dark abyss in which humanity is wallowing to-day, in the mad revelry of the flesh, rioting in masks, subterfuges, deceits and hypocrisies; then you may measure and try to estimate how great has been the fall; something of the nature of the effort needed to restore the race to its original estate.

Consider this. Linger over it in patient, sober contemplation until the revelation of its verity permeates to the marrow of your moral consciousness, then-and not till then-will you begin to comprehend the significance of what is meant by redemption through Jesus Christ.

I am not anxious to assume the role of a preacher. I have no theological axe to grind. Churches and systems, creeds and dogmas, forms and ceremonies, theologies and philosophies, and the thousand other factions and contentions which destroy the peace of brotherhood, are things of the past with me-left behind as contraband in the customs-house on the frontier.

But since I have been called to the ministry of intercourse across the boundary, I have a fellow-feeling with you who are left behind, and would faithfully transmit my findings to you in the light of the principles of the golden rule. In doing this, I shall not go wrong if I follow in the footsteps of the Master and just here I recall, how, in the parable of Dives and Lazarus, the erstwhile rich man, being in torment, and having failed to secure for himself the relief he sought, bethought him of those who were still in the flesh and cried,

"I pray thee, father, that thou wouldest send (Lazarus) to my father's home, for I have five brethren; that he may testify unto them, lest they also come into this place of torment."

If in the agony of purgation such a thought could cross a tortured soul, is it to be wondered at that one who finds himself more happily circumstanced, should be moved by an equal consideration and wish to reach down a helping hand to guide you upward?

Just one other moment. Someone will be wanting to ask me what I mean by "redemption through Jesus Christ?" I cannot do better, or be more brief in my reply, than by considering the Master's answer to one who asked Him the same question (Luke x, 25-28)-"Thou shalt love God and thy neighbour as thyself. This do and thou shalt live." For love is the fulfilling-is the satisfaction of the law if it is observed in practice. To believe it only will not avail. "The devils believe and tremble."

I was conscious, however, that there was something-perhaps much more in the vision than I had thus far discovered. The idea was suggested as my eye fell upon the three vacant pedestals, that they were no more than accessories suggesting an arc was out of the question. But how was I to solve the problem? Oh, for the presence of Omra or Rael to enlighten me! And for the moment, the sense of my loneliness and helplessness weighed heavily upon me.

The pressure of the silence, the vague uncertainty which enveloped me, the indefinable sense of invisible presences crowding around filled me with a trembling reverence, wondering what next would be revealed. How long would the tension last? My eyes travelled enquiringly, yearningly, prayerfully, from pedestal to pedestal, round and round again seeking a solution, until a softly sympathetic voice whispered in my ear:

"Rest in the Lord; wait patiently for Him."

That voice did more than break the tension. It immediately gave me the assurance that the period of waiting had been a necessary part of the proceeding-the trying interlude was not an accident, but had been carefully designed.

I was still within the Court of the Voices, and no doubt being prepared for clear and definite instruction from out the depths of that mysterious profound at greater length than hitherto permitted to hear. No isolated sentence could convey to me the explanation I sought, and which I now felt was awaiting me when I was in a condition to receive it. For I was now convinced that all the reason for my waiting was to be found in myself alone. I had no reason, however, to fear; since I had come so far; I felt assured that that which had gone so far would now be carried to completion. It only needed my yearning aspiration to reach the necessary height of intense desire, then the response would come, and I should be satisfied.

So it proved to be.

God never fails to answer the truly earnest and patiently waiting soul. That is one of the things God is not able to do. It may take a long time to bring the soul into such delicate tune with the Divine that it may be able to catch the sweet modulations of the sacred Voice, but it is certain to be heard, when the attuning is completed. Get away from the tumultuous discord without; find the way into the silent shrine of your own soul; wait-listen for Him in the sacred hush, and you will presently hear Him, as He spake to me.

The Voice came soft and soothing as a murmuring zephyr, sweeter than a love song, clear and musical as the chiming of a silver bell. I may never know from whence it came-it seemed to be within, without, around; filling everything to a measureless overflowing. It was like the anthem of the ages rendered in music that needs setting in all the accessories of heaven to be understood and appreciated. I cannot recall its poetry. It would be vain to attempt it, and yet it is essential that I set down, as best my memory serves me, something of the intimation it gave for my direction:

"In reaching the position in which you now find yourself, you have already passed two stages in the pilgrimage of life-an eternal course, and hence a goalless journey, of which the final stage the

mind can comprehend, is God. Here we encounter the inscrutable I and-pause, until some stronger, clearer vision shall enable you to scan some further stage. Let it suffice you for the present, that you have secured your release from the physical; said farewell to sleep and other psychic means for restoration from weariness, and now you stand at the end of your third stage where you must part with doubt and uncertainty.

The third stage."

Here the Voice seemed to take a reflective tone as if speaking in an aside.

"This raises the problem of the circle, and the whole mystical interpretation of numbers."

There ensued an interval of silence. Then, as if under the influence of another inspiration, the Voice assumed its original tone.

"Here we come face to face with another-one of a score of problems which converge on this centre. Problems you are not yet prepared to grapple with, but they will be separately and clearly explained to you before you will be able to pass the gate. In so far as this number three involves the re-interpretation of your idea of the Trinity, we must waive its consideration for the present. It is enough for now that it is forced upon your attention by the three pictorial reproductions of the child standing before you as an illustrative model, in the analysis of yourself you are about to witness. Let us explain:

"God created man in His own image'-a trinity of body, soul and spirit. Above, you see the child in its physical form-a trinity interblended into one. Below, on the three lower pedestals, you see the same child presented in segregation that, in its passing for judgment, every influence in life, whether for good or evil, may be carefully traced to its true source, and be rewarded or penalized as

justice demands. On the left, everything pertaining to the physical will be recorded and developed, commencing with an exact register of every disqualification or impediment with which the child is born. For all such defects, due compensation will be made in the award.

"On the right will be registered the record of the soul-the mental, moral and temperamental qualities with which the child begins and evolves. Here you will observe the analysis as to responsibility will be ruthlessly exact, in balancing between the weight of outside influence and resisting force, that justice may be done. On the centre canvas the spirit will stand before you stripped as a gladiator for the arena, an athlete ready for the contest, a wrestler for the struggle. There you will see and get to know your real self-not the robed and accoutred manikin that may have strutted as yourself-at any and every step of your journey. Your wish, your motive, your aim, your aspiration and your purpose will be laid bare to your inspection in the full light of God.

"But you will look in vain to see achievement represented there. You may recognize failure, but do not allow such discovery to dishearten you. Things are not always what they seem to be. He that endures to the end will prove to be the victor-many start who fall and are lost sight of by the way. Neither account the loneliness, obstacles, hardships and tortuous windings of the path as disqualifications or evidences of defeat. The most brilliant Victor who carried off the prize was so proclaimed after tearing through the briars of Gethsemane, toiling o'er the brow of Calvary, then dying of a broken heart as He exclaimed, 'My God, my God, why hast Thou forsaken me?' So watch diligently, and in patience await the declaration in hope to hear the award-'Well done!'"

That strangely recondite voice, and that equally strange vision, was but the Preface and the Prologue to the mystic volume I had yet to study. Most appositely does it bear the title of "The Judgment Seat." It is not a record. It cannot be transcribed, nor reduced to linguistic form. It is an actual experience every soul has to encounter, as certainly as birth or death.

The introductory scene and discourse enabled me to understand the vision clearly from the beginning. Man, in God's image, was created with body, soul and spirit perfected, balanced, adjusted to work harmoniously each in its own sphere, character and stewardship through obedience into the consummation of sonship. But the idea of service was irksome to the flesh. The brain conceived and planned a coup that failed, and the tragedy of sin resulted.

For the opening of the pageant the setting of the scene remained, with this exception-I saw myself, a child of tender years, standing on the larger pedestal, but oh! the appalling change I saw in the representation on the lesser. I knew at once how it was that I had been called a misanthrope. I understood, as neither Myhanene's explanation nor my own experience had made me comprehend the matchless providence that had arranged for the ministrations of The Magnetic Chorale.

I watched sin in its conception, sowing, cultivation and its harvesting, working through all its hideous subtleties, evasions, deceits and hypocrisies, as it wrestled to achieve its mastery. But the analysis was inviolate. By a law as ruthless as death, not only every seed, but every fraction of the harvest it produced was laid at the feet, to be garnered by whoever had sown it.

As I beheld, I sighed and asked myself, "Who then can be saved?" and instantly a whisper came out of the tense silence:

"Justice carries the key of the door of salvation."

It must be so, because it so proved to be at the end, but again I have to say, "Such knowledge is too wonderful for me." I watched that record of my life unrolled, analysed, dissected, criticized and laid bare, with all the eager anxiety of a criminal standing at the bar. From the first scene my conscience and memory had seemed to rise in evidence against me, quoting one and another warning, saying, "there is nothing covered, that shall not be revealed; and hid, that shall not be made known" (Matt. x, 26); or yet again, "Bind him hand and foot, and take him away, and cast him into outer darkness." (Matt. xxii, 13) But in response to these were other voices whispering in far more hopeful tones, "My thoughts are not your thoughts, neither are your ways my ways." (Isa. iv, 8)

So the examination proceeded. How long it occupied, I cannot say, for day and night have passed away in those latitudes.

At length we reached the scene where I rushed to the rescue of the little child in Whitechapel. I reached him-lifted him-a vapour passed over the scene. It lifted. All was changed! I was lying on the slopes, and in my arms I held-the child that had occupied the higher pedestal.

* * *

CHAPTER 6

A VERDICT OF REVELATION

Shall we think about moving now?" Omra's voice is equally soft, persuasive, and sympathetic as that of Myhanene, but, coming unexpectedly after the musical vibration to which I had been listening from the mysterious around, it aroused me to a recognition of his presence with something of a start. I was still in a state of dreamy uncertainty as a result of the vision, the last scene of which had transported me through the mists, and I was in a condition of bewilderment as to where, and under what circumstances I was environed for the moment-whether I was actually lying up on the slopes as I originally found myself, or lying on one of the couches in the Court of the Voices.

Omra's voice, however, speedily recalled me to a true sense of my surroundings.

"If you think it is advisable-yes," I replied, "but I am scarcely clear as to who and where I am for the instant."

"You need not apologize for that," he assured me with an indulgent smile. "A little action will soon help you to recover yourself."

"That is what I need-to recover myself," I answered. I am almost wondering how much of my old self remains for me to recover."

"Leave yourself in my hands, and we will soon determine that point."

"I would like to ask you one question, if I may." I ventured.

"Have you only one to ask?" he enquired encouragingly. "I anticipate you have many, and I shall be pleased to help you as far as in me lies."

"If I attempted to ask only a fraction of the questions the vision has prompted, I am afraid I should keep you engaged for a very considerable time."

"I have no doubt of that," he replied. "And when I had

reached the end of your enquiries, even then they would not have taken up a single pulse-throb of eternity. There is, therefore, no need for you to curtail your research. Where shall we begin?"

Such outspoken generosity at once placed me at my case. Here was another instance of the same spontaneous ministry I had everywhere experienced. If anything, it came with more rippling freedom from the lips of Omra than in others. Yet I had stood in awe of meeting him.

What an exposition he offered of the Master's words, "He that is greatest among you, the same shall be servant of all!"

With this encouragement, I lost no time in placing my first difficulty before him.

"I am more than a little surprised that in the end there was no-shall I say-decision, arrived at."

There was a suggestive pause, and then he asked,

"Where did the last scene leave you?"

"Lying on the slopes, where Helen found me, with the boy in my arms."

Another short silence.

"That seems to suggest another commencement rather than an ending," he answered reflectively. "It would be somewhat out of place to hear a decision in such a connection, would it not?"

"But what need was there to introduce the final scene? That is my difficulty."

"Every need," he replied laconically. "Was not your waking on the slopes the natural sequence to your falling asleep under the feet of the horses in the street?"

"Certainly! But-" I was at a loss how to proceed.

He gave a passing salutation to a friend at the moment; then quickly enquired, Yes? But ...?"

"Do you not understand my difficulty?" I asked.

"Quite. I only want you to recognize it as clearly as I do myself, if possible; then I will show you where the error lies," he said sympathetically.

"It seems to me that the accident introduced a perfectly

natural break in the course of events," I ventured to suggest.

"Where do you find the necessity for any break?" he asked, as he passed his hand through my arm and drew me closer to him in a gentle fraternal pressure. "Breakages are always to be avoided rather than encouraged. The eternal purposes of God are monumental testimonies to this great truth: 'Without variableness or shadow of a turning.'

"Where can you find room for the suggestion of a break? Let us review the accident and see if we can discover any reason for it. You rushed to the assistance of a helpless child-was knocked down-God's providence at once automatically leaps to the assistance and recognition of your ministry, and by the anaesthetic of a swoon, saves both yourself and child from suffering. The period of unconsciousness passes-you open your eyes-the scene has certainly changed, and, instead of finding yourself in a hospital, where you would have been under other circumstances, you wake to find that you are still holding the child in your arms, not only unhurt, but considerably advantaged by what has taken place. There has been a breaking away, most certainly, but it is the breaking away of a prisoner from his prison-house into the freedom of life. You have no doubt about you being the friend who ran to the assistance of the child?"

"Most certainly not!"

"So far, then, we are agreed. Now let me ask you to try to follow me, while I anticipate a little. I appreciate the feeling of novel uncertainty in which you find yourself, perhaps even more than you yourself are able to realize. The stream of events is, just now, so strong that you are scarcely able to keep your feet. Nor do I expect you to do so. If I may use an allegorical anachronism, I scarcely expect a child during the violence of its birth-throes to scientifically analyse the process. This you will be able to accomplish presently. In the meantime, let me indicate what is actually taking place as viewed from the position you will occupy when you reach the gate. For this purpose I need not trace the genesis of life prior to its human phase, a point at which it enters on a significant combination marking a legitimate starting point.

"The one point I ask you to bear in mind is that we are not starting at the origin of life, but at a spot where two streams meet, and joining, become a river which will empty itself into the ocean. Now, as we see it, the first reach of this river is the measure of the earthly course, or, to drop the figure, the physical life is nothing more than the infant stage of the soul's existence. The scriptures always use the characteristic terms of infancy-innocence, ignorance, and incompetence-as relating to the condition, and never use the terms of maturity. They are taught as in a nursery by means of pictures-stories-parables and allegories, and the only lesson they are expected to learn is, "Little children love one another." The whole span of the mortal life is spent in the kindergarten class of the school of the eternities.

"At the close of the term, the soul is passed on to whatever place the elementary examination of the class shows it to be qualified for by its practical application of the love lesson. The liberty conceded to children in the lower class allows the free expression of individuality, directed by the advice of under-teachers, but in the higher school, a more rigorous system prevails-law and order obtains, and the older child is subjected to the discipline of obedience.

"This you have been permitted to watch under the direction of Myhanene and his friends, and I hope the brief sketch I have given you has enabled you to get a better understanding of your position."

"Yes-it has in a measure," I replied with some degree of hesitation, "but where did the elementary examination you speak of come in my case?"

"That introduces another thought, the explanation of which will not be uninteresting to you. When I said that law and order was observed in the sphere through which we have passed with Myhanene, I did not mean a mechanical or iron-bound law that treats all alike without reference to circumstance or condition. Justice demands that each case shall be considered with that care and impartiality you have just observed in your own case. In many instances-your own for example-the evidences are so obvious that the examination is postponed until this point of your progress is reached. In those cases, a kind of roving commission is allowed under such guidance as you have received. In this pursuit you have seen much, heard much, learned much; your eager, enquiring soul has been bountifully fed. Your hunger for maternal love has led you into enquiries which have revealed even a greater love than you set out to find-a love which has constrained you to leave the lesser for a moment and press on in the sure and certain hope of reaching the one ideal which still lies on beyond. Is this not so?"

"It is not only so, but it is considerably more than so. I have, in laying aside the physical, lost something, but I remain the same personal living entity, and in place of that which I have lost, I have received abundantly more than a compensation. All this I am compelled and ready to acknowledge, but still I am without an answer to my question, 'why has no decision been given respecting the analysis of my life?'"

Those softly penetrating, liquid eyes looked compassionately into my own as I pressed my point, and his silent lips grew into a lingering, patient smile.

"Were your ears heavy and your eyes holden that you did not hear and see the verdict?" he enquired almost in a whisper. "Or was it that such judgment was too divinely sweet to be entrusted to the outer senses? I have already told you that our proceedings are not marked by mechanical formality, hoping that, acting on that suggestion, you would look around and recognize the glorious recognition you received when the verdict was pronounced."

"When the verdict was pronounced?" I repeated with a gasp.

"Yes," and he smiled so indulgently. "But perhaps I am inclined to expect too much at a time when the birth-throes are making such a claim upon you."

"Why do you veil your speech in mysticism?" I pleaded. Will you not speak plainly?"

"I will endeavour to speak plainly," he answered with quiet deliberation after a brief silence, "but let me answer your first enquiry by a word of explanation. What you are pleased to call mysticism is the native language of the soul. That it is not understood by you is due to the fact that, so far, you have not been liberated from the final influences of the earth-you have not yet entered into the full freedom of the spirit. I mention this because you will presently be looking back in an endeavour to discover and trace the gradual progress by which you broke away from this bondage to the flesh, and the far-reaching effects by which the soul is followed into its new abode. My object in this respect has not been to mystify, but rather to instruct you.

"Now let me explain when and how the decision you seek was given. To understand this as clearly as I would like you to do so, I must ask you to bear in mind three points I have already explained. Life is essentially eternal, varying in its mode and scenes of manifestation, but in continuity it is indestructible; in its human expression, revelation has classed it allegorically as the stage of infancy; and, compatible with this condition, the only law the individual is responsible for observing is the one most natural to this stage-thou shalt love. Do you understand me so far?"

"Perfectly," I replied.

"That being so," Omra continued with measured deliberation, "all the mysticism of the vision's allegory vanishes from your understanding, and you will now be able to gather up its conclusions and see them in the light in which they appear to me. The vision did not cease at the instant you rushed to the rescue of the child. It carried the action forward to completion. You saved the boy, and recovered your consciousness to find him in your arms on the slopes. An illustration of the fact I affirm of the continuity of life. It had not experienced a break, but merely changed its scene of operation. The idea of death is altogether out of the question. I think this will explain to you why the vision was carried over."

"Yes, I can begin to see its purpose and meaning now."

"If that is so, there remains little more for me to say before 'the light that shineth in darkness' shall reveal to you the true finding of that analytical vision. I will again remind you of the two latter points I mentioned in reference to the earth-life-its infancy stage, and the solitary lesson it was expected to learn and apply. I am quite willing to share your opinion that, when that scene in Whitechapel was introduced into the vision, the analysis may have shown that a balance was due from you. If the decision had been given then, that decision might have been as in the case of the Babylonian monarch-'Thou art weighed in the balances and found wanting.' But God, being both just and merciful, it is not to be wondered at that He should concede that which a mortal would allow, and permit an act that was in progress when the fiat went forth, to be considered in the award. What was the value of that last effort you made? You apparently lost the analysis of it as presented in the vision.

"Let me tell you what the record was. You saw the child's danger! Instinctively you rushed to save it-was trampled down, and, together with the child, was crushed. What prompted the instinct to save? The carefully nurtured humanitarian habit of your life? This was so strong with you that the thought of your own safety never crossed your mind in your desire to save the child. In other words, you had so learned the lesson of your standard that it had become part of your life, constraining you to obey the command of the Christ: 'Follow me.' 'He gave Himself for us.' You did likewise when you laid not yours, but yourself, upon the altar of sacrifice in your desire to save that child. Thereby in losing your life you found it, and the dénouement of the vision-your waking as you did with the child still in your arms-is the award, 'Well done!'"

"But your explanation leaves me even more bewildered than the mystery itself," I gasped in an abandonment of surprise. "Do you mean me to understand that by a single unpremeditated act such as that, it is possible to reverse the effect of a life -say of careless indulgence?"

"I am not astonished at your surprise," Omra made reply, "though I may remind you that it is not the first you have had since your arrival. Surprises have been your constant companions since you met your old friend Helen, and now you are entering on a new environment-taking your place in a somewhat more advanced class in the schoolroom of life-and here, you will find them crowding even more thickly around you, until you are able to use the new faculties and powers with which you will find yourself endowed.

"I must, however, say one word in reference to what you call 'a single unpremeditated act' and its effect. You have yet to recognize and bear in mind that the brand of heresy is not necessarily an infallible guarantee of ungodliness. The Nazarene is the Field-Marshal of the army who wear that heresy mark of liberty. That one 'unpremeditated act' was not so foreign to your nature and daily life as you may imagine-it was rather the well matured harvest of a carefully cultivated sympathy you had encouraged for those who, like yourself, had experienced the hunger for an affection and companionship which was beyond their reach.

"To stretch out a helping hand, to give a sympathetic glance, to breathe a compassionate word, to help to bear a soul-crushing burden, came more naturally to you than you would be inclined to admit, but these unnoticed nothings of earth are carefully cherished and garnered here against the day when the Lord makes up His Jewels; they are precious assets which are laid up where moth and rust does not corrupt! Mustard seeds sown by the wayside-cups of water supplied to the fainting and the weary-grains of kindness thrown compassionately to the unknown and the outcast-tears of sympathy shed in secret which the Lord has preserved in His bottle for recognition and reward in the day of His reckoning. In the mass of heterogeneous miscellanies scattered along life's highway by heretics who were not considered worthy to be recognized by the so-called Church, your 'one unpremeditated act' will be found to be preserved, and the value at which heaven's experts will estimate it has been already indicated, when I tell you something you failed to recognize..."

"What is that?" I interrupted him to inquire, my soul aflame with wonder at the volubility of his findings of treasures hidden in the apparently barren fields of life.

"Surely there can be nothing more you have to reveal- nothing more that remains to be said!"

"So far I have but spoken of the seeds which have been sown by those labourers of 'whom the world was not worthy.' I have made no attempt to estimate the value of the harvest they shall reap in due time, whether it shall be thirty, sixty, or a hundredfold. I am interested just now in pointing out to you how justice values that 'one unpremeditated act' by which you threw off the physical and found admittance into the higher life. This was an instance where, in the losing of your life you found it, and the child you brought out with you was..."

"Was-yes," I gasped as he made a momentary pause.

"The child that stood on the greater pedestal in the prologue of your vision, whom you imagined to be the Christ child. 'Ye did it unto Me!'"

The announcement filled me with speechless amazement, and the silence broke into a benediction of revelation.

* * *

CHAPTER 7

OMRA'S FIRST LESSON

We had been moving leisurely hither and thither about the Court and its precincts while Omra had been thus discoursing. The beautiful balance of harmony which existed between the scene, the companionship and our communion, so fascinated me that more than once did I find myself wondering whether heaven itself could possess a more restful peace than I was then enjoying. I recalled Rael's assurance that the subtle charm of the Court would remain and draw me back again and again, even from the distant ages. I did not appreciate his meaning then, much as I felt the soothing influence of its initial caress, but I was beginning to understand what he meant more fully now. God does not display His court regalia in the unprotected windows of earth's marketplace to attract the cupidity of passing adventurers. He hides it deep in the secret of His presence where thieves do not break through and steal.

Omra knew well enough where the attractions lay, and we came across them one by one just as their lights were needed to illustrate some particular point he wished to make.

And as with the Court, so it was with my companion. It needed acquaintance to be able to appreciate his value. On first impressions, I spoke of him as another Myhanene. That was my ideal of an angel so far as my experience had carried me at the time; nor would I say that the comparison would fail me even now, had Myhanene's ministry continued through the scenes where Omra led me.

It would, perhaps, be helpful here for me to point out in what respect the ministry of Myhanene and his friends differed from that which Omra rendered and in doing so, I do not think I can do better than state my position in Paul's familiar allegory:

"We know that if our earthly house of this tabernacle were

dissolved, we have a building of God, a house not made with hands, eternal in the heavens, for in this we groan, earnestly desiring to be clothed upon with our house which is from heaven; if so be that being clothed we shall not be found naked. For we that are in this tabernacle do groan, being burdened; not that we would be unclothed, but clothed upon, that mortality might be swallowed up of life." (2 Cor. v, 1-4)

The Myhanene group of ministers discovered me just as the old tenement had fallen away. With wonderful kindness and infinite patience, they set to work to clear the site of all unnecessary, undesirable and foreign debris in anticipation of the new tabernacle that was to be erected under the superintendence of Omra. Many of the old foundations had to be removed, false limitations swept away, enlarged boundaries had to be ascertained, disqualifying conditions to be revised, and the new outlook to be determined in accordance with the true laws of life.

Omra's ministry commenced by ascertaining how far these drastic requirements had been complied with, the result being declared in accordance with the critical decision of the vision that had just been afforded me. That the result was found to be so far satisfactory as to allow Omra to proceed, scarcely needs to be recorded here.

Rael, the pioneer of my advanced teachers, had found me standing in uncertain wonder on the threshold of the Court, and with fraternal welcome, led me to await the coming of his chief. Omra, at once-even in his approach-inspired me with a sense of homeliness exceeding that which I experienced when I met Vaone. He led me at once into his rich treasury of knowledge, and proceeded to set before me a refreshing feast of good things for which I had long hungered. Shall I ever forget or cease to appreciate the delicate caution with which he began his ministry? How unostentatiously he broke a seal here, unlocked a mystery there, or, by some subtle magic, cleared some distant cloud away, as he wished me to catch a glimpse of problems I had to solve under his guidance, each as occasion arose.

He drew me nearer and nearer to him at each step as he led me down the soul-transforming corridor of the revelations he had to make. Like a super-physician, he foresaw an incipient need, aroused a hunger for the remedy and then supplied a superabundant feast.

It is impossible for me to speak of the pleasure with which I looked forward to the term I hoped to spend under such coveted tutelage.

But great as were the ever-increasing beauties of the Court-delightful as were the prospects of my association with Omra and his friends-I had before me a rising promise of something far surpassing either or both combined, if only the promise blossomed into fruition.

This consciousness of the hope dawned upon me during the watching of a very curious and mysterious coincidence. Usually, concentration of thought is necessary to trace a logical sequence or arrive at a clear understanding of such a matter as Omra had been expounding; but while he had been so engaged, I had not only been able to follow him with close attention, but at the same time to critically observe, admire and appreciate the numerous surprising beauties of our surroundings.

And more.

Below the horizon of this divided, though strangely complete consciousness, the superior light of another and more far-reaching dawn gave signs of rising. Another, an interior eye, was first awakening to discover that a new and yet unknown universe was in existence eastward in the boundless expanse of the soul's domain. As yet I could neither see the orb, nor the new creation it was destined to illumine, but the opening eye could catch the herald rays that darted in ever increasing brightness to break the long, lingering gloom of the region that is yet to be. A little longer, and those rays of glory would form a royal road over which my soul would pass and reach its rightful heritage as a son of God.

I knew it. I needed not that Omra should tell me. That awakening organ of vision was more than an eye-it was more than all the rudimentary faculties of sense combined-it was the true mirror of revelation that was to enable the oneship with the Christ that had just been born in me, to catch and reflect the image of our Father-God. A little while, a brief period of Omra's instructions as to how to use my newly-found faculty (for from hence all the senses are now merged and comprehended in one), a period of superintendence while I throw aside the hindrances that even now beset me-while the scars I have sustained in my battles and struggles are effaced-while I am being made ready for the position I have to fill-and then I shall be able to play my part in the grand orchestra of life, and thus glorify the God who created and called me into being.

"Omra," I gasped, "are you aware-do you understand?"

"I know," he quickly responded, drawing me just a little closer to himself. "Be not afraid. All is well."

"I am not afraid-except that in my ignorance I may be guilty of some inadvertence."

"Even those are excusable until the twilight has passed, and the unclouded light bathes your soul in its wonderful fullness."

His calmly sympathetic but unobtrusive presence was like a mountain of repose on which I rested in that eventful crisis. We seated ourselves on the basin of the fountain, and while I fell into a reverie over the lilies, Omra held communion with one and another of the friends who found him there. It was soon evident that I was not singular in valuing his companionship. Who, having once feasted at the table of his angelic generosity, as I was now permitted to do, would lightly wish to pass him by without a look, a smile, a word, a benediction? Ah! Happy state indeed where the azure skies of love are never shadowed by a passing cloud of doubt and the sun of loving-kindness marks the eternal noon of truth that is incorruptible!

Take heart, poor, weary, fainting, struggling, tempted, outcast soul. There is such a haven of repose awaiting thee on before. With your eyes blinded by tears, you may not now be able to behold it with your heart grown callous with the storms of deceit and betrayal through which you have fought your way, you may find it hard to believe it-soul-sick and faint by the vanishing of a thousand hopes, each but the mocking laughter of a mirage, you may feel that you have not strength to travel further-but take heart and make another effort.

I have travelled through the self-same wilderness-I have hungered and thirsted, limped, friendless, with bleeding feet, fainted and fallen by the way, been the sport of mocking cruelty, the jest of heartless buffoons, and the distracted shuttlecock of fate-but the night for me has ended.

The morning breaks. The dark, black, wilderness lies behind me now, and on before I see the land flowing with milk and honey-the homeland-the Father's house-the ring, the robe, the welcome that awaits thee also, only a little further on before. Take heart-dry your tears-just one more effort. Take heart!

In the course of my reverie I presently found myself wondering what the next step in my career would be. I am not conscious of its being more than a thought passing through my mind, and yet my lips may have responded to my thought and involuntarily uttered the words, since Omra turned at once to reply.

"When you are quite ready," he said with a significant gesture of leisurely consideration, as if anxious not to disturb me unnecessarily.

"When you are quite ready. I am absolutely at your disposal to assist you in getting into alignment with your new vocation."

In my eagerness to ascertain what my new duties were, I was on my feet before Omra had finished speaking.

"Shall we proceed at once?" I asked.

Omra smiled indulgently.

"Yes, there is no reason why we should not," but the deliberation with which he signified his acquiescence was in marked contrast to the vigorous verve of my suggestion. It contained no trace of a reproof-the half-veiled humour I caught in his askant look assured me of that-it was more an experiment to test how far I was able to use one of my newly-acquired powers by reading his mind as he had so recently given me an example of reading mine. Under similar circumstances, Myhanene would have laid a gently restraining hand on my arm, and said, "My brother, God never hurries." Omra gave the same intimation by his own significant code.

It was my first attempt to decipher such a message, but I evidently accomplished it with some degree of success.

"We will now turn our faces towards the gate," he suggested, and in an instant my impulsiveness would have cried, "And shall we go through?", but I was able to repress the enquiry just in time.

"We may approach, but you will find that you are not able to pass through the gate just yet."

"May I know wherein lies the inability?" I enquired. "The way is open and unobstructed-is it not?"

"Yes, the way is open and unobstructed, but you will discover that, for the present, you will lack the power and confidence to walk in the way. You are not yet master of the new powers you have received. You are not yet acquainted with their nature, purport and possibilities. How, then, can you be expected to use them with that conscious familiarity which is demanded of all who pass that gate?"

"Do you wish me to understand that heaven is not so accessible as I have been led to believe?" I enquired, perhaps, with a suggestion of anxiety.

Omra answered me with a glance of eloquent reassurance even before I had finished speaking.

"Not inaccessible-the Homeland can never be inaccessible," he replied, "but it is inviolably safe-guarded against the admission of all that is unworthy or unprepared. So absolutely is this enforced, that though you have been found worthy of admission you must needs tarry while you gain such command of your newly-acquired faculties as to enable you to make the entrance. That is why, when you asked me whether we were going through the gate..."

"The idea simply passed through my mind as you suggested turning in that direction," I ventured to suggest.

"I am fully aware of it, my brother," and the tone and look with which he replied assured me that I had rather pleased him than otherwise by my interruption. "I am fully aware of it, but you have now to discover that henceforth thought and speech are equally audible-it is one of the multitude of revelations you have now to become conscious of, and effectively learn to employ in the new sphere of life to which you are about to be introduced.

"When you raised the question of the gate, it at once became necessary that I should indicate the existence of reasons for some delay in reaching the consummation of your hope. In doing so, I had no design of exciting the very natural doubt you experienced, and I can easily make my reply to it the point from which I may proceed to introduce you to the studies you have now to undertake in order to equip you for your new mission."

"For my new mission?" I enquired.

"Yes. You have already elected to associate yourself with Myhanene's mission to earth. So far you have done this under certain restrictions owing to your lack of certain knowledge you will now be in a condition to acquire, and thereby widen the sphere of your influence. It is to this end that I am hoping to be of assistance to you. It was in relation to this work where the doubt arose in your mind while I spoke of the searching scrutiny in front of you before passing the gate. So we will begin with the consideration of the question of accessibility of heaven.

"Bearing in mind the object Myhanene has in view in his ministry, it would be well to take a brief glance backward in order to pick up and connect the idea of the continuity of life. The approach to heaven is made through the vestibule of mortality. 'There is a natural body, and there is a spiritual body ...Howbeit that was not first which is spiritual, but that which is natural, and afterward that which is spiritual.' The mortal stage in comparison with the everlastingness of life is Biblically compared (and when interpreted by its own key, the Bible is the only authority by which we may safely proceed), the mortal span is compared to the infancy stage of existence, the similes used to indicate its duration are a 'vapour,' or man's entrance and exit are likened to coming 'forth like a flower...he fleeth as a shadow'; the one lesson he is expected to learn and apply during the mortal span is that which is peculiarly natural to infancy- 'Thou shalt love'; and when he is old enough to enter school and begin to study the alphabet of being, the curriculum is strictly confined to allegories and parables."

"I do not wish to break the thread of your discourse," I ventured to say, but, if I may, I would like to ask a question in relation to the allegories you have several times referred to."

"I can well understand the thousand queries that are bubbling up in your active mind," Omra returned with a very pleasant touch of sympathetic forbearance. "You are like an enquiring child, fresh from the playroom, catching his first glimpse of a manufacturing hive-you wish to ask, all at once, the 'How?' 'Why?' 'Where?' and 'What?' of everything. But if we are to understand anything, we must confine our attention to one thing at a time and go slowly. The allegories will be reached presently, and will then be explained and interpreted so that their purpose and scope will be clearly understood, but for the moment, I have another reference to make to the infancy stage of existence.

"So far I have spoken of the compass of the mortal span of existence-life in the physical-in its comparative contrast with immortality. I have now to hint at-it is impossible to do more than offer a mere suggestion-the nature of the surroundings in which that nursery stage of existence is passed.

"In his physical aspect, man is the capstone and crown of creation-a thinking and reasoning animal-the instinct of the brute has evolved into a moral consciousness. But still, the physical man formed of dust of the ground, is of the earth earthy. 'Dust thou art, and unto dust shalt thou return,' because 'flesh and blood cannot inherit the kingdom of God.' But before this superb organism, so fearfully and wonderfully made, was dispensed with, the all-wise Creator had another and higher purpose for it to fulfil. The invisible, complex and mysterious forces which had been unfolding in and operating through this crowning glory of creation, were to be interblended with the breath, the spirit of the Divine-the mortal casket was to become the matrix in which a new race of sons of God should be moulded; and in the mortal man became enshrined a living eternal soul.

"For the production, nurturing, and protecting of this race of immortals through the primary stage of their existence, God, in His foreknowledge, had already fashioned and called into existence an earth and surrounding heaven, fitted and in every respect arranged to meet with and supply every requirement to ensure the purpose He had in mind. The earth and surrounding heaven were provided with every necessity and qualification for producing and conducting through its initial phase a race of beings who shall be worthy of its high calling.

"It is impossible for me here and now to do more than take this most cursory glance at the way by which you have approached the stage of life on which you are about to enter. You will have ample means and time at your disposal to make an exhaustive study of the whole subject presently, when you have finally broken away from the last effects and influences of the physical condition."

"The last effects of the physical condition!" I gasped in utter amazement "Why, surely, I did that long, long ago"

"No-that is where some of the greatest mistakes concerning the nature of the spiritual life are made," Omra made answer; "and the great object I have had in taking this retrospective view has been to remove this misconception.

"Let me now, as far as possible, drop the use of metaphor and try to make you understand something of the position in which you at present stand. But in attempting to do this, I shall be driven to the use of illustration in order that you may grasp my meaning. I will take a common case that will reduce my difficulty to a minimum. In the physical, a person suffering from a zymotic disease, after the malady has been combated and conquered, the patient has to be most carefully isolated to avoid spreading the contagion."

"That I perfectly understand," I answered, as Omra made a

significant pause.

"Sin, disobedience, and wrong-doing are among what I may call the zymotic diseases of the soul, and if mankind, who at best are only in an infantile stage of being, find the necessity of isolation in such cases, should it surprise you that a state of quarantine should be established here?

"That precaution is rigorously taken where you are now standing. Convalescents from the flesh may come so far-then comes the analytical examination to which you have been subjected. Yonder is the gate admitting to the confines of the city of life eternal, but, "-and here Omra spoke with a deliberate and measured emphasis-" 'there shall in no wise enter into it anything that defileth, either whatsoever worketh abomination, or maketh a lie; but they which are written in the Lamb's book of life.' (Rev. xxi, 27) 'Blessed are they that do His commandments, that they may have right to the tree of life, and may enter in through the gates into the city; for without are dogs, and sorcerers, and whoremongers, and murderers and idolaters, and whosoever loveth and maketh a lie.' (Rev. xxii, 14-15) The great line of demarcation is not drawn at the laying down of the physical body at the barrier beyond which neither medical nor theological practitioner can be of further avail. But the loving-kindness and tender mercy of God are still available through the regime-of correction, it may be-certainly through convalescence and quarantine the more effectual ministrations of God's truly ordained assistants are available-as you yourself have experienced-to guide and direct you hither.

"Thus far but no farther. Here all that is of the earth must be laid down-'flesh and blood cannot inherit the kingdom of God.' Now, in order to pass, 'Ye must be born again.' The in-breathed God can no longer lie concealed in its casket-the angel must be divorced from the human-then, and then only, when your name has been recorded in the Lamb's book of life, will you have the right-the power-to pass through the gate into the kingdom.

"The period you are now closing, with all its irksome limitations, futilities, mysteries and incapacities, has not been life as you imagined; it was only the gestatory period of the life everlasting upon which you are now about to enter as you reach the precincts of the gate.

* * *

CHAPTER 8

I MEET WALLOO-MALIE

There were fifty questions arising out of what Omra had been saying that I wished to ask, but since he had told me that he was simply glancing at the way by which I had come so far, and also assured me that an opportunity would come for me to study the whole course in detail, I restrained my desire until that more convenient season should arrive. Much that he said I had heard before from others, but each one had his own way of putting things, and each, according to his own point of view, gave more or less colouring or emphasis to one or another detail, so as to give a freshness and value to each and every exposition. Still, these variations were never suggestive of contradiction. In no sense were they opposed. If they were not in unison, they were perfectly harmonious, and each new note only added more volume to the choral effect. More noticeably so was the deep, clear, resonant, but unimpassioned statement I had just heard from Omra.

The one subject to which he had closely confined his remarks, others had treated in a somewhat superficial manner, but it had now been placed before me as a foundation fact upon which the whole superstructure of the life everlasting rested. And though he refused to be drawn away from his theme, in all he had said he never professed to be doing more than glancing at an outline of his subject. What, then, would a full and explicit discussion of the question mean? Two very important thoughts relative to this, I very much desired to ask about, but he brought his observations to a close, somewhat abruptly, and the consciousness of it led me to restrain my desire, in deference to what I felt to be his wish.

In our communion we had drawn near to the upper end of the Court, where we stood looking across a most entrancing landscape towards the gate which lay, perhaps, half a mile away. Atmosphere, light, colour, perfume, everything combined to make an ideal prospect in which, for once, the presence of visitors seemed to add a final touch of perfection.

I can well imagine it might have been some such scene upon which the eye of Baxter fell, giving him the first suggestion of the Plains of Heaven, and in his sleep the genius of dreams filled in the wondrous details.

But this was no dream. I had long since bade farewell to sleep. Had not Omra told me in very surety that yonder gate was the entrance into the Homeland? Was not this the sacredly-appointed trysting place to which tear-dimmed eyes have looked uncertainly forward, and where broken hearts would have covenanted to meet; had not that icy grip suffocated speech as we slipped into the arms of the long silence? Yes, this was the place of the great reunion! No wonder it was bright and happy and vibrant with music that was more than sacred-Divine! The whole environment was peace; the atmosphere instinct with strength. The unconventional freedom that was everywhere observable among the company before me was eloquent with fraternity; age, care, sorrow, doubt, sickness, weakness, and all the usual undesirables of the flesh were obvious by their absence, for every soul displayed the full vigour and beauty of dawning maturity.

It was in the observation of this fact that I discovered another wonder. I had always been more or less familiar with the idea of types of beauty, but the possibility of its almost infinite variety had never been even suggested to me before; I saw and understood it now, and why should it not be that beauty is as capable of diversity as ugliness?

The comparison was suggested to me by the presence of one who first attracted my attention by the peculiarity of the robe he wore. Not that it was assertively distinctive; on the other hand, its delicate tones were as if it modestly shrank from observation, but at the first recognition of it, my memory recalled what had been written of One who once would have humbled and made Himself of no reputation, but "He could not be hid" (Mark vii, 24).

History repeats itself in the case before me. In a casual glance he vesture had somewhat tile colouring of a deep creamy pearl, but a closer scrutiny revealed its strikingly unique character. It throbbed with a shimmering iridescence of colours of which I neither knew the name nor description, but the delicate modesty with which they manifested their existence blended exquisitely with the condescending grace of their princely wearer. There was no danger of his being lost in a crowd-his exalted rank needed no frigid isolation or hauteur to proclaim it; he could afford to be, and was genuinely lavish in his urbane companionship. Yet he was essentially a prince among his peers, even in that exclusive gathering.

As I contemplated the varied aspects of the scene before me, it seemed to be so wondrously idealistic-so perfect in every feature and detail-so far beyond any realization I had ever known, that I was tempted to doubt its reality; found myself questioning whether it was not a vision which had burst upon me, a vision which would just as suddenly disappear.

The doubt presently took such possession of me that I determined to refer it to Omra who evidently did not wish to disturb or interrupt my musing.

"I am in a quandary," I said, scarcely knowing how to tell him what my difficulty was. "Will you help me to clear up a doubt?"

He turned his large brown eyes upon me with a benignant smile.

"I know-I understand," he replied encouragingly. "But it will help you more if I let you frame the difficulty in your own way."

"It is something of a relief to know that you regard it in the light of a difficulty," I answered. "But-well, to put it briefly. Is all this a reality or only a vision that will presently fade away?"

"What makes you doubt its reality?"

"Well-because-I wish I could find the words to express what I feel. I could understand it if it simply impressed me with a feeling of home and reunion, and left me to enter into the full enjoyment of it as a member of such a highly-favoured family. But it does not stop there. It is too much. It is all I could desire it to be, and a thousand times more, until the fullness of it comes upon me with all the force of a tidal wave and carries me, I know not where. That is why I ask-is it a reality or a dream?"

"You have expressed yourself splendidly," Omra declared as he took me by the arm and led me forward into the slightly-rolling plain. "The superabundant sense of homeliness which you mention is the great attraction I have already spoken of, which makes this place a rendezvous where souls of every rank in the heavenly hierarchy are continually to be met and communed with. But beyond this stupendous advantage, there is also a personal matter of importance which we must not miss, since it constitutes the chief feature of the incident. In the transition of the second birth, you must naturally come into possession of higher faculties adapted to the requirements of the eternal condition. For instance, the doubt you feel as to the reality of this experience is due to the fact that you have arrived at a conclusion without being compelled to reason the process; or, as we should put it, Revelation has assumed authority and Reason henceforth occupies the subordinate position. Grasp that interpretation and accustom yourself to obey the higher power, then there will be no further room for doubt."

"Oh, that the way to act upon your advice were revealed to me now!" I cried with ardent longing.

"Have a little patience. When once the vanguard ray breaks through the darkness the morning glory is not far away," responded Omra.

"You mentioned the coming here of members of the higher hierarchy. I have noticed a most attractive and commanding personage, clad in a robe of most unusual tints, moving among the varied groups. Is it possible that he may be such a one?"

"Yes. It is Walloo-Malie. There are two circles between this and his own. His has been a very remarkable career. In his earth life he sounded the deeper depths of sorrow with a heavy plummet, which has qualified him in a special manner to minister to souls who stand in dire extremity."

"Is he ...?" Then I stopped myself, astounded at the audacity of the question I was about to put.

Omra gave me a humorous but encouraging smile.

"Yes?-is he?"-he queried.

"The thought of my presumption stopped me, or I was going to ask if it were difficult to approach him."

"From your observation of his movements would you imagine it to be difficult?"

"Not in the least. In my eagerness perhaps I was- "

"Hoping to exchange a word with him," Omra came to my relief by suggesting. "Well, that may be easily accomplished."

It was-more readily than I imagined, for Omra had scarcely uttered the words before I was greeted by a kindly hand laid on my shoulder from behind, and a most musical voice saying:

"So we meet again, Aphraar; and, I hope, under more happy circumstances than before."

"Again?" I asked in blankest astonishment.

But before I had spoken-before I had time to face him, he had turned aside and was speaking to one passing on the other side.

"Ah, my brother Cresvone, and so you have found your way so far from the midnight of your Gethsemane towards seeing the sun rise over the hill of Zion. I will speak with you presently. I am most anxious that you should hear and appreciate the sweetness of the music breathed by those cypress trees, as you would enjoy it now that the sob of your agony is over."

"Shall I wait for you?" enquired the friend.

"Yes, do."

Then Walloo-Malie turned to me with as calm a look as if he had been all attention to my response.

"Of course I said 'again!' Has Peter Stone, the Putney boatman, been quite forgotten? Has the memory of Clarice faded into forgetfulness?"

The quite deliberate enquiry was made with a most searching look, but it was marked by more persuasive sympathy than accusation.

"Do you seek to open that old wound again" I asked, wondering at the drift of the strange questioning.

"Is it still a wound?" he queried with a curious smile, as of astonishment. If so, I can scarcely understand your presence here. And, were it even so, I would only re-open it to pour in oil and wine. Did you not hear what I said to our brother Cresvone about the music of the cypress trees? In case I found upon you even the scar of that wound, I would ask you to come with us thither and hear how that one-time dirge of agony has now become a song of soul-inspiring thanksgiving. But you have already heard the thrilling rapture of its strains."

He avoided any difficulty as to my reply by instantly and adroitly addressing himself to Omra.

"Aphraar, or Frederic as it was then, had just discovered his heartless desertion by one who was more to him then, than life itself, and came to the conclusion that the cross were too heavy for him to bear. He staggered beneath it to the river side. But I was on duty there that day; we had a talk during which the burden grew so much lighter that he promised to try and bear it, and I think he has bravely succeeded."

Then, turning back to me, he continued; "I think it was about two months after this that you met poor Philip Ranger, sadly in need of a friend, down in Whitechapel, and in helping him you had an introduction to the Little Bethel where you found a congenial sphere of labour among the helpless, erring and fallen."

"Was it as much as two months after?" I enquired. "I thought it was scarcely half so long."

"Ah!" he responded, with a smile that carried a world of sympathetic meaning. "The cross must have grown lighter to allow the time to slip by so quickly. Yes; it was a day or two over the two months, before our second meeting."

"'Our second meeting'?" I re-echoed with incredulous astonishment.

"What do you mean? Surely you would not insinuate..."

"No, my brother, I need not insinuate anything. The time has arrived when I may boldly declare-when the veil may be lifted that you, in looking back, may be able to understand some of the mysteries in which your earthly pilgrimage was occasionally enveloped, and recognize now, all unknown and unsuspected, 'God has given His angels charge concerning thee' to keep and guide thee on the homeward way. You read and believe that such a ministry was in operation in the patriarchal day; you profess to believe in an unchangeable God, who is the 'same yesterday, to-day, and for ever,' and yet your teachers tell you this all-important ministry has long since ceased. It is no wonder that the mysterious burdens of life grow too grievous to be borne. The need for our ministry, under the circumstances, is greater now than ever before, and it is still as available as ever.

"Your desertion by Clarice was due to no sin or shortcoming of your own. In the sight of heaven you esteemed her above your own life, which you would have gladly laid down in your loyalty when you lost her. Such fidelity is far too rare to be lightly dispensed with among the sons of men; therefore when you went to lay your sacrifice on the altar, the saving ministry of Moriah-where Abraham would have offered Isaac-was called into operation, and I was the boatman sent to your deliverance. But the work was only half-completed when I bade you Godspeed at Putney. The worker thus preserved from destruction had still to be directed to a field of labour where his talent and fidelity could be employed in the Master's vineyard, and when the opportunity offered again, following in the Master's footsteps, I took on 'another form,' so that in the guise of Philip Ranger I could introduce you to a field where the labourers were few and badly needed. In that sphere you have been as faithful to God and your fellows as you would have been to Clarice.

"You are another seal added to my ministry for the Master-that is why I am here to greet you now. The fruit of your own labours and the bouquet of souls you have gathered from that mission as your offering at the dear Master's feet will be shown to you presently. But even now your work is not complete. You have voluntarily associated yourself with Myhanene's mission, and are returning to earth in a desire to do for others that which I have been entrusted to carry out for you. May our Father, God, make you equally successful. Only be as faithful in this as in your former sphere, then great will be your reward. But I have here a special case in which I would ask your sympathy and assistance, if I may. I am speaking of poor Clarice."

I started with surprise, but he took no notice and went earnestly forward. "She was but a moth, and then not a rare one. She saw a mate with brilliant colouring, which she wished to make her own. She was burnt fearfully; fell into a labyrinth of trouble from which she can find no way out. Will you go to her? You will be able to do for her by your forgiveness and sympathy in return for her perfidy, far more towards redemption than any other soul I know. Will you go?"

"If you think I am capable of helping her, there is no service I would rather be entrusted with," I answered, but I felt doubtful-very doubtful of my success.

"All I need is to know your willingness to go; God will undertake the rest with such a minister."

With this he turned, moved away to join Cresvone, and was gone.

* * *

CHAPTER 9

FAITH'S SUPREME TEST

My eyes followed Walloo-Malie longingly, almost enviously, as he went on his way; and yet why did I wish that he had remained? Had he not fed me bountifully; had he not given me food for thought and meditation, like the overpowering effect of the scene of which he formed a part, and constrained me to appeal to Omra as to its reality, because of its overflowing fulness? Had he remained striking other chords on the harp of memory, entrusting me with other commissions in the Master's service; would he not have overloaded me with the result that something would be lost? How thoughtful of him; how superlatively kind thus to consider my capacity.

He had shown me a single instance of divine intervention on my own behalf, working through the medium of his personal ministry, with a suggestion of the result thereof which I should presently behold. For his illustrations, he had taken hold of the darkest disaster of my life, then rending the mysterious veil which had enshrouded it, had made it clear that the Divine hand had so overruled the catastrophe as to make it to be the progenitor of life's crowning blessing. He had taken the insignificant mustard seed of an apparently chance meeting and demonstrated how, in God's providence, it had blossomed into an ark of salvation which had borne my own soul to the heavenly heights of the Ararat on which he had found me. Then-oh, most faithful and loving disciple of Him, who was "the Way, the Truth, and the Life" with matchless skill and Godlike force he pointed out the application, "Go thou and do likewise!"

So far, the miracle of grace was only half-complete. Were there not two souls involved in the wreck from which he had rescued me? The other,-whose perfidy had been the occasion of the disaster, was still battling with the fury of the storm- helpless, bruised, despairing! Was her soul not of equal value to the God who gave it as my own? To leave her to her fate would be to make myself a partaker of her sin. She had done wrong to me, but God had intervened for my salvation; ought I not now to offer myself as the agent of God's saving grace to her, and in the forgiving outreach of my hand perform my part in the completion of the miracle as a manifestation of the love that never faileth?

So did I muse as I watched Walloo-Malie and Cresvone passing leisurely into the distance. With the recognition of their going, I could almost hear the indefatigable angel as he cast the life-giving seed of some appropriate germ into that other soil, and I thought how like a God is the method and fascination of his teaching. Then I recalled a favourite passage from Shakespeare over which I had often pondered, beautiful in its sentiment, while irritating to me in its theological interpretation; but in the light of what I had just heard, it came back to me in a better and far more accepting aspect:

> *Why, all the souls that were forfeit once;*
> *And He that might the vantage best have took*
> *Found out the remedy. How would you be,*
> *If He, which is the top of judgment, should*
> *But judge you as you are? O, think on that;*
> *And mercy then will breathe within your lips,*
> *Like man new made.*

It is not among the least of the advantages of this larger life that, when one desires to retire within himself for such meditation, as I had now been enjoying, the mood is always noted and never disturbed. In Omra's superior station, of course, my wish would be more clearly known than to myself, so that he allowed my thoughts to run their course, and only when it was evident that they had taken a turn, did he venture to speak.

"Well, and have you been able to decide the question for yourself?" he enquired pleasantly.

"What was the question?" I asked, not quite certain as to what he referred.

"Whether Walloo-Malie is approachable," he answered, leaving the enquiry significantly incomplete.

"You must forgive me," I replied apologetically. "I might- I ought to have known from the experience I have already gathered, that no one who is unapproachable could be found in these latitudes."

"There is nothing to forgive, my dear Aphraar. Everyone you see around you; everyone you will meet with as you pass onward, has travelled by the self-same way that you have come; has learned as you are learning; has asked as you are asking. The impress of our own ignorance is clearly made upon the memory of each of us, and the recollection of it helps to make us considerate of those we are permitted to assist."

"'Permitted to assist'. There again is breathed that spirit of unlimited generosity which I find in almost prodigal profusion at every step I take. I have seen it, watched it, and been perplexed by it from the first conscious instant of my arrival and the question I have asked myself again and again is whether it is not possible to carry this practice of generosity beyond all reasonable limits? I am speaking purely in the light of reciprocal obligations. Take my own case, for instance. Look at all the attention, advantages, and consideration I have received, not only since my arrival on this side, but Walloo-Malie has begun to carry the account back into the days of the flesh, and while I am wondering to what extent it will be continued, I almost tremble as I ask myself how my obligation is going to be discharged. Do you understand what I mean?"

"Perfectly, and I should like to answer you by quoting one of the analogies used by the Master to illustrate the case, but at present I have not been able to explain the use, purpose and extent to which analogies are to be carried, therefore I will meet your enquiry by a more personal illustration furnished by Walloo-Malie. In the extremity of your own need, Walloo-Malie received a commission to assume a mortal resurrection body in order to save you from the result of the aberration of despair. He succeeded. What has resulted? I will confine myself to the one case which you are already familiar with-that of Helen. Your ministry to her saved her from a far worse fate than a death by drowning, when you come to remember the value the dear Master attaches to the soul-'What shall a man give in exchange for his soul?' Bear in mind, I am not taking into consideration any other work you may have done after the rescue I have spoken of-that work has not yet been made manifest to you-but when Helen's case is placed to the contra account of your own indebtedness, how much have you yet to pay to discharge the balance?"

"That goes a long way towards clearing my difficulty, but at the same time it suggests another I should like to hear you explain."

"And that is ...?" he enquired.

"Would not such an interpretation on earth foster the idea that every man is his own Saviour?"

Omra looked at me with a most indulgent smile.

"What a triumph it would be for truth if the world could get through the dust and debris of theological invention and reach the native bed-rock of revealed truth," he answered more in a meditative tone than as if desirous to destroy a fallacy. "It stands sadly in need of being led back to the original rock from which we were hewn-and that rock was Christ'. He is 'the way, the truth, and the life'; the way all must walk, the truth all must follow, the life all must live, the great Example all must imitate and copy. It is not enough to believe-'the devils believe and tremble'-but they who are saved 'work out (their) own salvation with fear and trembling'.

"When the flesh fails them at the time of the great unclothing, they make the discovery that only 'their works do follow them'; then 'whatsoever a man soweth that shall he also reap, he that soweth to the flesh, shall, of the flesh reap corruption; but he that soweth to the spirit, shall, of the spirit reap life everlasting.' Work, toil, sorrow, anxiety, doubt-almost despair sometimes, contending against the un-numbered forces and enemies peculiar to the agricultural life. Work, work, work-ploughing and sowing in the spring; watching and expectantly tending through the summer; reaping the harvest in the autumn, some thirty, some sixty, and some a hundredfold'. But what of the man who followed the self elected teachers, simply believed? You will find him outside with the cautious miser who hid his talent in the field, bemoaning his fate.

"So it was that the beloved John saw it-'And I saw the, dead, small and great, stand before God; and the books were opened...and the dead were judged out of those things which were written in the books, according to their works.' "(Rev. xx, 12) Then, rousing himself to a recognition of my presence, as it were, he concluded-"That being so let us take heed to ourselves, as 'workers together with God', that we may allow no opportunity to slip by; no open door to close; no hungry soul to turn away until we have faithfully discharged the obligation which has been laid upon us. That is the one great lesson you have to learn here at the gate."

"Here at the gate?" I re-echoed, almost forgetting the value of his exposition, in the now familiar mysticism by which he closed one subject and opened the door of enquiry into another.

"Yes," he replied, still wearing his indulgent smile, which appeared to be almost a resident feature of his placid, olive-coloured face, "I have to be more insistent than I would, because there is so much that might be said, so much that one in your position wishes to know in relation to everything we meet with, while there is also so much that is absolutely essential for you to accomplish in order to pass the gate, that I must pass the non-essentials with but a cursory notice in order that the necessary ones must have the attention they demand. It is for this reason alone, I thus remind you that we must pass along."

"And I am afraid that I am a very laggard companion, when I am tempted by such a plethora of treasures."

"But even then I must hold myself responsible for counselling you," he insisted.

"Will you then explain to me the significance and importance you attach to the gate?" I asked.

"I have already mentioned how it marks a line of demarcation beyond which nothing unworthy is permitted to pass. This provision is rigorously carried out by a system of defence which, although undiscovered by yourself as yet, lies between ourselves and the gate, over which it is absolutely impossible for an ineligible to pass."

"That seems almost incredible," I answered as I critically searched every foot of ground I could see between us and the gate.

"You will see it presently, and when you do come to it, you will understand how incomparably God protects the boundaries of His domain from the invasion of the unready. In connection with the safeguarding of the spiritual domain, the precincts of the gate are made available for the guidance and assistance of all who would legitimately enter, and equally a safeguard against all who have no right, being void of the necessary qualifications for passing."

"Will you pardon me?" I appealed to my companion as, in the intensity of my desire to know; I came to a stand and laid my hand upon his arm.

"This surging of revelation-sometimes visible to my understanding, but often far beyond my comprehension-is growing too overpowering for me to sustain. I feel so entirely insufficient for it, that I want to shrink away into some retreat, where I may try to recover myself before it carries me away into a vortex of confusion from which I feel there will be no escape."

Again Omra met my perturbation with his calm, complaisant smile.

"There is no need for you to fear any untoward result arising from the experiences you are bound to encounter just here, nor need you give way to doubt because you do not fully understand any preliminaries to which your attention may be first directed. The ordeal you are approaching is the test of your faith or confidence, which exists in you towards the inviolable perfection of God. I would ask you to recall Paul's definition of faith, then, by a clear, calm acceptance of the standard raised, straighten yourself and touch the height victoriously-'Faith is the substance of things hoped for, the evidence of things not seen.'

God's ways are not altogether as man's ways, but if you will only recall the vision of the Court, you will see that mysteries are afterwards revealed.

"Walloo-Malie has also given you an instance of the same certainty, nor will you be asked to wait very long before you will be put in possession of the solution of this present mystery, as to how the unworthy find it an impossibility to pass that apparently undefended gate. I can understand and I do most ardently sympathize with the feeling of perturbation of which you speak. But for the brief space you are called upon to endure it, you may take whatever consolation may be derived from the knowledge that it is not peculiar to yourself, but is rather the common experience of every soul that passes this way. It is not natural, or intended that it should be so; it is due entirely to the false credentials, instructions, and advices which are carried hither from unauthorized agents by too-confiding travellers. Every passport has to be presented, examined and vised before the bearer crosses this frontier; the why, the wherefore, and the eligibility of every person seeking admission has to be carefully ascertained; the manners, customs, and the laws governing the kingdom have to be declared and subscribed to; the freedom from taint and contagion, or disease, has to be satisfactorily established in each and every case before anyone is allowed to pass.

"This circumstantial examination is ignored, even denied, by the purveyors of denominational certificates on earth, who assure their patrons that membership in their fraternity avoids any further trouble and provides an immediate and abundant entrance into the kingdom. And though, in your own case, you could not conscientiously accept such assurances, you had largely imbibed the spirit of the idea, and even now the taint of it lingers over you, creating the confusion of which you speak. So potently abiding and deep seatedly ingrained are unsuspected inherited ideas found to be in the revealing powers of the light of the borderland, that not even the influences of the probation you have passed since you threw off the physical, has been sufficient to eradicate the final stain without which it is still impossible for you to reach the gate."

"I understood you to say that the decision of the vision's analysis indicated that I might?"

"And you understood me correctly. You have the right to enter as soon as you have lost the taint of doubt which at present would prevent you from carrying the right into effect. So very sensitively is the entrance to our inheritance balanced."

"I can scarcely comprehend the distinction you make. It almost seems to be drawn out to the attenuation of a quibble," I replied.

"But I can assure you that it is a very solid and stern reality. Let us go forward and put it to the test."

We quickened our pace and turned directly towards the gate. I have said that the ground had a slight undulating surface, and our course had an almost imperceptible rise. It was as we were reaching the top of this undulation that I began to understand the fullness of the force of Omra's statement.

Between ourselves and the gate there lay a yawning gulf, its depth lost in profound darkness, and its clear-cut sides as sheer as a wall. Its width might be something like a hundred yards- which I suggest simply to convey some idea of its dimensions- and at no place could I discern any bridge or means of crossing. I staggered with consternation at the first sight of it, and it was only after an interval, in which Omra went boldly 'forward and stood upon its brink, that I was able to accept his invitation, and the firm support of his hand, to go forward and look into the dismal void.

I looked with speechless awe and bewilderment upon the appalling chasm, then turned a questioning glance upon my guide. His face, now, had lost its usual smile. In the presence of that awful bulwark of protection against invasion, his magnanimous soul was too sensitive to the occasion to dream of the crushing victory he had achieved. In such a place, under such circumstances, any thought of elation would have been a profanity. It was a contrary thought that held his mind-the sense of the catastrophe that would crush any attempt at invasion. And, as I scanned his face, I could read an index of the depths in which his generous sympathy was moving.

Still, he had brought me to the spot to show me the reality of the distinction he had drawn, and he was too faithful to his duty to leave it undischarged. He accomplished his purpose with wonderfully inoffensive tact. He gave me a liberal allowance of time to investigate every feature before he ventured to address a word to me respecting what I thought, and when at last he did hazard a remark, it was to give me a most surprising bit of information.

"We are standing here upon the confines of one world, and looking across the chasm that divides us from another. They are related to each other as planet to planet, but they are just as separated as the planets are. Now, if you were required to pass from one to the other, how would you propose to accomplish it?"

It was in propounding this problem that he approached the explanation I myself was seeking.

"Has it to be crossed?" I enquired, at a loss to make any suggestion.

"It is the only way of reaching the gate," he replied.

"The only way that suggests itself to me would be to get someone to carry me over, as Myhanene once conveyed me to his home.

"That would not be allowed," he answered. "Whoever passes through yonder gate, must reach it by crossing the gulf on foot."

"But where is the convenience for so doing?" I enquired.

Then the familiar smile took possession of his face again.

"It is there now-a bridge across the chasm linking the two worlds together, but at present your eyes are holden that you may not see it. That is where your unreadiness exists of which I spoke. You have the right to pass over and enter, but you await the sight by which you will be able to cross. Let me try if I cannot help you to make out something of the connection between the two sides."

With this he placed his hands over my eyes for a few seconds and when he withdrew them I was able to distinguish a shadowy outline of a bridge as though it were constructed of the gossamer fibres of a wintry hoarfrost, and it appeared to be as dangerously unstable.

"Now can you see your way?" he asked.

"Would you venture yourself on that?"

Certainly, I have crossed it frequently. See, there are several friends about to come towards us from the other side! They show no sign of fear or trepidation. The sacred joy they find in their communion is not disturbed as they set their feet on what you imagine to be an unsubstantial structure. Their roadway might be across the solid shoulder of a granite mountain. See, they even venture to pause midway, lost in the sweet enjoyment of the theme which they discuss! They have no more consciousness of the yawning gulf beneath them than you had when Walloo-Malie held you spellbound by his speech. Now they move forward again, but not with haste as if to escape; 'tis rather the reluctant step of lovers who are not anxious to reach the end of their journey."

I watched the coming of that sauntering group of unalloyed happiness with a feeling dangerously near to envy. It was so clearly evident that they were moving under the indolent impulse of a blissful happiness that refused to be disturbed. In their wide and bright horizon there was not so much as a fleck of doubt, suspicion, care or risk to cause even a ripple on the bosom of their complacency; nor had need the semblance of authority to control their action.

"Tell me, my best of friends," I pleaded, in my intense yearning to acquire that which divided me from the enviable advantages these glorious immortals possessed, "what is it that holds me back and keeps me out of the inheritance they enjoy?"

"Confidence-faith that is securely set in love," Omra quietly responded.

"The passage of this gulf is faith's supreme test. As I have already told you-and the chasm confirms my words-in proceeding beyond this point, you break away from the very last thread of influence the flesh and the earth have upon you. So far the mental, moral, and even the physical habits of the earth have been able to follow and influence you, as for instance, the doubt of your ability to cross by this bridge. This must be removed here and faith will take its place. Here you have to learn how rigorously absolute the dictum of Job is carried out 'Naked came I out of my mother's womb, and naked shall I return' (i, 21). The last contention we have to combat here is one you will not put forward, because you have never learnt your sanction to any of the various orthodox religious sects. But every formal adherent to these institutions makes a firm stand to carry their tenets forward until we remind them that, 'whether there be prophecies, they shall fail; whether there be tongues, they shall cease, whether there be knowledge, it shall vanish away' (1 Cor. xiii, 8), 'for by grace are ye saved through faith; and that not of yourselves; it is the gift of God.' (Eph. ii, 8) It is for this gift that you are waiting. Your feet stand here before you are truly ready to receive it, and that because there is something more for you to learn before the call to cross the bridge can be heard.

* * *

CHAPTER 10

THE LIVING TEMPLE

Omra's hand was almost imperceptibly withdrawn from my arm, to creep round my waist in a gentle insinuation that we should move away, but every impulse of my soul was urging me to find some means to reach that other shore. Never before had I felt such an all-consuming desire as I had to reach that gate which stood so near and yet so far away.

Again the gentle pressure of Omra's intimation suggested our departure, but still my obedience was paralysed by the force of that irresistible attraction.

My companion waited for me with more than patience. He did not speak. The only argument he employed to induce me to yield to his suggestion, was the silent pressure of his compassionate sympathy. He himself had passed that way heretofore and he knew-he remembered-and being touched with the feeling of the same infirmity in the presence of a like occasion, his soul clave to mine in its reluctance to leave, even though he knew the better way to reach the goal.

We stood for a considerable time watching many passing to and fro over the now invisible bridge-for the power which Omra had loaned to me had now been withdrawn-but I was rooted to the spot as though I was part of the native rock which walled the gulf.

Presently Omra spoke to me, not with the voice of one glorying in the demonstration of an argumentative victory, but as a sympathetic teacher congratulating a pupil on the solution of a somewhat abstruse problem.

"Now you will be able to understand something of the impregnable nature of the bulwarks of the kingdom," he said.

"I understand," I replied laconically. There was much more I should like to have added, but something whispered that it would be inadvisable to do so just then. Instantly memory flew back to that striking scene which so interested me when I was standing on the Mount in the company of Eusemos, and again I watched the unsuccessful attempts of that resolute woman to travel one of those invisibly inaccessible roads, until at length I lost her in one of those dismal caves she had been so anxious to avoid. Again I listened to the explanation of Eusemos as to the constraining cause of her failure-she must needs go to her own.

In the light of what I had seen and heard since that incident occurred, I now understood his meaning in a newer, clearer, more forceful sense than I could then appreciate. There were points of likeness as well as difference in the comparison of her case with my present position; but the advantage seemed to be to myself, and especially when I remembered, in all who passed her by as she made her vain endeavour, 'there was not one who volunteered to give her a word of advice or direction, while I was favoured, not only by the advice and direction of a greater than Eusemos, but by his companionship to guide me in the way that I must go.

How could I go wrong or make a mistake? Why should I demur to follow where he proposed to lead? I answered him, "I understand", but how much more did I understand the next step my feet must take, than she comprehended at every turn she was self-compelled to take?

Omra again came to my relief with all the tender consideration of an elder brother, and in doing so I received another incidental reminder of the precise knowledge he had of whatever was passing through my mind.

"In attempting to institute an analogy," he said, as if we had already been discussing the subject, "you must be very careful not to try and carry the illustration beyond the particularly obvious point of resemblance. I will speak more fully of this directly, because the failure to observe this necessary rule is one of the great sources of ignorance and error you will have to combat in your mission to our brethren in the flesh. For the moment, I wish to make a personal application of the rule. In the comparison you are making between the woman you are thinking of, and yourself, there are certain points of resemblance, but they are very superficial and cannot be reasoned upon.

"For instance, both of you are unable to pass by a chosen route to a goal you desire to reach. So far the two cases are parallel; but directly you ask 'why you are each unable to proceed?' you find that you are divided as far as night and day. She, because of misdeeds for which she must first atone; you, because being found worthy, you have taken your stand in readiness, but your eager soul has been called upon to perform a preliminary duty before crossing, in learning that 'they too serve who only stand and wait!' Prompt response, obedience to the word of command, is the first sign of fidelity, whether that command be to go 'Forward' or 'Stand still,' and blessed are they who stand in such sympathetic relationship through love, that command and response work in automatic union, leaving the 'why?' for the future to reveal. Even the angel who stands in the very presence of God only knows in part, as he is commanded to 'Go!' When he reaches his destination, he may find further instructions awaiting him, but only after his return can he hope to know what the harvest of his commission has yielded.

"As for yourself, I counsel you to rest in the assurance of the 'Well done' you have already received, and try to wait with contented patience whatever commission may next be entrusted to you. Be it enough for you to know that The Great Architect of the universe has called you into existence, and brought you thus far to fill one spot in His superb design which cannot be occupied by any other soul in all His vast creation."

"Is that not fatalism?" I interjected, but instantly added, "Pardon me; I do not desire to controvert your affirmation, but I would be glad to hear how this predestined purpose can be harmonized with the contrary declaration of man's free will."

"There is no necessity for any excuse, my dear Aphraar," Omra replied with characteristic urbanity. "It is quite enough that there seems to be an inconsistency somewhere that needs to be cleared out of your way. To affect this clearance we will recall what I have already stated to be the starting-point of man's conscious eternal existence and in doing so, I wish to speak as a man, because it will be necessary to present it to you from that point of view. We have the authority of the Christ for speaking of the physical stage of existence as a state of infancy. Let us now add to this the reminder of the fact that God is 'our Father'; then we may go on to enquire what is the attitude of a parent towards a child who is not yet able to discern between the evil and the good. Is it one of arbitrary discipline, or one of sympathetic tolerance, so long as the child respects the authority of 'Yes' and 'No'? Here you have set before you the sphere of action, the scope, and the limitation of free will.

"We may even carry the figure to a more mature illustration if you will, and say the husbandman in the winter may determine and arrange for the sowing of his land in prospect of the coming harvest, but having once planted the seed he has renounced his free will, and is bound to reap the harvest of what is sown. The child, likewise-infancy gone-enters upon a school career, where the former leniency gives place to discipline, in order that he may be fitted to take his destined place among men. So, when you come to compare the imperfect regime of men with the perfect law of God, the former bears a shadowy resemblance to the latter. There is no conflict-the ascent to success is made through three stages-may, must, and will. In the flesh you have free will, and may do as you will within certain limits.

"When you throw off the flesh, you may enter upon a course of discipline demanded by the use you made of your free will; this discipline will be continued until all the dross, stain and contamination are purged away; all stubborn defiance broken down; until the remorse gives birth to repentance and the soul submits and cries for mercy. Then, purified by affliction, it will submit to the Father's guidance and presently reach this hallowed spot, and pass forward through the gate.

"If I have made myself understood in this, I think you will see your ogre of Fatalism drop his sombre garb and reveal the Father's welcome Messenger of Love."

"Yes. It is so. I always blush at my audacity in venturing to ask such a question as led to this, but in the end I am always more than glad by reason of the difficulties the answers clear away."

"Then let me advise you not to blush any more: though, let me tell you that the blush is only a sensation of earth, not yet relinquished. You cannot blush here," he said with a humorous glance. "But though you may not blush, continue to ask whenever you need information. When I myself am called into the higher circles, I find that I have more and more questions than it is needful for me to ask."

"I wish I knew some way in which I could do something to repay your amazing generosity. I am positively bewildered to think why I should receive such attention."

Omra laughed outright as he witnessed my discomfiture.

"Don't allow that to disturb you, my dear brother. However great your past obligation may be, it is always fully discharged by your asking the next question. You will scarcely be able to understand this at present, because it is one of the rules of the school you are about to enter, where it is provided that every soul shall feed upon the essence of that it furnishes to another. If you will think that over, you will see how that ensures that we give you of our best, and also how every enquiry you make affords us the opportunity of attaining to something better."

"That is beyond me. I will not try to answer it," I responded, for such an argument was far above my reach.

"Then I may return to that of which I was speaking that roused the idea of fatalism in your mind. I was assuring you that the Great Architect of the universe has called you into being and brought you so far on your way because He has a particular spot in His edifice which you, and only you, can fill. That being so, there is no reason for you to fear as to your being able to reach it. God 'will have all men to be saved' (1 Tim. ii, 4), and He, being omnipotent, is able to carry out His will. Rebellion may delay, but it cannot frustrate the Almighty's plan, so, in His own good time, the redemption shall be found to be as universal as the fall, and 'in Christ shall all be made alive' (1 Cor. xv, 22).

"Now, in this higher home of the soul into which you are waiting to be received, God is raising to Himself a glorious temple of the Church of Christ of which the Master Himself shall be the capstone. Think of it! He whom the teachers, preachers and priests of earth found not to be worthy to live, shall here be acclaimed of God, and 'mid the plaudits of heaven be set as the pinnacle of the seven-fold holy sanctuary of the Most High. You will understand how such must be 'a glorious Church, not having spot, or wrinkle, or any such thing, but that it should be holy and without blemish.' (Eph. v, 27) Built upon the foundation of the prophets and apostles, the whole structure raised of living stones quarried from east and west, and north and south, of 'every kindred, and tongue, and people and nation.' Who can anticipate the grandeur of its magnificence?

"Oh, who can picture the beauty and the splendour of that edifice when it shall be completed?-or who, on the other hand, can estimate the endurance of the agony those living stones have passed through in the shaping, dressing, and embellishment necessary to qualify them for the positions they hold! 'They were stoned, they were sawn asunder, were tempted, were slain with the sword; they wandered about in sheepskins, and goatskins-being destitute, afflicted, tormented'; others had trial of cruel mockings and scourgings, of bonds and imprisonments; other have been gathered from inhuman fields of torture; the rack, the fire, the lions, and every other fiendish device a counterfeit Church could invent, through which these heroes of the faith have boldly and triumphantly followed their Lord, and now they are glorified together with Him in the city of the Great King."

"And will all who follow Him be built into that wondrous temple?" I enquired.

"Not all. No! Only those who are found to be worthy of the supreme honour. But still there will be almost unlimited facilities for the employment of others in the furnishing and garnishing of the temple, and after that for all in the choirs and among the great multitudes who will worship Him therein. Sometimes the thought of that incomparable fabric takes possession of me, and I go away where I may indulge my soul in the contemplation as to what it will be like when the Master has given it its finishing touches, and the glory-light that plays about the throne shall shine upon it. I try to conjure up the vision until I lose it in the blaze of light that is radiated from its purity. I picture its myriad gems-souls of heroes, victors, saints, who have unflinchingly braved all the malicious powers of hell-the struggle over, the victory won, set as an aureole around the Bright and Burning Star, drinking in and reflecting His eternal glory for ever and for aye.

"Round about the walls pulsates with living mosaics of scenes through which He moved sowing the seeds of His kingdom as He sought for the lost and wandering sheep, or hunted for the unfortunate who had fallen into the hands of robbers by the way. Into all such masterpieces of love and forgiveness, I could see a mystic interblending of those who had chosen to follow Him in these rugged and briar-strewn paths. I have sat and watched with enraptured wonder how He will reproduce His Gethsemane there.

"It will reflect the darkness and the agony in richer and more suggestive colours, in which the far-off dawn will cast a prophetic tinge of a hope the heart of man has not yet dreamed of. Nor will He be there alone. I can see from out the vague and shadowy background, a vast procession marching towards Him to share and help Him to bear His agony. I hear their consecration prayer, like the music of a summer sea breaking upon the shore to the rhythmic throb, throb, throb of the bloody sweat- 'Father, Thy will be done!' And so, through all the roll of the ages, the great paean runs-Bethlehem, Nazareth, Jordan, Gethsemane, Calvary of the long ago caught up, linked and interblended with the New Jerusalem where 'the stone which the builders rejected...is become the head of the corner'."

"When I hear you speak with such feeling and enthusiasm of that which lies before us," I said with some hesitation, as Omra finished what seemed to be more of meditation than a reply, yet it admirably answered all I needed, "I can well understand that only a few-a very few-can ever hope to be included in such a sacred combination. Few indeed can hope to be found worthy, but blessed indeed will be they who are permitted to enter into that city and look upon the glorious vision."

"I am glad to hear you make that declaration, because it will help you to understand how absolutely impossible it is for the slightest taint or stain of earth to pass over the dividing gulf."

"That suggests to me another thought I would like to mention."

"You are wondering whether the gulf would have existed if sin had not been introduced into the world."

"Yes!"

"Yes. The breach does not exist because of sin; it is the natural division that lies between the flesh, matter and spirit. These two are as diverse from each other as light and darkness, and cannot be interblended. They may be connected by means of the bridge as light and darkness are linked together by means of the twilight. Had man not fallen from his first estate, the approach to the bridge would have been by a far more attractive route, which is even yet available but, alas! it is never used."

"Might it still be used?" I asked.

"Certainly. But existing circumstances make it almost impossible. It may, however, be made available for assistance."

"Will you tell me of it?"

"Yes. If you will come with me I will point it out and explain it more fully than you have yet been able to understand.

* * *

CHAPTER 11

MORE NEW FRIENDS

Omra's purpose was evidently not to be so promptly carried out as he had intended. I lifted my eyes to take another yearning look across the bridge, when I espied Eilele, Myhanene, and a group of other friends, known and unknown, coming as if to meet us.

Eilele and the sister she was conversing with at once came forward to meet me, while I reluctantly had to await their approach.

"May I hope that Dracine and I are the first to welcome you as you reach this favoured spot?" she enquired, thus introducing her companion.

"Scarcely the first," I replied. "Both Omra and Rael have already spent some time with me, and I have also had an interview with Walloo-Malie, which I shall never forget."

"Then you have indeed been fortunate to have found Walloo-Malie here on your arrival."

It was Dracine who answered me, taking both my hands in an impulsive outburst of welcome, contrasting markedly with Eilele's calm and self-contained greeting. Then, having so expressed herself, she turned to another of the company as yet unknown to me, and continued, "Tasha! Aphraar has been speaking with Walloo-Malie." Then, to me. "Did you not think him to be the most perfect reflection of the Divine love you have, so far, met with?"

"You need not ask that," Tasha made haste to reply.

"Did you ever meet with anyone who, having been in his company, has doubted it?"

"He certainly touched a depth of feeling in me that had never been stirred before, and drew my soul to him in a closer, more sacred bond than even Myhanene had," I replied.

"I can understand that," said Tasha, "perhaps better than most that know him, since it was my good fortune to be with him, have the charge of him in the days of the flesh, and the bands of affection which bound us together then have never been disturbed or weakened through all the intervening ages."

"Were you his sister?"

"No! I was his mother's slave-a fact that in itself declares the native magnanimity of his soul, which asserted itself so nobly as to lend to his barbaric nature almost an aureole of saintship."

"Was all the excellence found in Walloo-Malie?" I enquired, "or did he catch something of its beauty by reflection from Tasha."

"You are not the first to ask that question," Dracine was delightfully prompt to interject, "and as you know Tasha better, you will not be surprised to see what children such a foster-mother can give to the world."

"But you must carry your quest further back if you wish to discover its source," modestly suggested Tasha. "Had it not been for the treatment I received from La-yong-la's mother, I should not have been the nurse I was. So, in the end, the brightness of my life was but the reflex of what I saw in my queen-mistress, while all the beauty of La-yong-la's disposition came to him in his blood."

"Why do you call him La-yong-la?" I enquired.

"Because I was speaking of Walloo-Malie in his earth stage, when that was his name."

"Is it not somewhat confusing to use different names for the same individual?"

Myhanene, who had been speaking with Omra, joined us as I asked the question.

"Not in the least, my dear Aphraar," he replied. "On the other hand, it frequently saves much explanation when we are referring to any particular stage in a personal career. Even on earth you adopt titles to mark your social or political progress; why, then, should it be confusing for us to use a change of names to designate the stages we have passed. Here you will never find two persons bearing the same name, and yet we are all of one family, and it is possible for any one of us to be the possessor of at least ten names at different stages of our ascent, and yet in all the assembly of the universal family in heaven there will not be two souls in any condition who have borne the same name.

"You had one given to you when you arrived here; when you pass the bridge over the great divide you will change it for another, but in all the ages to come, when any reference is made to your experiences in this early school career, you will always be spoken of as Aphraar. So will Walloo-Malie. In his earth life he was La-Yong-la, but in the stages he has passed through here he has borne the names of Areta, Caerell, Walloo-Malie, by which we always speak of him here, but he has yet another name connected with a yet higher station, which name is never used except in what may be called an official capacity."

"May I know what he was and how long he has been here?"

"Nations, like individuals, are born, mature, and pass away, and Walloo-Malie is the child of a nation that has passed away and was lost before the foundations of Babylon and Chaldea were laid. A nomadic tribe of herdsmen had found a fruitful and congenial home in an upland valley among the Altai Mountains, where they discovered gold and stones which brought the small community almost untold wealth. Their home was in a secluded dale, where they were easily able to defend and hide themselves from whoever sought to discover their retreat or exploit their treasures. Under the successive control of a line of queen-mothers, the little community developed into a noble race of barbaric fraternity, until the reptile of envy crept into the royal circle, bringing ruin and devastation.

"Walloo-Malie was the only son of the last queen-mother, and the story of his sufferings under the diabolical machinations of his traitress relative has become one of the cherished classics of heaven. I would advise you to ask Tasha, at some convenient season, to tell you the story, for she is better acquainted with all its details than Walloo-Malie himself or his sister Vedrona. Yes, get Tasha to tell you the matchless epic, and you will at once understand the sacred veneration in which we hold Walloo-Malie." Then, turning to Tasha he went on; "Do you hear the ministry I am outlining for you, Tasha? I know it will be one of love, and so I have not much doubt but that you will generously perform it!"

"It is not the first time you have asked it, nor does it come upon me as a surprise," she answered with her vivacious winning smile. "So for your sake, as well as for my boy's, I will find some opportunity to do as you desire."

"I knew you would." he replied, "and I almost envy Aphraar hearing the story from such an authority, for the first time."

"How does it feel, Aphraar, to be swooped down upon and swallowed up by such a family circle without any consent or permission?" appealed Dracine as she thrust her hand through my arm and led me away.

"I am not at all disposed to offer any violent opposition to it." I returned.

"Do all new arrivals meet with such a reception?"

"I anticipate they do. It would be an absolute impossibility for anyone to reach the Court and cross the plains unattended. And every one of us has so many companions that it is not difficult to raise a party to extend a welcome. Myhanene mentioned to us, at Eilele's, that he was coming to meet you, and we all at once suggested that we should bear him company."

"But you did not know me."

"The more reason we should come to meet you since you were coming to join us. We are no longer strangers and foreigners to each other-not even fellow-citizens-but members of the self same family. If by reason of our wanderings, misunderstandings, or even reported death we have been isolated or forgotten, is that not still a more empathic cause for our rejoicing at the heralded return? Every addition to the family increases the volume of its happiness, and makes the glory of heaven just one degree more radiant. Hence, from its battlements, its bulwarks, and its towers, the innumerable multitude of the family who have reached the Homeland would cry, until the echo of the invitation should reverberate to the darkest corner of the lowest hell, 'We are waiting for your coming to make our joy complete!' We did not know you, but we know you now, and in that knowledge we have each discovered that heaven had a certain sweetness we had not tasted before. Come! Let us go back to the Court and again recount the treasures our Father has lavished upon us."

I shall make no attempt to record what took place in that memorable reunion. Such sacred festivals lie outside the boundaries of eloquence, have a wider horizon than imagination can scan, need the employment of more enthralling figures than poetry can devise, and the use of warmer colours than love has ever dreamed of before one would venture, even with unshod feet, to attempt to tell the story of the bread of life that was broken in that communion.

The record is immortally written on the walls of the holy of holies-the secret inner sanctuary of my soul, where none but God and myself can see to read it. So will the record of such a communion be written for you my brother, my sister, when your feet shall reach those hallowed precincts-when you shall be ready to bid your final farewell to the last influences of the earth-when by the gate you are able to meet the cherished kindred of your soul and receive their welcome home. You need not despair. That time must come for you as it had come for me, since 'God is no respecter of persons,' and 'He will have all men to be saved,' so that 'as in Adam all die, even so, in Christ, shall all be made alive again.'

When we had reached the Court, we disposed of ourselves in simple Arcadian abandon, and my interview with Walloo-Malie struck the keynote for the communion in which we so rapturously indulged to the accompaniment of a deep melody of thanksgiving. Almost every one had some reminiscence of interposition to relate in connection with that established ministry which needs not to rend, but just divides the tendrils of the veil that falls between the domain of the spirit and the flesh, as the screen of foliage hung between the compartments of the Court in which we were gathered. The universe of God is not a concourse of rival and antagonistic nations brought by conquest under the sway of a victorious sceptre.

It is the palace of a King in very truth, but every soul that passes across its threshold is a natural son or daughter of the Monarch who sits upon the throne. It is the residence of a single family, not the rendezvous of a conglomerate rabble. In the perfection of its arrangements it has, necessarily, provision for any and every demand that may be made to ensure the security of the home life which has been commanded by the King; but from the highest tower to the lowest basement, from the banquet hall to the nursery, from the audience chamber to the corrective cell, there exists no barrier to a free and open communication according to the direction of the Father.

There are still numbers of wayward, prodigal, self-willed and rebellious children who, taking advantage of their Father's great loving-kindness and tender mercy, have wandered into forbidden and defiant associations. After such, the unchanging Heart is ever yearning, and from the palace, messenger-members of the family have gone-are ever going east and west, and north and south, crying, "Come home! Come home!" and from mountain, sea, plain and city they are constantly returning, bringing one and another repentantly back. Nor will that Father's yearning cease until the last missing lad or wayward girl has been restored to the anxious breast.

This was one of the visions that passed before my mind as I listened to the recital of providential interpositions by one and another of those around me. Interpositions such as I had encountered, which had saved me from suicide at Putney, that had led me into a new walk and ministry at Whitechapel. Interpositions of gratitude in obedience to the impulse of the golden rule, such as had constrained me to break the silence of the grave and rush back again to earth to shout the blest evangel "There is no death", and tell how much better were even the approaches to the palace of the King, than had entered the heart of man to conceive.

Oh! that I had ten thousand voices that could cry with an echo that should never cease against the blasphemy of those who lie to men in their ignorance of the immutability of God in His dealing with men as Father, as they picture Him in His capacity as judge. Did He ever send a single angel, under any circumstances, back to earth upon any mission, no matter when or where or how-whether it was to save Hagar's child or to roll away a resurrection stone, does not matter-whether to eat Abraham's cutlets at Mamre or to destroy the cities of the plain, is of no consequence-I only ask, did an angel ever come back to earth with a commission from the beyond? Answer that. If so, "The thing that hath been, it is that which shall be; and that which is done is that which shall be done, and there is no new thing under the sun." (Eccles. i, 9) If you answer that you don't believe an angel ever did return, then I pray you to be honest and cease to prate about a resurrection. Better far to be an avowed agnostic than a wilfully blind hypocrite.

So ran my mind, in dual action, as I contrasted the confident assurance of the "blind leaders of the blind", with the testimonies of those who were around me, and I had scarcely reached my somewhat indignant conclusion when Eilele began to discourse upon the theme that had so moved me, but with a far more concise and trenchant enquiry than mine as she asked:

Know we the heavenly anthem
Soon as the organ rolls
Forth the symphonic prelude
That thrills our inmost souls?
Know we the noontide glory
When first the eye of day
Opens from night's deep slumber
Kissed by the vanguard ray?

Would you permit the novice
Who fails to find his way
From Alpha to Omega
Greek classics to inveigh?
The landsman, who is making
His nauseous trial trip-
Say, would you trust his knowledge
To navigate the ship?

And so, earth's mighty giants
Of intellect and mind
Are freshmen in the schoolroom
Which God of yore designed?
Imperfectly they master
The first two letters yet-
Philosophy and Science-
In His great alphabet.

How, knowing not two letters
Can they the volume read;
Or solve the hieroglyphics
Without a key to lead?
And, if the book defies you,
How can you comprehend
The sources of that wisdom
That Nature's volume penned?

Eilele's contribution to the testimonies that had gone before only served to change the key of my meditation. Or, perhaps, it would be more correct for me to say that she appeared to widen the cleavage of consciousness in my mind, so that I was able to follow two distinctly separate streams of thought, each with an added critical attention. I did not venture any attempt to analyse the strange phenomenon. I had enough to do to listen to the accompaniment she played, to the vision that was flooding my soul with a light that was expelling the shadows that had hitherto refused to vacate.

So far, in spite of all that had been said to me, there had been a lingering doubt, a failure to understand the drastic, almost vindictive prohibition with which any attempt to pass the gate was defended. Already several times had I been reminded that "there shall in no wise enter into it anything that defileth, neither whatsoever worketh abomination, or maketh a lie." Whenever I had heard it, it had seemed to me like an unnecessary going out to find some cause of objection which did not really exist, but in some curious and not very probable circumstances might come into existence; and the idea of it gave me a certain feeling of injustice, I vainly tried to get rid of. It recalled the uncontrollable feeling of aversion I had always felt towards God when I had read that command which Samuel gave to Saul, "Go and smite Amalek, and utterly destroy all that they have, and spare them not; but slay both man and woman, infant and suckling, ox and sheep, camel and ass." (1 Sam. xv, 3) Where was the justice of such a command that was reconcilable with everlasting loving-kindness?

The answer lay buried deep in the kernel, not in the outer shell of that command of the prophet. God is not only the only King who writes His dispatches in cypher, that they may not be understood by His enemies. For they who have eyes to see and ears to hear-equipments which are bestowed for loyalty, fidelity and valour-they are as a lamp to the feet and an unfailing guide through the Egyptian darkness, while to the enemy they are the snares and pitfalls which entice to destruction.

In the parting of that stream of consciousness, I was carried down the broad channel of revelation where the light of God shines to the elimination of the last shade of doubt. In that allegory of Saul and Samuel lay the mystery to the enemy of righteousness-the clear solution to the heirs of the kingdom. There the light shone upon my darkness, enabling me to read and understand. The Amalekites were a race who had sprung from the seduction of the sons of God by the daughters of men, who in their marauding expeditions had entered and remained in the land, promised to those over whom Saul had been made King. They had introduced their defilements into a land that was to be holy to Israel's God, and therefore, the command. The land must be purified, its atmosphere must be cleansed from the taint of leprosy, the last trace of contagion must be eliminated, the roots of epidemic must be plucked up and destroyed, not even a breath of contamination must remain within its borders.

The earthly Canaan was the antitype of the heavenly, hence the drastic command given by the unimpeachable wisdom of the King-"there shall in no wise enter into it anything" that is capable of producing or tempting to defilement.

I was pondering the revelation in a dream of profound thanksgiving when Dracine aroused me by asking:

"Have the influences of the Court been too much for you?"

"I should scarcely like to say that," I answered, making an ineffectual effort to recover myself. "I should rather suggest that at present I am scarcely strong enough to carry such a weight of glory, as Paul expresses it."

"Perhaps it would be well for you and I to take our contemplated trip while you recover yourself," Omra volunteered.

"I am by no means anxious to break up such a gathering, I can assure you," I replied.

"You need not think of that," Dracine assured me.

"Our reunions are not so easily disturbed. We are expecting Avita, and when he arrives, we shall be well provided for until your return, if you are thinking of coming back."

"Then we will rejoin you, so that we may cross the bridge together," Omra paused, and, not without a shade of reluctance on my part, we left that first communion in which I had been privileged to take part.

* * *

CHAPTER 12

DOES GOD ANSWER PRAYER?

We were nearing the end of the Court. Neither Omra nor myself had spoken since parting from our friends. How could we speak? The whole place seemed to be wrapped in the embrace of a "Hush" under which it felt like a sacrilege to attempt an utterance, even in the execution of a duty. I looked at my companion under the growing impulse of an awesome fear, but he only raised his hand with a gesture of silence, while he reduced his deliberate pace into a mere suspicion of movement. Then a breath of coral perfume trembled across the stillness, like the echo of a strain of music from the so-far-away as to vibrate in the depths of cognition with the sweet rapture of a fairy dream. Under the influence of its hypnotic constraint we stood, listening to the scarcely perceptible flowing crescendo that rose with the perfect movement of a cloudless dawning until the vocal and instrumental elements could be distinguished as some still invisible procession neared, and the words of the great anthem rolled in volumes through the Court with the proclamation that, "The path of the just is as a shining light, that shineth more and more unto the perfect day."

When the recession was accomplished, and my arrested powers released, my mind went back to the music which had once held me spellbound in that early Chorale. What a revelation was then made to me of the powers, influences and restorative possibilities of music, in comparison with the elementary ideas of it, with which the earth is acquainted. But now I had discovered that, in the Chorale, I had done no more than behold the phenomena of music; it had been reserved until I had entered "the general assembly and church of the first-born" on the threshold of heaven for me to discover and know what harmonies are laid up for the homecoming of the children of God in the sacred sanctuary of the soul of music, where all and every separate element of creation are brought together, purified, tuned, fitted, interwoven and interblended in accordance with the Great Composer's theme, then strung to concert-pitch to sound one chord of revelation, in which the Trinity of Heaven-Father, Love, and Home, will be unified in God.

As we left the Court, Omra turned in an oblique direction across the plain towards the gulf which enabled us to reach a delightful wilderness of flowering shrubs through which we wandered leisurely, catching an occasional glimpse of the precipice which lay on our left.

"What did you think of the prophetic benediction by which our departure was accompanied?" Omra asked me presently.

"I am almost afraid to venture an opinion," I replied hesitatingly.

"Revelation rolls over revelation with such an overpowering bewilderment that it requires more effort than I seem to possess to form any real conception of anything. I am something like a man surfing in a sea that defies you to keep your feet-I must leave my opinions until I am more at liberty to quietly review my experiences."

"And when you are thus able to review what now appears to be a chaos of turmoil," he answered in a calm but resolute confidence, "you will see that this seeming confusion has been governed to its minutest detail by a marked and most beautiful precision."

"I am, in a way, prepared for that, but is it not strange that the confidence I feel that it will be so, only helps to increase my perplexity?"

"No. It would rather be strange to me to find it otherwise." He responded with quiet encouragement. "You are somewhat in the position of a sensitively-strung pupil confronting his first lesson on an organ-the array of technicalities he has to master, the impossibility of his reaching such efficiency that eyes and fingers and feet may act in automatic conjunction to bring out every note of Handel's 'Hallelujah' which lies open before him, appals and makes him tremble at the thought. But if the lad has once been permitted to hear the music, the spirit that dwells in the organ sings to the soul she loves, the mastery of the technicalities will be forgotten-impossibilities will no longer exist-difficulties will take to themselves wings and fly away-his eyes, his fingers and his feet will no longer doubt their capabilities, and he will woo the invisible angel until the organ will reciprocate his soul's devotion, and sing to him songs sweeter than Mendelssohn ever heard or Handel in his rapture-dreams composed. So shall it be with you. But just now, you are in the transitional stage. Old things are passing away-all things are becoming new. Hitherto you have been dreaming-now you are waking up to what real life is to be, and you are not only perplexed, but absolutely astounded to discover that in your new life, the fundamental essentials of your past are not only unnecessary, but actually non-existent here. As a theory, you have been conversant with the formula that 'flesh and blood cannot inherit the kingdom of God', but the formula was nothing more than a theological phrase for the benefit of experts, and meaningless to the ordinary man in the world. When the rising sun of eternity banishes the vapour of mortality, the soul is startled to discover that with the discarding of the flesh and blood, the whole philosophical equipment of the wise has been cast aside with the non-essential debris; that the spirit works by means of a higher faculty than the brain-a reflecting mirror by which all truth is heliographically transmitted from the central sun and needs no intermediaries to interpret or translate it.

"Can you trace the analogy I would establish between yourself and the boy in front of the organ? But in that case I had to introduce an 'If', and in doing so, made the figure cease to serve my purpose; therefore I must change it in order to convey the lesson I desire you to learn. I said, 'If the lad has once been permitted to hear the music,' but that quality of uncertainty no longer applies to you. Like the wise men of another parable, you have seen the light-you have followed the star and coming to worship and adore, you have brought gold, frankincense, and myrrh to lay at the Saviour's feet, and the offering has been accepted and acknowledged. For the rest you need have no further concern. That misgiving does not arise from your unpreparedness to cross the bridge and enter in, but rather from the overwhelming sense of the magnitude of the inheritance into which you are entering. As soon as you are able to realize your joint-heirship with Christ in the kingdom, and feel that in Him 'all things are yours', you will have confidence to cross the bridge and enter upon your own."

While Omra had thus been speaking, we were wandering among an unspeakably entrancing floral display with that perfect appositeness which characterizes every detail of this higher life. This sense of completeness meets you at every turn-nothing lacking or out of place-nothing to be desired that is not immediately available-nothing available that you wish to dispense with or would change its location or rearrange. In this, as in every aspect of existence where the Creator's design has not been disturbed, one can always re-echo the Psalmist's avowal, "The law of the Lord is perfect, converting the soul." Not for the first time in my experience did I find it so as I listened to the soothing assurances of Omra, and when he ceased speaking, I stood still, with a feeling of gratitude I knew not how to express, and taking both his hands in a grip which I hope expressed more than my words, I said:

"And let me say that I hope one of those realizations will be the power to express how much I am indebted to you for all your patient forbearance in my weakness."

"Say no more of that, my brother," and in tone and returned pressure he was far more eloquent than in his words. "It is always pleasant to find one's services are appreciated, but let us say no more about it. In what I have done and said, I have been what I am-I am what God has made me; and if aught that I have done has been in any wise helpful, it is a testimony that God has not laboured upon me in vain. To him be all honour and glory."

"I shall not attempt to argue the point, much as I almost wish I might," I answered his self-repudiation in the matter. "But merely for the sake of information I would like to ask if this is not a case where it might be said that you are a 'worker together with God?"

"Not in the slightest degree!" came the prompt and definite reply.

"When occasion serves, in the review of my past, I shall be able to convince you that when I threw off the physical I was not wearing the aureole of a saint. My free will had been considerably exercised in the wrong direction, I can assure you."

"But do you forget that the earth life is only the infancy stage of existence?" I asked alertly.

"...in comparison with its everlastingness," he added as completing the sentence I had left unfinished-and he turned his eyes on me with a self-congratulatory gleam as he made the correction. "I have anticipated and watchfully waited for you to make that slip. I knew it must come, and did not wish it to occur when we were in the middle of another subject. It naturally raises the question as to how far parables, analogies, and allegories should be limited or pressed in their illustrative employment, because from a failure to be discreet in this direction, very many of the errors and misunderstandings of our friends on earth arise.

"In comparison with the endless duration of life, we are quite justified in using the figure employed by James (iv, 14) and asking, 'What is your life? It is even as a vapour, that appeareth for a little time, and then vanishes away.' Or we may use a more extended illustration, and say it is the infancy stage of being, when we link with duration the comparative amount of knowledge we can possibly acquire. In this aspect of life the mortal man is so circumscribed in his actual knowledge that the greatest of all the mysteries around him is himself. Nothing more vividly displays the impotence of the human intellect than this incontrovertible fact, for while it is impossible for a man to know himself, how can the predicate be logical that claims to comprehend that which is beyond him? It is from somewhere along the line of the recognition of this great truth that God regards the infancy stage of the race-it is here where He first reveals Himself in the character of Father. 'He knoweth our frame; He remembereth that we are dust,' and in his inviolable wisdom and justice, He adapts His requirements from man to the feebleness of the situation and says, 'Love one another! Do this and thou shalt live.'

"The mortal stage of existence viewed from such a standpoint, in comparison with the expansion and duration that is to follow, is very appropriately symbolized by the figure, a 'vapour' or a shadow.

"But in that Paternal command-'Love one another'-there lies the germ of another aspect of existence regarding which we have to institute a very different comparison. Here the scale of comparison and contrast is not the finite with the infinite, as in the previous case-not mortal with immortal-infancy with manhood-or ignorance with wisdom. In this wider aspect, we have a family living under a wise and loving Father whose wisdom, justice, and consideration may be carried forward from the previous illustration. The Parental rule of life is the very natural one-'Love one another,' to which is added an encouraging promise with the shadow of a sinister negative result for disobedience, 'Do this and thou shalt live.' Now, in watching the daily round of the nursery life, the judicious observer must be prepared to see the manifestation of every shade of infant idiosyncrasy, the immediate results of which, in many cases, are poignant, crushing, terrible-but with the kindly attention of the nurse, and a Fatherly kiss, the tempest is soon over and the incident forgotten by the sufferer. Not so the Father, whose rule of life has been disobeyed, and who has the future career of the sinner to consider and his own authority to uphold;-The sufferer may not be made aware-the occupants of the nursery may not be witnesses, but the offender has had to reap the harvest of the viciousness he sowed, and, in doing so, has learned that he cannot break a single law of his Father with impunity, and the remembrance of the penalty will not only save him from further disobedience, but will also inspire him with a filial love that will be stronger than the operation of any moral law.

"In my reference to this particular phase of life I have purposely confined myself to the use of the nursery term, though I wished you to remember that it embraces not only the natural span of three-score years and ten, but also the period of correction which follows the throwing off of the physical. I have adopted this course because, while it serves on the one hand to show that from the lower view, in comparison with the ambling gait of sorrow, the duration seems to be almost an eternity in passing, on the other hand, it emphasizes the view we take of it, and brings into glorious prominence the immutable loving-kindness and tender mercy of the Great Father of us all.

"If I have been half as successful in my explanation as I have desired to be, you will now be able to understand how very careful it is not to press figures of speech beyond the obvious limit for which they have legitimately been used."

"I can clearly appreciate the necessity for the distinction you point out, and can see at once where the neglect of it may be- and often is-a misleading and fruitful source of error. I am, however, especially grateful to you for the helpful light you have thrown on the Fatherhood of God in the retention of the nursery figure in the latter part of your remarks."

"That must appeal to you with more than usual forcefulness, because it is the view from which you will now regard it. It will have all the force of a new revelation breaking upon you."

"That is just how I feel it to be. There is, however, one point in relation to this that I am not clear about. It is in relation to the efficacy of prayer. We will retain the figure you have been using, and suppose a child has been disobedient. When the Father is about to administer correction-or anticipating that He will do so-suppose a nurse intercedes on behalf of the child. Christ promises that 'if ye shall ask anything in my name, I will do it' (John xiv, 14)."

"Yes," he answered, with marked deliberation, but there is a world of meaning and effect in the "If" with which the promise is prefaced. It is a condition too often so completely ignored as to be omitted altogether in connection with the covenants of God, and yet it is the only key that will open the door that leads to the desired fulfilment of the prayer. In this case it raises the question of the fidelity of the nurse. Let me repeat the same promise to you in its fuller form-"If ye abide in me, and my words abide in you, ye shall ask what ye will, and it shall be done unto you" (John xv, 7). To ask in his name is the equivalent of abiding in Him and His words abiding in us. Can you imagine one who stands in this relationship to Him, asking Him to abrogate or suspend His own law to save a contumacious child from correction? Would anyone having personal acquaintance with an earthly judge dare to do so to defeat the ends of justice? The difficulty in your mind is due to another confusion of the figure, which in this instance is out of place in the nursery, because no true nurse would feel it necessary to plead with the Father on account of a child, seeing that he would be both better informed and far more willing to forgive than the nurse would be. There is no need for intercession unless a law has been wilfully and deliberately broken, and the act was committed well knowing the punishment it incurred; or, to put it in another light-it is no use after a husbandman has sown oats to pray that he may reap wheat."

I had hoped that when started on this most important and very disputed subject, he would have gone on to a full exposition of it, a desire I was evidently destined not to have satisfied just now. It was not that I had any robust doubt about the efficacy of prayer in my own mind-I had never seriously faced the question in my earth life with a view of attempting to settle the matter either one way or the other. I had, more as a matter of habit than conviction, knelt down and said my prayers- occasionally when I thought about it, and had the time-but now it assumed a somewhat different aspect, and I wanted to hear Omra's method of dealing with one who was uncertain on the subject.

"Your reply is pregnant with suggestion," I replied, "but I was hoping it would lead you on to give an answer to the oft-repeated question, 'Does God really answer prayer?'

Omra's immediate answer was by one of those playfully

mischievious smiles I had seen so frequently on the face of Myhanene.

"Of course such a question would only be put on the earth side," he remarked, "and if it were put to me, I should reply by asking a question in return; 'If on entering a room you were to press the electric lever, would you obtain a light?'"

"Of course you would, if the installation was complete and the fittings in order," I answered. "How could it be otherwise?"

"Exactly! You see everything depends on the conditional 'If' I have already pointed out. Let me repeat the promise, 'If ye abide in me, and my words abide in you, ye shall ask what ye will, and it shall be done unto you.' Could anything be more clearly expressed?"

"But it is so very seldom that a direct answer can be traced," I urged.

"I know it, still no doubt exists as to Why it is so-there is no light in a disconnected electric bulb-there is no fruit on a branch that is broken from the vine-there is no reply from God to the cry of a soul that does not abide in Him. It need not be so. Find a consecrated soul, and ask him if God answers his prayers? Then let the earth ponder over his reply until it learns the meaning and significance of it."

It had not required a lengthy argument, but Omra was unanswerable.

* * *

CHAPTER 13

THE HEAVEN AND THE EARTH

Not the least of the consolations we enjoy in this higher life is the perfect freedom on which we enter from the limitations of time. Oh, the liberty, the relief, the rest, the rapturous satisfaction of the realization of it. All that partakes of pain, sorrow, trouble, weariness or affliction eliminated, and every ideal for which the oppressed has sighed attained-what greater consummation could be wished than for time to be dispensed with and for the released to enter upon the full enjoyment of the rest that remains?

Think of it-dream of it, poor disconsolate and overburdened soul-the full realization of all that it meant to the poor weary cottager who told her friend that her idea of heaven was to be able to put on a clean apron and sit down, with no one able to say get up and do anything until she was tired of resting.

It was with some such sense of gratification that I meandered among the fadeless flowers of that Paradise as I conversed with Omra. The heart of time had ceased its beating-I stood across the boundary in the eternal Now. The 'Then' of yesterday was a dream-memory from which I had awakened, and the 'There' of tomorrow was an undiscovered impossibility, because the eternal day reaches beyond the sunset home, so that the night of Regret could never return again.

Under the fragrant benison of such a consolation, what need had we to hurry forward?

"Shall we make the crossing by another bridge?" I presently asked my conductor.

Omra slowly shook his head.

"No! There is only the one way to reach that other side," he responded.

"I am not sorry. I am not at all impatient to turn my back on such an attractive retreat."

For a brief interval there was no reply to my remark-my companion might not have heard it-he appeared to be particularly engaged in the examination of a most beautiful flower he had just discovered, and his face wore a most complaisant smile. Arousing himself, he said:

"Now we begin to feel the exhilarating air wafted from the other side. You will soon feel the benefit of its stimulating effects."

"Do you think we should return?" I enquired, under the impression that there might be a hint of such a suggestion in the remark.

"Not for the present. Before doing so, I want you to take a glance at the great earth circle, so as to enable you to understand something of the various atmospheres and influences which surround it, and help you to a clearer comprehension of what has befallen you on your way here. Will you come?"

"I have no other desire," I replied, "but to leave myself absolutely at your disposal. Do with me as you will. You know the way I ought to take-the things I need to know-the mysteries I fain would solve-the goal I desire to reach. Lead me in the way I should go, then I shall be content."

We paused for an instant, not on the verge of the chasm where I had previously stood, but on what seemed to be the outer edge of everything, with the boundless void of space reaching away into the infinite. Then Omra took my hand, and in a flash we were poised somewhere in the vast profound, and before us lay a majestic orb, like a tri-coloured moon, which at once recalled to mind the prismatic landscape I had previously beheld when standing with Eusemos on the Mount of God.

The connection had scarcely been suggested to my mind before Omra proceeded to confirm it.

"I have already intimated to you," he began, "that hitherto your attention had been engaged almost exclusively in the observation of externals. All your interests, studies and occupations have naturally been concerned with the varying changes and appearances that have been presented on the surface of the great ocean of life-you have had no power to penetrate its depths, to explore its secrets, to examine its mysterious forces, to solve the problem of its origin and nature.

"Children are always more interested in the sands, shells and paddling on the seashore than in the problems of tides and currents, and winds and navigation. Such questions are for older heads, for more mature minds, for those who have been educated and trained, and qualified to deal with such subjects. Childhood is the time when the opening life is allowed freely and joyously to expand, and the joint responsibility for the form it assumes rests upon the shoulders of the parents and guardians.

"You do not find diamonds already cut, polished and mounted, scattered around on the African veldt; nor profound philosophers and expert scientists on the lowest form of an elementary school; nor accepted theologians in the cots of a foundlings' crèche; nor white robed saints in flesh and blood.

'There is none good; no, not one.'

"I multiply these illustrations and reiterate the same idea, because the time has come for you to permanently grasp the essential fact that the mortal span of life is no more than the infancy stage of existence, and it is important that you recognize the transition you are making.

"When you first saw the prismatic landscape, it appealed to you by its attractive grouping of colours, but you were blind to the mystic significance of its arrangement; nor did Eusemos make any attempt to explain it. Even now-after all you have seen and learned through the ministry of Myhanene and his friends-the idea suggested to you by the vision of the orb which lies before us is that of an immense tri-coloured ball- green, and grey, and pink-like, but larger than a ball that children toss about in their play. You have no conception of the world of revelation that lies hidden beneath its surface.

"Let me break the seals, lift the veil, and help you to understand something of the beauty, perfection and adaptation with which God carries out His great designs."

With this Omra again laid his hand upon my arm, and instantly we stood in the workshop of the Infinite, where a gigantic coloured diagram of a vertical section of creation, comprising both "the heaven and the earth" (Gen. i, i), lay unrolled before us.

I have included a coloured frontispiece, (sectional diagram above), in order that my readers may more easily follow my interpretation, and only regret that it is not possible to reproduce it in the varied tones of colour in which I saw it. A word of explanation will make it clear why this is so.

The colour, shade or tone is not an artificial or arbitrary arrangement, but an atmosphere exhaled by condition. That such an atmosphere or odour is exhaled from the physical body is a point that needs no argument, but whereas in the physical, its presence is occasionally evident to the olfactory nerves, in the discarnate state it becomes equally evident to the visual member, its quality being distinguished by the colour. This emanation of the real self clings around and forms the clothing of the soul, by the colour of which it is "known and read of all men." (2 Cor. iii, 2) "This is the Lord's doing," and in the great scheme of creation we shall see that in His inscrutable wisdom, provision has been made that not only the traitor Judas (Acts i, 25), but every soul that passes through the portal of death might find his own place prepared for him.

Such a perfectly adapted scheme-not primarily for punishment, but rather for the administration of justice and the elimination of all vindictiveness-is the silent, but eloquent declaration of creation that its Architect and Builder is a God of love. His purpose in calling a world into existence was not to consign its great majority of men to the agonies of hell, but knowing the inescapable weaknesses and frailties of the flesh through which His new race of sons must pass to reach perfection, He so planned and arranged that even though man, in the blindness of his folly, should wilfully determine to make his bed in hell, in the blackness of its darkness he should find a guiding hand that would eventually lead the prodigal home.

I know I am heretical in my conclusions, but I am a humble follower of one who was crucified for the same offence by those who were orthodox, and if Paul was speaking rightly when he said that prophecies may fail, tongues may cease, and knowledge pass away (i Cor. xiii, 8), would it be very surprising to discover that theologians might be mistaken concerning things which eye hath not seen nor hath the ear heard? Therefore let us turn to our diagram and carefully compare its revelation with those things we have been taught to believe.

The one object Omra had in calling my attention to this subject at this particular time was to clear my mind of certain false ideas that were hindering me from crossing the bridge. My purpose in recording it is to make it serviceable to my readers at a much earlier period of their pilgrimage; because I realise the great assistance it would have been had I been equally fortunate. This is the whole of my desire and wish. I am not aspiring to the dignity of teacher or leader in the purpose I set before me. I simply wish to stand at a somewhat doubtful point of the way like a finger-post proclaiming-"This is the way," because I, myself, have already been benefited by the information.

Take out your Guide-Book and compass; study the diagram I offer for your perusal in the light of what you profess to believe as to the intentions and disposition of the Father; then, if you agree with me as to the way, walk ye in it; if not, follow your own idea. You will make the great discovery by and by. You have a perfect right to exercise your Freewill until your feet reach the edge of the gulf where I have stood; there you will find that your Freewill will have to be exchanged for Must, as the Great Teacher has declared-"Ye must be born again."

Now we are in a position to examine the details of this particular mansion of the Father's universal house in which he who has declared Himself to be "the way, the truth, and the life", has said He will prepare a place for us.

The circular form which is stamped upon every detail of its construction, at once declares that its "builder and maker is God" without beginning or end, the emblem of eternity. And yet it has a beginning-a microscopic centre expanding toward an infinite circumference.

On beholding the plan, the eye is at once arrested by an upper and lower group of interblended circles (1 to 7), slightly divided at the middle, but clearly suggesting the figure 8. If I had time and space to enlarge upon the mystical reason for the employment of this particular symbol in this connection, we should find it to reveal more than a coincidence. In the spiritual realm, numbers have a significance and meaning far beyond a scientific and commercial value, in exposition of which a whole library might be written without exhausting the subject. I shall attempt no more than an indication of one of the meanings of the figure 8 as suggested here.

It requires no elaborate argument to prove that 7 and its multiple is used in scripture to denote completion of varied circles-the week, and the jubilee year will suffice as illustrations. But while one circle is so completed on the one hand, there are three of the ten numerals left unemployed before the circle of ten becomes complete. In accomplishing this, we institute an interlocking of circles, in which the 8 becomes "the first day" of the new week-the resurrection day, of which the symbol in our diagram is prophetic, revealing a glimpse of the purpose that presumably lay in the mind of the Creator in laying the foundations of the earth and its adjoining heaven.

Outside this central group of circles we have three larger divisions, most curiously arranged to fill up the remaining space in the great circumference, and at the same time, retain a connection from side to side. It is these divisions that give the tri-colour aspect (viii, green ix, grey; x, pink) we observed from the distance.

To prevent unnecessary confusion, it is necessary here to explain that the diagram before us shows neither the Physical (except for the suggestion of the relative position of the earth by the small dotted circle) nor the Spiritual, but simply the Psychic stage of man's progression, and in order to prevent any confusion or uncertainty as to my meaning in the use of the word Psychic, let me explain the sense in which I employ it.

I accept as my Guide-Book-not as a Manual of Doctrinal Theology-the Scriptures of the Old and New Testaments. I do this because I have found by extended experience-since I have learned so to use them-that they form the most helpful and reliable directory I have so far met with. They tell me that "God created man in His own image," a triune being of "body, soul and spirit." Not three personalities in one being, but three clearly defined stages in the career of the one person, which stages I will name as physical, psychical and spiritual, just as we have in the mortal the corresponding stages of infancy, youth and manhood. This particular idea is so familiar to every reader of the scriptures that one can scarcely wonder at the theologians pressing it into service to support the accepted doctrine of the trinity, but I ask nothing more from it than what must be undeniably patent to every unbiased mind, that if, in the economy of God, suitable provision has been made for the needs and growth of both the physical and spiritual natures of man, we are equally warranted in assuming that the same consideration has been given to the psychical.

Creation's prophetic reply to the arrogant assumption of the priest, of power to open the doors of the kingdom of heaven to whom he would, and close them against whom he would not allow to enter, was pronounced from the foundation of the world, by God interposing an intermediate-a psychic state between the natural and the spiritual, just as He placed a daybreak between the darkness and the light, and allegorically, a Wilderness of Sin between the Egyptian bondage and the Promised Land.

Let us now examine our diagram and see how it reads in harmony with the idea of a Psychic, or transition stage from the Physical to the Spiritual.

The opening sentence in the Handbook we are using reads, "In the beginning God created the heaven and the earth," and a little lower on the same page (v, 8) it says, "And God called the firmament heaven." There are other heavens. We are told that Paul knew a man who was "caught up into the third heaven" (2

Cor. xii, 2); but we are now concerned with the particular heaven that immediately surrounds the earth.

The small dotted circle (E) in the centre of the plan marks the relative position held by this cradle of our existence. Our entrance at birth is at the microscopic point from which the radius of the heaven is struck, and every child steps upon the stage robed in the garb of innocence. This we have upon the authority of Him who declared Himself to be, "the way, the truth, and the life." When He was appealed to as to the terms upon which the purely spiritual stage of existence could be attained, He replied, "Except ye be converted, and become as little children, ye shall not enter into the kingdom of heaven." We are warranted, then, in assuming that the newly-born child is the standard of innocency required for entrance into the spiritual kingdom, and in support of this, may I not recall the condition demanded of Nicodemus, "Ye must be born again."

I shall deal further with this presently, but for the moment, another development demands my attention. If, then, the Nazarene speaks with authority, every child enters upon life free from the taint of personal impurity, and retains that freedom until it is old enough to "know to refuse the evil and choose the good." At that point it begins to shoulder the responsibility for its own actions, and, in accordance with the choice it makes, moves from the neutral condition it has occupied so far from birth.

What a tremendous decision to rest upon such a delicate and incompetent balance! Is it? Perhaps so. But when we say so, are we not taking a too narrow view of the situation, just as we are also forgetting to point out the significance of the inter-blending of the circles in the diagram we are considering?

From that central point where we enter upon the stage of being, to the infinite expanse of life's circumference, "none of us liveth to himself and no man dieth to himself." The Human Race is a family name that embraces every inhabitant of earth, whether, black or white, yellow or red; God "hath made of one blood all nations of men," and of every soul it is required that he shall recognize the obvious fact and each perform a brother's or sister's part to another, wherever needed. If this duty were fulfilled, how carefully would the child be guided, shielded and encouraged in making its initial decision?

Then the question arises, "Who is to bear the blame if the child stumbles and falls?" This is one of the problems respecting which the Master advises us to "judge not;" that is a question that will be decided in a court of assize where absolute justice will be meted out. What we have to bear in mind here is the warning we are all too apt to neglect, "Be not deceived; God is not mocked; for whatsoever a man soweth, that shall he also reap." For the present, children may have to bear the burdens, effects and certain penalties of their parents' sins, neglect and indifference, but in the great assize, a just compensation will be awarded to the innocent sufferer, and the guilty one will have to atone until the last farthing is paid.

Let us see what provision is made for this. We dismiss for the moment all extraneous ideas of neglect, and allow the deliberate action of the freewill. The child chooses to be disobedient. This is the very sin upon which the doctrine of the Fall is based. Having disobeyed the command of God, and seeing how the sin had stained the innocence which had robed him, and hearing the voice of his Creator calling to him in the garden, Adam, in the consciousness of his shame and guilt, for the first time tried to hide from God.

The first step of disobedience taken, the downward road becomes easy; momentum increases, till, at length, the crash comes, and the reckless prodigal finds himself hurled amongst the swine (the Egyptian synonym for devil), smirched, fouled and wallowing in the filth of the pigsty. He is lying in the lowest hell a child of earth can reach (1) on the verge of the "uttermost," in the way of death, but he cannot die. God has foreseen and made preparation to meet and overcome such a dire catastrophe. The sin is great, but God is greater-Almighty- and He, whose word cannot be broken, has promised, "I will ransom them from the power of the grave; I will deliver them from death." (Hos. xiii, 14)

Let me sound this trumpet call of hope through the darkest and deepest abysses to be found in hell; God the Almighty- the everlasting and immutable-has decreed that, "He will have all men to be saved, and come to a knowledge of the truth" The penalty of deliberate wrongdoing must first be paid-the contumacy of rebellion has to be uprooted, and its effects made good-the fidelity of the regenerated must be satisfactorily assured-and then, the prodigal, coming to himself, shall arise and turn his face homeward. As the ladder of his dream pointed out to Jacob-the homeless wanderer-the way from earth to heaven, so from the pit of the nethermost hell, God has raised another ladder with its feet resting in the filth around the swine-trough, that the victim of temptation, when he wakes from the stupor of his drunken orgy, may yet be able to struggle back again to the ring, the robe, the kiss, the welcome.

And now, having taken a glimpse at this, the lowest depth to which a soul may sink in evil-doing, let us glance at the various stages by which the redemptive ascent is made.

This need not detain us long, since we shall find that we have already made a visit to each of the other stages in the journey, as Myhanene, or one of his fellow servants has carried me hither and thither in answer to enquiries I have made, or to illustrate some point in the instruction I have received.

One word of explanation may not be out of place here for those who have already become acquainted with the fact of communion through the evidence afforded by spiritualistic séances. This group of conditions we are here considering (1 to 7 in our diagram), are the seven spheres so often alluded to by the varied controls. So far as I am aware, what I now propose to do is the first time they have been placed in orderly sequence, so as to enable the student clearly to understand their arrangement and relationship to each other.

Leaving their lower depth-where the soul might sink to extinction and cease to be, but for the everlasting arm upholding it-in the second sphere we catch a glimpse of the ceaseless strife and combative struggle which goes on in the endeavour to escape the scorpion-lash of an arousing conscience, where the watchful ministry of Ladas and his band of helpers are waiting to render the first possible assistance that may be afforded towards restoration.

In the third stage we learned the story of a very typical case of this condition as we listened to Marie's recital of the Harvest of Jealousy, and were instructed as to the means that are used to lead such souls from the poignancy of their agony and the darkness of their despair into the light of freedom and hope.

Reaching the fourth sphere, we emerge from the subterranean dens and caves in which these scenes of the soul's first purgation are situated, and find ourselves at the foot of the Mount upon which I stood so soon after my arrival. Not far away we can see the Mists which envelop the earth. How near to the earth we are, I shall speak of when I deal with the contiguity of it in relation to this sphere and Section IX of the plan, as the whole of these three states wear the same grey atmosphere. Had there been sufficient light to have seen the colours in those caves we have left, we might have seen them change, as we came along from the muddy filth of the depths, through the range of browns and khaki till we reached the grey. From hence, as the soul rises in its approach to the Spiritual, the grey will change and lose itself in the prismatic shades, growing lighter, brighter, and then translucent as it rises into the true light of God.

It is seen at a glance that this sphere (4) holds the central position in the general scheme. It is the only member of the group that presents a perfect model of the whole design-a complete circle, divided into upper and lower divisions by a corridor, suggesting the allegorical balance in the scales of Justice. But perhaps the most suitable illustration we can use to indicate its varied features would be that of the main or ground floor of a building, used as a custom house on the frontier of two kingdoms. All who seek to enter must needs pass through its examination hall for preliminary inspection. Here is made a strict scrutiny of properties, that all contraband goods may be confiscated, passports are carefully viséd, letters of credit authenticated, all currency ruthlessly tested, and finally a satisfactory condition of health established or a term of quarantine is demanded in one or other of the basement wards.

The rigorous ordeal of this scrutiny is most appalling to the majority of immigrants, who find they have been misled, misinformed, or advised by unauthorized experts as to the conditions of entrance. Especially is this the case in relation to the law regulating simplicity of dress which is demanded. It is in this respect where the affluent, the proud, the vain and the arrogant come to grief; while the poor, the humble, the modest and the diffident pass by with surprising consideration. This question of dress is determined by law upon the peculiar basis of what a man is in himself, without the slightest reference to what he has, or any position he may have filled in the kingdom from which he arrives; and the character of the robe he assumes determines his present destination and the conditions under which his new life commences. This frequently constitutes one of the most startling surprises of the soul's transition. I shall record a case of this kind presently.

In the upper part of this sphere (4) we reach the first buildings that are to be found in the spheres-the Home of Rest, where we heard the Magnetic Chorale; and such institutions as the Home of the Assyrian; then, as we cross into the fifth, we reach the City of Compensation.

It was just across this border-line that I reached the home of my mother-Vaone, in which, for the time, I found the great ideal of my heart's lifelong desire. From thence I have had your company, my patient and indulgent friends, and you have been able to learn something of the teaching I have received; have looked upon the illustrations that have been placed before me; have, with me, been surprised at the wonderful revelations that have been made, as I have been led forward to the Court of the Voices. Now you are waiting to see me cross over the great divide. I, too, am anxious to be rid of the last of the earth's influence which prevents my doing so. What this particular infirmity is, I have not yet discovered, but the one great point I am anxious to stamp upon your consciousness is the fact of the far-reaching effects of even the weaknesses of earth, and the inexorable demand for the removal of the last taint of sin, even to "spot or wrinkle," before the power is acquired to reach the other side, and the soul is truly born into the spiritual kingdom of God.

So we conclude our enquiry as to the processes at work under the provision and ordination of God for bringing rebellious souls back from their wandering into the inheritance He has set apart for us. But the Shepherd has told us, "Other sheep I have, which are not of this fold; them also must I bring, and they shall hear my voice; and there shall be one fold, and one Shepherd." (John x, 16)

There are still three other sections of our plan unnoticed. A brief consideration of these will not only complete the study of the circle, but gather in all the other sheep to complete the fold. We have seen what provision has been made for the civilized, cultured and morally responsible races, but He who has commanded that the fragments shall be gathered so that nothing shall be lost, holds the heathen, uncultured and degenerate souls to be intrinsically of equal value as the cultured and has therefore made just as suitable, considerate and appropriate arrangements for their perfection as has been made for others.

These forlorn, despised and contemned people, though in their depravity, they "are of the earth earthy," in moral rectitude they are nothing more than irresponsible children knowing nothing of any standard of right or wrong. Therefore He has prepared a place for them (VIII) on the level with, but free from the influences, penalties and contaminations of cultured recklessness and depravity. In this safely protected reservation, they have given to them a ministry perfectly adapted to their every need to bring them finally into the one all-inclusive fold.

Section IX, in position and colour corresponding to the fourth sphere and the earth, with only the slightest of veils dividing it from either, is the condition into which the souls of those still in the flesh enter for instruction during the hours of sleep. The body cannot lose its consciousness until the soul vacates it, and this condition was designed by God, in order that, while the body slept, the soul might still continue an unbroken communion with those who had assumed the immortal, and so obviate any suspicion of death. (Job xxxiii, 14-17)

History, both sacred and profane, is crowded with the evidence of this apparently stupendous fact, but interested organizations, which could not exist side by side with such an open communion, have laughed at the idea until it has been relegated to the region of superstition, and the multitude of men return from their sleep with the memory of its incomparable ministry drowned in oblivion. But God never leaves Himself without a witness to the truth. I have learned of a striking illustration of this in connection with my own attempt to carry the news of this fact back to earth, and a little further on I will record an incident of an assistance I received from one of my readers which was rendered to me in her sleep.

The final section of the plan which I have now to deal with (X) is one calculated to bring a message of joy and comfort to many a sorrowing heart. How many of the sons and daughters of earth sorrow that their only child was still-born or passed away immediately after. Listen! "Comfort ye, comfort ye my people, saith your God."

This last apartment we have to look into, in connection with "the earthly house of our tabernacle," is the corner of heaven for which you have been sighing and seeking, even as I sought all through the days of my flesh for the unknown love of my mother. At length, when the veil was rent, I found her. "Seek and ye shall find, though the conception of the idea so far surpasses the human thought and hope that it "hath not entered the heart of man" to imagine what God has provided for in this connection. The stillborn child has lived if there has been one separate, deliberate movement of the foetus in the womb that was the birth throb of the new soul, which can never die.

From that initial struggle into life until it knows "to refuse the evil and choose the good," by the exercise of free-will, that soul is in the nurse care of some particular angel who has been appointed to the office, therefore, said the Master, "Take heed that ye despise not one of these little ones; for I say unto you, that in heaven their angels do always behold the face of (the) Father, for of such is the kingdom of heaven." Carried away from earth in their personally unsullied state, it is not meet or necessary for them to pass through the refining stages of even the higher spheres, and so the wisdom of God has provided another way of ascent in which they may be instructed and prepared for the Spiritual realm beyond.

Is it possible that such souls do need any preparation? Yes; and by this we may be able to grasp a connection of the scrupulous rigour that is observed, to ensure the purity of the soul ere it can pass from the Psychic into the Spiritual Kingdom.

In the child there may be-is-the seed, the germ, the taint of hereditary vices, or there may be psychological vibrations and impressions received from circumstances to which the mother has been subjected; these have to be absolutely removed, and the possibility of any after-effect rigorously provided for. The agency at work to secure this we have seen at work more than once in our visits to Cushna's children's home.

With this I leave our review of the great scheme of creation and the wisdom it displays for the evolution, education and purification of the soul during the infancy and childhood of its existence. Surely, as the review is thought over, meditated upon and intelligently considered, we shall be able to take up the declaration of the Psalmist, and say, at least in relation to this corner of the universe, "Such knowledge is too wonderful for me; it is high. I cannot attain unto it."

* * *

CHAPTER 14

A WORD OF CAUTION AND HOPE

Having summarized-far more briefly than I could have wished, or the importance of the subject demands-the new interpretation of the heaven and the earth as placed before me by Omra, I am not sufficiently unreasonable as to ask for its immediate acceptance as true on the authority of my own unsupported declaration. No person, whether he is in the body or out of the body, has the right to make such a demand, and far be it from me to raise even the suspicion of such a course. I am simply recording that which has been revealed, made known to, and fully approved by myself. In the light it has afforded, I have been able to solve many problems, have broken the seals of hitherto inscrutable mysteries, have been able to test the value of many insistent authorities, freed myself from the burden of weighty superstitions; and have gained a nobler and more consistent idea and conception of God. In the days of my incarnation, I claimed the right to exercise my free-will-I might use it, or misuse it, as I neglected or determined, always subject to the just penalty I incurred by my action. You have a right to the same freedom I claimed, and I would be the last to restrict it. In the ultimate "God will have all men to be saved, and come to a knowledge of the truth." The question for every man to consider is-What are the best means of reaching the goal in the shortest time and under the most favourable conditions? There is very little, if any dispute as to the essential qualification for success; all the difficulty arises when we come to interpret the rules by which the qualification is to be secured. The Guide-Book (scriptures) we have at our own disposal for help and direction tells us that these rules are so plainly and simply set forth therein that "the wayfaring man, though a fool, shall not err therein." Would you ask me where these rules are set forth? The great Shepherd, who declared Himself to be the

Way, condensed them into a simple, unequivocal sentence; "Therefore all things whatsoever ye would that men should do to you, do ye even so to them; for this is the law and the prophets." (Matt. vii, 12) A life so lived is anointed by the Holy Spirit-the Christ-life-and cannot come near death. But to be so it must be consistently lived, not merely accepted as a form of belief. Habit of life produces character when the cloak of the flesh is thrown off; character manifests itself as a clothing for the soul in gradations of colour ranging from white to deepest crimson, and every shade of colour must occupy its legitimate station. "Order is heaven's first law." You can find no filthy rags of unrighteousness among the white-robed throng before the throne.

Again I wish to remind you, that, though I am speaking to you from where faith has been changed into sight, I am not insisting on your accepting my word if it does not commend itself to you; but I have suggested, and I again repeat my advice to think, ponder, meditate on these things, and "let every man be fully persuaded in his own mind," as to whether I am speaking the words of soberness and truth or not, and then let him act accordingly. For-and in what I am now about to say, I am not speaking lightly, nor in ignorance of the awful consequences of the result, but boldly and lovingly declaring the truth as it has been revealed to me, and as I have spoken-if in the issue you do discover that you have made a mistake in not accepting the advice I am offering, you will find the error is not irremediable.

You must reap what you have sown; must go to the identical place for which you have prepared yourself; must pay to the utmost farthing the penalty you have incurred, and you will be compelled to endure whatever treatment is necessary to take out every stain and taint you have contracted, but wherever you may find yourself located, you will, as I have already pointed out, always find efficient and sympathetic ministers of God to help and direct you, whenever you, having discharged your liability, turn your thoughts and desires homeward. And though you fall to the lowest depths-horrible thought, from which may you be preserved-remember that the "man after God's own heart" has declared, "if I make my bed in hell, behold, thou [God] art there." God, who has promised, "I will ransom them from the power of the grave; I will redeem them from death; O death, I will be thy plagues; O grave, I will be thy destruction" (Hos. xiii, 14); and this because His love is everlasting, and He "will have all men to be saved."

Once again I invite you to ask yourself the question whether such an evangel as I set forth does not make an appeal to your affections and consideration that prompts the soul to respond with, "I will arise and go to my Father," and thus avoid the inevitable results of disobedience?

But I also want you to think for a moment of the soul that wakes up too late to escape the penalty; or the one that finds itself the victim of blind leaders of the blind-the soul that opens its eyes to discover that the promises and assurances of the professional priest are worse than valueless in the customs house of the hereafter. The victim of a confidence trick may not be responsible for the robbery that has taken place, but he has to suffer for his neglect to take precautions against falling into the trap that brought about his downfall. It is sad indeed to watch the bewildered victim as the stroke of disillusionment falls upon the unprotected shoulders, and the conscience is smitten with remorse as it is reminded by a tenderly sympathetic voice, lamenting: "How often would I...but ye would not." Yet out of the wreckage there comes a salvage gleam of hope. All is not lost. The dictum of the hireling was equally false in both directions. If he had no authority to promise a crown upon false terms, neither had he the right to affirm an eternity of punishment.

Presently-no matter to what depth the weight of personal responsibility has sunk the soul-it will come to itself and review the condition in which its culpable conduct has justly placed it. At such a crisis it will not find itself alone. Near at hand will be found one of the authorized angels of God to whom charge has been given to render such assistance as I received at the hands of Myhanene's band, which you have been able to follow, and to whose instructions I have afforded you an insight. After having profited by such a divine ministry, I never see or hear of such a one as I was, but I yearn to find him, that I may speak to him of what I have experienced.

Poor pilgrim brother, like the man who went down from Jerusalem to Jericho, you have indeed fallen into the hands of adventurers by the way. But you are in the hands of true friends at length. Hear them, commune with them, go with them, for, in the spirit of the dear Master, they will cause your heart to burn within you by the way. Oh, how I would love to whisper in your ears something of the consolations I have received from such a ministry from the time when first the suspicion of what had occurred began to suggest itself as I lay bewildered on the slopes at the time when Helen found me! Omra has said that the Court of the Voices will fascinate me through the whole course of the ages. It may be so-the spell it weaves is only beginning at present to envelop me in its wondrous charm, and, it may well be that I am not competent to form an opinion as to the attraction it will have in the ages to come-but, at present, I cannot conceive of heaven producing a fuller, sweeter, holier, or more soul-soothing chord of music than the simple declaration Helen made in answer to the doubt as to whether acts of love and sympathy were, in themselves, of any value here.

"Why, 'God is love'," she answered me. "That which is born of love is born of God. That is all we know about Him."

I did not catch the fullness of the music of it at the time-my ears were too full of the sounds of the shock that had thrown me over the border, to hear anything but words. I have been able since then to catch and listen to the theme, also to sound something of the depth of that evangel, and I tell you that you need not despair, "though your sins be as scarlet, they shall be as white as snow," even though you are compelled to make your first bed in the lowest hell, because He who "will have all men to be saved" is able to carry out His purpose to the uttermost, whether that uttermost be of distance, time or depravity.

We may not know the way by which your salvation will be accomplished, but the Architect who designed the house is Himself conversant with every means of communication, and should it at last be found that He has failed to bring only one soul to its appointed goal, in that one failure His almightiness would fall short of perfection. Therefore be of good courage. You have heard the call, "Come unto me!" Your sins may have delayed your answer to that call, but you will not be forsaken-you will not be left to find your way alone. In whatever darkness and uncertainty you may meet with you, will have the assistance and support of an authorized guiding hand. You will come through many vicissitudes, it may be, but rest assured that in the end your feet will cross the Paternal threshold, and your final rest will be in your Father's home.

Such is the prospect which lies before my eyes. You, who are still in the valley, may not be able to see it, but take courage-climb the upward, onward path, which lies at your feet; listen to the whispers of hope that fall like echoes from the hilltops; ask yourself where all those are going who are toiling up the ascent, and following in their footsteps you will soon see, as I am seeing now, and hear the music that I am hearing-the heavenly chorale which Helen sang to me when I was standing where you are standing now, but which I failed to appreciate then as you are failing to understand the evangel I am commissioned to proclaim to you.

But let me breathe one word of caution against a danger it is possible, but not probable, for you even at this time to fall into. Do not attempt to form any estimate of how long it will be before you reach the goal you were promised to reach just through the veil of death. Behind you lies the Yesterday of the flesh, but now you stand in the eternal To-day, to which there is no To-morrow. Time has ceased to be. And God, who is perfect in all Its works and ways, will now perfect that which concerns yourself. Into His heaven there can nothing enter that defileth, and before you cross its threshold you must be without spot or wrinkle. As I think of it, I recall those lines of Eilele:

Oh! 'Tis not as men would teach us-
Just one step from earth to God;
Passing through the death-vale to Him,
In the garb that earth we trod;
Called to praise Him while a weary;
Or to sing, while yet the voice
With love's farewell sob is broken,
Could we, fitly, thus rejoice?

No! We must wait until the last trace of an earth stain is removed, till the final indication of the weight that did so easily beset us is lost, and the soul becomes so buoyant with the indwelling of the spirit as to be able to tread with a firm assurance the gossamer fabric that spans the gulf, and with the step of a conquering hero, enter upon its reward.

For by far the greater majority of pilgrims the path leading to such a consummation lies through the valley of Hinnom rather than over the brow of Olivet. But fear not-"If thou seek [God] with all thy heart and with all thy soul," thou shalt find Him, though He be compelled to bring thee through a Babylonian furnace, and not so much as a smell of burning shall be found upon thee, when the deliverance is accomplished.

Do you, from the earth plane, ask me; "Why must this be so, if God will have all men to be saved?" I reply, "Because God hath decreed that every soul that hears and responds to the invitation, 'Come unto me,' shall enter into the kingdom through the 'strait gate' which is always at hand, leading into a highway-'The way of holiness; the unclean shall not pass over it' (Isa. xxxv, 8), and it leads, without the shadow of a turning, direct from the spot where the wanderer is found, to the long-lost home. If the valley of Hinnom lies in that direct line, it is the Sin, not God, who is to be blamed. But the wayfaring soul need not be afraid of the vicissitudes by the way for he shall hear a still small voice of love and encouragement behind him saying, 'When thou passest through the waters, I will be with thee...when thou walkest through the fire, thou shalt not be burned; neither shall the flame kindle upon thee." (Isa. xliii, 2)

Still, though the ultimate victory is assured, it is not yet attained, and, particularly in the early stages of the soul's redemptive career, there are dangers to be encountered, which I am anxious not to pass by unnoticed. There are lions in the path, as Bunyan saw in his famous allegory, and it was never more necessary than now for some Porter to be on the watch to assure pilgrims not only that the lions are chained, but also to explain and advise as to other devices and obstacles which have been placed in the path to turn others aside.

Just here I can fancy that I hear a voice from one-it may be more-of my nervous readers who are watching and rightly so-for any sign of heresy, or mayhap the cloven hoof, in my teaching, asking me if I have forgotten that I am supposed to be speaking from beyond the river, and whether I am not somewhat mixed in my allusions?

I thank you a thousand times for the reminder, dear friend, and pray you to go on occupying the watch-tower, and shouting whenever you discover any sign of danger. We are all safe, so far, however. In the use of your dogmatic field-glasses you are resting your eyes on the foaming, turbulent Jordan over which,

> . . . *timorous mortals start and shrink*
> *To cross,*

but I, in further explorations, have found the place where the "Israelites passed over on dry ground, until all the people were passed clean over Jordan" (Jos. iii, 17), and having learned, in the home beyond the dried-up river, what Christ fully meant when He declared life to be "everlasting," therefore indivisable, it is all one whether the dangers and difficulties arise a little earlier or later-they do occur, and have to be surmounted.

The rediscovery of this dry-shod passage-for it has existed from the beginning-and the re-establishment of communion, which is now as conclusively demonstrated as any natural facts of existence, entails upon every individual who ventures to profit by the advantages it offers, very serious responsibilities. The establishment of any relationship always demands circumspection, and satisfactory guarantee against mistakes, even in the commonplace connections of a commercial life. Where the relationship contemplated is that of a closer and more enduring kind, a correspondingly more severe scrutiny is demanded. But where we are establishing an intercourse with an outlook ranging over the eternities, how necessary it is that we only enter into relationship with those whose credentials are unimpeachable, authoritatively established, and being well-tried are presently proved to be in every way efficient and trustworthy.

It is in relation to placing yourselves in the hands of unknown and voluntary guides and counsellors to instruct you in connection with this latter and most important aspect of life that I wish to offer another word of caution.

Please let me be understood at once. I have no axe to grind, and with all the reverence I am capable of, I say; God forbid that I should attempt to disparage the meanest effort that has been put forth by the least of God's little ones to bring the truth of a continued existence home to the mind of the most unworthy mortal, whatever form, or however apparently ridiculous that effort might take in its demonstration. The Lord of hosts- if the incident is faithfully recorded-has been known to make use of the vocal apparatus of an ass, and in His omnipotence has magnified His revelation thereby quite as gloriously as when He elected to break the bondage of Israel by the intervention of a destroying angel. Therefore that which God has chosen to employ, I have no right or wish to traduce. At the same time-and this is the position I wish to take-because God may have used Balaam's ass upon a most extraordinary occasion, it would be foolishness to argue that the braying of every ass is to be accepted as the voice of God. The master-key of Sin is a travesty of Truth. For this reason, it behooves every man to "believe not every spirit, but try the spirits, whether they are of God; because many false prophets are gone out into the world" (1 John iv, 1), and this is why I wish to offer this word of caution and explanation.

Sympathetic attraction is the most potent influence in life, whether that attraction be towards good or evil, and it is probably more dominant in the region of the soul than in that of the flesh. Prayer is the wrestling yearning of the life for the object of its desire, whether that desire be pure or vicious. A request may be clothed in the mask of a verbal formula, but the soul will instinctively shrink from appropriating an uncongenial favour. Therefore "everyone that asketh [in accordance with this law] receiveth."

Christ lays this down clearly, "If"-mark this emphatic qualification for success-"If ye abide in me, and my words abide in you, ye shall ask what ye will, and it shall be done unto you." (John xv, 7) On the other hand; "If a man abide not in me, he is cast forth as a branch, and is withered; and men gather them, and cast them into the fire, and they are burned." (John v, 6)

Now, prayer-or yearning desire-is the wireless installation by which the call to communion is first made, between the incarnate and discarnate estates of the soul, and every heart, which is the instrument of despatch-as a man "thinketh in his heart so is he" (Prov. xxiii, 7)-is sympathetically connected with one or the other of the only two existent exchanges which exist-either the God-appointed centre (whether you call it Christ or by any other name), or that of the enemy. You cannot hold the two connections.

When, therefore, one determines to make an effort to establish a connection for communication with the discarnate, the all-important prelude is for a man to examine himself and come to a clear understanding as to the quality of soul that will respond to his call for intercourse.

Be not deceived. It is a vital necessity, if you wish to come to a knowledge of the truth, that a man should rather undervalue himself in this estimate than otherwise, for righteousness cannot meet on equal terms with unrighteousness; light will not hold communion with darkness; Christ hath no concord with Belial.

The law controlling this lack of attraction the one to the other is just as certain in its operation as that which warns against playing with matches in the presence of gunpowder.

* * *

CHAPTER 15

CONCERNING SPIRITUAL INTERCOURSE

It is a common but very natural fallacy that, granted a means of communication can be established between the so-called living and the dead, it would be most readily achieved between members of the same family than with strangers. Such a supposition is based upon the idea of the continuance of blood relationship; but "flesh and blood cannot inherit the kingdom of God," and the only relationship that survives is the sacred bond of pure affection. In the spiritual realm there is only one family which embraces "every kindred, and tongue, and people and nation. "One is their Father, even God, and all are brethren."

This may be a hard saying for you to consent to receive, and you may doubt the truth of what I say. Well! I am simply telling you what I have myself discovered. If you prefer to wait until you discover it, the result will not be fatal. All mistakes will then have to be corrected. Whatever their nature or extent-venial or mortal, they must be expiated and atoned for. But no matter where the prodigal may be when he comes to himself, he will then learn that there is a way home from the ground whereon he lies, and someone near at hand to lead him to it.

Still a little reflection and forethought touching the question of opening up communion may not be out of place. Whether a man is or is not a believer in the immortality of the soul really makes little or no difference to the fact that when he stands by the bed of a beloved one and watches the vital spark flicker to extinction, so far as the physical is concerned, he stands face to face with the most awfully solemn experience of life. Standing there, clasping the almost unresponsive hand, watching the stealthy, almost visible approach of death, who is there who does not feel how appropriately it might be said, "Put off thy shoes from off thy feet for the place whereon thou standest is holy ground" And is not the sacredness equally profound when, under the insatiable longing of that widowed heart, an attempt is about to be made to stretch a telephone wire across the grave and speak once more with the beloved, and so shatter the unbearable silence? Tennyson spoke with true prophetic caution and advice when to such he said:

> *How pure at heart and sound in head*
> *With what divine affection bold*
> *Should be the man whose thought would hold*
> *An hour's communion with the dead.*
>
> *In vain shalt thou, or any, call*
> *The spirits from their golden day,*
> *Except like them, thou too canst say,*
> *My spirit is at peace with all.*
>
> *But when the heart is full of din,*
> *And doubt beside the portal waits,*
> *They can but listen at the gates,*
> *And hear the household jar within.*

Communication between the physical and the spiritual states of being is not only possible, but natural, uninterrupted and free; free as the oceans are to shipping, or the air to aircraft. The only limitations by which you are conditioned are to be found, not in any imaginary obstructions which are supposed to block the way; everything depends on the character and capacity of the vehicle in which you make the attempt. No man would try to cross the Atlantic in a rowing-boat, nor to pass from Europe to America in a gas-balloon. These are both useful, convenient and desirable for insular and local purposes and necessities, but must needs give place to greater and more enduring powers where the effort is made to unite or bridge the great divide that lies between continent and continent.

As the instinct of the animal has evolved into the reasoning power of man, and intellect unfolded into the higher power of inventive genius, these impossibilities of the ancients have become not only possible but commonplace. But great as the human intellect is-suggestively omnipotent as it appears to be, it has its bounds and limitations beyond which it may not pass, because it is yoked to the physical, and presently must reach a point where a higher power is heard saying, as to the sea when its doors were shut, "Hitherto shalt thou come but no further; and here shall thy proud waves be stayed." (Job xxxviii, 11) The mightiest ship that ploughs the ocean will never be able to cross the land, nor will the most superb aeroplane that genius can perfect have power to cross the void between the planets and visit Earth's nearest neighbour. And the reason why I am able to speak so confidently as to this is, that there lies a condition between the planets, mysterious, unknown, unexplored, unconquered, in the presence of which, intellect, science, human wisdom and achievement are both dumb and powerless.

As the intrepid aeronaut ascends, he finds the conditions by which he is surrounded become absolutely impossible for physical existence to endure. He reaches the fatal boundary beyond which flesh and blood may not trespass. In the heights he finds, as in the depths-a grave. And yet that No Man's Land is not an unconditioned void. What is it? Is there no analogy in nature that will enable us to gain some fore-gleams of its use and purpose? I think so. Turn to our Guide-Book again. "And God called the light day, and the darkness he called night. And the evening and the morning were the first day." (Gen. i, 5) This supplies all our need-evening and morning, darkness and light, in creation; and in man, physical and spiritual. But in nature, in between the two estates, we have the twilight, which serves the purpose of inter-blending or handing the night to day -the darkness to the light. So man is a creature of body, soul and spirit, and the Psychic or soul condition is the transitional agent between the Physical and the Spiritual.

It is in the highest degree important for me to point out just here that, though the line of demarcation between the physical and psychic or psychic and spiritual estates is a very fluidic one, as the tidal mark upon a sloping beach, yet it is always the higher condition that reaches down to and embraces the lower. The physical has no power to invade the psychic sphere, nor has the psychic the slightest claim to cross the frontier of the spiritual. It is the waiting to get rid of the final trace of the psychic that kept me from crossing the division that hindered my reaching the Gate when I first beheld it. Here is made apparent the wisdom of God in designing the Sleep-state as a school in which the temporary discarnate soul might be prepared and qualified to higher heights on entering the discarnate than if only subjected to the intellect and teachings available in the physical.

This brings me back again to the consideration of the opening of communion. No enquirer has ability to influence another who stands on a higher spiritual plane than himself. Then-

> *How pure at heart and sound in head,*
> *With what divine affection bold*
> *Should be the man whose thought would hold*
> *An hour's communion with the dead.*

Is not the attempt to approach such an interview treading on holy ground? Would you care to break the silence of death in company with a captious critic, or scientific agnostic, or occult prospector, or one in search of an afternoon-tea sensation?

Incredibly startling and revolting as it may appear, the ordinary séance not infrequently presents such features. Do not misunderstand me. I am not objecting to enquiry, or asking you to believe without the most drastic proof. You cannot reach the inner shrine without first passing through the portal. You must first find the soul for whom your heart is aching, before you can enter upon the hallowed communion you wish to re-establish. You must be fully assured in your own mind that this mystical path is not a delusion and a snare. This you have a right-nay, more, it is demanded that you should ascertain, and the preliminary phenomena by which you may be assured and led forward into the deeper revelation is placed at your disposal. "Seek, and you shall find." "It is not hidden from thee, neither is it far off. It is not in heaven, that thou shouldest say, 'Who shall go up to heaven for us, and bring it unto us, that we may hear, and do it?' Neither is it beyond the sea, that thou shouldest say, 'Who shall go over the Sea for us, and bring it unto us, that we may hear it, and do it?' But [it] the word is very nigh unto thee, in thy mouth and in thy heart, that thou mayest do it." (Deut. xxx, 1114) But what I counsel is that you make and keep your preliminary enquiry a sacred part of your private or family prayer or worship, and guard it as solemnly, as was the parting you are now seeking to annul.

I wish to be very clear and emphatic here, because great issues are necessarily subject to equally great risks. I have already pointed out how closely the fourth sphere is allied to the physical in more than one aspect, notably; it is the portal through which the passage is made. Its occupants are, for the most part, new arrivals, and therefore very little better acquainted with the new life than they were before the transition. I say for the most part advisedly, because those who have returned to this condition after purgation, even though they were enquired of, would naturally be very reticent as to their experience; neither would they be so likely to be sought after by personal friends as those who had more recently passed over.

It naturally follows, then, that this fourth sphere becomes the great centre of demand and supply between public séances and those presided over by professional mediums, and I ask all who are acquainted with such, to recall how many of the replies to enquiries as to the condition of the communicants are to this effect-how seldom they bear of one who speaks from the fifth.

As an instance of the kind of authority and knowledge with which they speak, I take a characteristic illustration from a volume written by one of your most respected and eminent scientific authorities and refrain from offering one word of criticism. I only ask, "Is it worth while to break the silence of the grave to gain such information?"

One word of explanation may be necessary. If the reader has carefully followed my description of the diagram, he will be able to verify the position from which the communication is given. It comes from a soldier, who had been killed some ten weeks earlier, who finds himself still wearing khaki, and does not speak himself, but through "a little Indian girl." The message is to his father, and the subject under consideration is houses and clothing in the beyond. These things, we are told, have to be manufactured, "just as you manufacture solid things." The question is-"How?"

"...Everything dead has a smell, if you notice; and I know now that the smell is of actual use, because it is from that smell that we are able to produce duplicates of whatever form it had before it became a smell. Even old wood has a smell different from new wood; you may have to have a keen nose to detect these things on the earth plane.

"Old rags," he says, "cloth decaying and going rotten. Different kinds of cloth give off different smells-rotting linen smells different from rotting wool. You can understand how all this interests me. Apparently, as far as I can gather, the rotting wool appears to be used for making things like tweeds on our side ...My suit, I expect, was made from decayed worsted on your side."

I do not criticize or deny the validity of the communication itself-most probably it is perfectly correct as to its source and transmission. My point is this-Souls who occupy any position in the fourth sphere, whether they have recently passed over, or have perforce been through the lower conditions, are not in a sufficiently advanced stage to speak with any degree of spiritual authority as to the discarnate life. Yet these are the souls most easily attracted by séances and professional mediums.

Are you beginning to wonder where I am leading you? Whether I have dared to open a door of hope for your tear-dimmed eyes to catch a glimpse of the scene for which your aching heart is yearning, only to shut it again and laugh at your trusting credulity? God forbid!

Where you are standing, I have stood. The sorrow which is darkening all your life, I have felt and endured. The agonizing enquiry you are making-"if a man die, shall he live again?"-I have toilsomely followed, praying for some response, but all in vain, until my wearied head dropped upon the pillow of the grave. I know how sacred is the quest-am conscious of the awful solemnity of the place as we approach the burning bush, and I have no other wish or desire but to preserve its sanctity. There are those who, in their search after the wonderful and hidden, would "rush in where angels fear to tread." To all such I would sorrowfully say, "Turn back, my brother, we are about to enter the secret place of the Most High, where you will find yourself most miserably out of place." But to the heart-broken, weary and heavy-laden, who are seeking light in life's darkness, the oil of joy for their mourning, I reach out the hand of fellowship and say, "Follow me, and you shall find that death is swallowed up in victory."

As I am about to open the door, let me again remind you that in crossing the threshold, we pass from the physical realm to the domain of the spiritual, and, to ensure the success you seek, you will be required to place yourself to the utmost extent of your powers, in harmony with the conditions of the spiritual life. You may not be pure and holy-but a consciousness of your shortcoming and a sacred resolve to honestly aspire to such a condition will be tentatively accepted if suitably presented. Therefore no really hungry soul will be turned empty away. No wonder that the outcast Jacob, when he realized all the possibilities and blessings that were spread out before his eyes and ears, when he passed across this threshold, said, "Surely this is none other but the house of God, and this is the Gate of Heaven."

Now let us enter. And, having shut out all contact with the physical, in our aspiration, let us place ourselves in harmony with the new conditions with which we find ourselves surrounded. In this strangely new light we are each and all seen and known and dealt with as we are, not as we should have others think we are.

We here wear only the garments our lives have woven to hide our nakedness. We are all naked here in the presence of our Father-our God. No one need be afraid. Simply, humbly, sorrowfully, it most probably will be, let us pour out our desires before Him-lay bare the wound that Death hath made-plead with Him to heal the open sore and to restore the broken communion, confident that He is the vanquisher of Death. Then leaving our petition at His feet, "rest in the Lord, wait patiently for Him," and He will give you your heart's desire.

The royal, natural, heaven-constructed way for restoring communion between the mortal and the spiritual is not by means of the séance room and the medium-these accessories may be, are frequently employed upon occasion, but they should be regarded as exceptions and irregular rather than the rule-the highway in which the wayfaring man shall not err, be deceived, or led astray, is through the ministry of Death's twin-sister, Sleep. Byron was right when he said:

Sleep hath its own world,
boundary between the things misnamed
Death and Existence.

Let us consult our Guide-Book; "He giveth to His beloved [in] sleep." (Ps. cxxvii, 2) "In a dream, in a vision of the night, when deep sleep falleth upon men, in slumberings upon the bed; then He [God] openeth the ears of men, and sealeth their instruction, that he may withdraw man from his purpose, and hide pride from man. He keepeth back his soul from the pit and his life from perishing by the sword." (Job xxxiii, 15-18) Men have wandered from the way and have lost sight of this, the most precious part of the function of sleep. It has a far greater purpose in the economy of God, than giving rest to a weary body. It was used from the beginning to make Adam know that he had a spiritual, as well as a physical nature; to show the outlaw Jacob the way to the spiritual home; to reveal to Joseph the future concerning Egypt, and instruct him concerning it; to bestow the gift of wisdom upon Solomon; to open the vista of the future ages to Daniel in Babylon, and give him the interpretation of the king's dream, and it gives the promise that the divine ministry shall be restored again in the latter days-a promise that is even now being fulfilled on every hand.

Another glance at our diagram will show that an open corridor exists between the earth and the sleep-state (IX), but-and here lies the power of the bondage into which man has been ensnared-were this free and uninterrupted passage left as God had first designed it, there would never have been a cult of priest-craft (hireling shepherds) possible. Under the teachings (emphatically plural) of the Babel of Theology, man has learned the sad truth of Isaiah's pronouncement, "My thoughts are not your thoughts, neither are your ways my ways, saith the Lord."

Still, the way is free and open for whoever has courage and desire to use it. If Revelation needed, or cared to ask the confirmation of Science, it would easily be procurable that the body is vacated by the soul during the hours of sleep. Where, then, does the soul go? The answer is not far to seek. We have already seen that in the discarnate, every soul goes to its own place. Should it be surprising that there should be a prepared place for those who are temporarily set free? Is it not what we might expect of a God who is perfect in all His works and ways, to provide a place where the sorrowing ones might meet with the loved again? Even man allows such occasional interviews with prisoners, and God is more merciful than man. So this night school of the soul has been designed to demonstrate the fact that, "There is no Death."

There has been no interruption of its service since the time that Adam is recorded to have learnt therein that he was a spiritual as well as a physical being. But, under the teachings of priest-craft, man has allowed his memory of the lessons he has received to be laughed and ridiculed into oblivion. The regaining of the faculty of memory is a personal matter entirely, which every soul must achieve for itself. No third party has any authority, right or necessity, to intervene. Proxies, advocates, or representatives are altogether out of place when a child wishes to make an acknowledgment or to ask a favour from its parent. Therefore, I say, when you seek to open this communion, which is your birthright, proceed according to the law of the kingdom, "when thou hast shut thy door, pray to the Father which is in secret; and thy Father which seeth in secret shall reward thee openly." The memory of the communion with the absent loved ones will dawn upon you. You will find it has never ceased. Only your memory has been at fault. You have simply changed the hours of your intercourse from the waking to sleeping, and they are a thousand times more precious to you now in their higher life than they were before. Or, should you find them reaping what they have sown in a lower sphere than earth, you will find that your love can still be of assistance to them, an instance of which I will record for your instruction presently.

But someone will tell me that what he requires is a demonstration in the objective rather than in the subjective. This also is provided for, and is to be far more reliably reached by the course I am advocating than by any other process devised by man.

Man is not a machine made up of standardized parts that may be exchanged and replaced as occasion may require. He is not simply a brute swayed and prompted at the impulse of instinct. He has been created in the image of God, and is a most mysteriously complicated being, actuated and directed in accordance with the working of a Spirit within him which, as yet, he is scarcely in a position to recognize, and certainly not able to comprehend. Hence the greatest and most profound mystery of creation which man has to face is-himself. Nor will the solution over be reached until man knows his Father-God. In all the great family of mankind there are no two that are in every respect identical, consequently that which is good for one may be injurious for another, and this applies to every aspect and walk of being, as it is found in its infancy or physical stage.

Here arises the necessity for the school which God has

provided in the sleep-state, thoroughly equipped and furnished with teachers who are competent to teach and say, "This is the way," and then guide their pupils into the appointed way of life. This "way" is most accurately suited to every individual need of the particular life under direction.

The wisdom that has arranged for a soul in the hours of sleep to ascend into the region of the discarnate has also provided that its tutors and guardians shall have equal access to council and direct in the more needful hours of its physical environment. "He shall give His angels charge over thee, to keep thee in all thy ways. They shall bear thee up in their hands, lest thou dash thy foot against a stone." (Ps. xci, 11-12) But the sources of intercourse these angel guards have at their disposal are as varied and numerous as the circumstances and needs which call for their intervention. It is a fallacy of the most childish imagination to suppose that communication with heaven is limited to séances and trance mediumship. You might as well contend that the free winds of heaven only blow through the kitchen bellows. The former, as the Master said, "blows where it listeth," and the latter is equally without restriction suited to the occasion, the individual, and the circumstance in connection with which assistance is required. Hagar, in the wilderness, needs clairvoyance to enable her to find the water necessary to save her child's life; Jacob first learns the way to heaven from earth in his sleep-but later he is granted, not only to see, but even to wrestle with a materialized spirit; Moses is permitted to commune with the "direct voice," "face to face, as a man speaketh with his friend;" to Abraham three angels, as men, appear and converse as he sat at the door of his tent; to Elijah, a fire display is granted, in answer to his prayer, burning up his offering; to David, automatic writing and drawing is granted; to Elisha, the resuscitation of the dead, but why need I further prolong the list? God's laws are to-day as they were in the beginning, without need of change or correction.

Therefore, in seeking to open communication, is it not far better that the aspirant "should seek unto his God" for all his supplies, needs and guidance direct, rather than apply to those who stand as interpreters of the beyond by means of séances and familiar spirits?

God has perfected His own plan and design for reaching and directing every individual soul that comes into existence. Each one has his own appointed place to fill which no other soul can take, and God has His own appointed and prepared method for bringing every soul to its appointed goal. From where the call to "Come" reaches a man, he is directed to take the Straight course, turning neither to the right hand nor to the left in pressing homeward. Then every spiritual gift that is necessary to his assistance and edification will be granted to him as he proceeds. But let a man beware-he who determines to choose by what method or manifestation he will be directed and advised, will soon find himself out of the way, and ultimately in the dungeon of Giant Despair. The prophet of the Lord who has been called to clairaudient, hear the secret plans of the King of Syria spoken in the monarch's bedchamber, and will not be instructed by means of a tipping table; he who has to decipher the mysterious handwriting on the wall will not need to resort to a clairvoyant for his interpretation; Daniel needs not the aid of a palmist to read the prophecy of the future; Peter needs no assistance from a trance medium to get free from his fetters and pass through the open door of his prison. Spiritual gifts can be as numerous as the mercies of God, and be equal to every occasion and need, if they are sought according to spiritual direction. Be sure that the instructions are observed, then "everyone that asketh receiveth; and he that seeketh findeth; and to him that knocketh it shall be opened."

* * *

CHAPTER 16

THE FOURTH DIMENSION - "THERETH"

I was alone-afloat on the shoreless sea of a boundless revelation. Every breath of wind, every musical ripple of the sea, seemed burdened with more and more incomprehensible beauty, majesty and perfection. Existence was but a single volume-an incomparable poem of faultless rhythm, unity and harmonious conception that had been born of a love-dream in the heart of God and executed by the matchless pen of grace Divine. Afloat on such a mystic sacred, rapturously pregnant flood; no wonder that my soul was vibrant with the music which would tax the agencies of the eternities to find expression in colour, sound, perfume and light, as a rainbow of life encircling the sanctuary of the Throne.

I was alone-afloat, dreaming; lost in the maze of revelation that spread out before me, no matter in what direction I turned my wondering, opening eyes. Each zephyr as it touched my cheek, each ripple as it kissed my bark, each sound as it caressed my ear, each spray of perfume as it refreshed my soul, expanded into some new and yet more wonderful revelation than its predecessor, until, at length, I yielded and, resting my head upon the bosom of ecstasy-I dreamed.

* * *

Rael aroused me.

"Shall I recall you with the Prophet's cry of 'Awake, thou that sleepest,' or by the Psalmist's declaration, 'When the Lord turned again the captivity of Zion, we were like them that dream?'" he enquired.

"I feel as if I would rather sleep on and continue my dream," I replied.

"I have no doubt but that you do. Sleep, however, is for children of the night; we who are of the day must be up and doing. Omra has asked me to accompany you in revisiting one of the earlier scenes you met with after your arrival. Shall we go?"

"That must be as you will. I am entirely in your hands. I am so overwhelmed by the revelations that crowd around me that I am incapable of anything but bewilderment."

"I can quite appreciate and sympathize with your difficulty. A village schoolboy suddenly thrust into metropolitan activities is a very inadequate figure to represent your case-there is no simile that you can imagine that would justly express it; that is why our ministry has been provided to assist you until such time as you are able to walk alone. Shall we go?"

Without waiting for my reply, he gently laid his hand upon my shoulder, and in an instant-without a conscious movement of effort-we were standing on the crest of the hill where I had first met Eusemos-standing at the hub of creation, the centre of the fourth sphere. Behind us lay the slope whereon Helen found me; to our right the bank of mists I crossed with Cushna on my first return to the earth, and before us, the prismatic landscape with its ever-changing, animated scene.7

Hitherto, when by means of flight I have been carried from place to place, I have always been conscious, not only of the act of travel, but also of receiving the necessary assistance to do so from whoever accompanied me. In this instance I had not the slightest idea of either. Rael touched me as he asked, "Shall we go?"-and, as by the wave of a magician's wand, we were at our destination.

"What has happened?" I gasped, as soon as I could command an utterance.

Rael's smiling composure was like a calm "Peace, be still" to my perturbation.

"We have simply taken another step in the path of your unfolding," he replied. "In the number of new interests and occasions with which you are being surrounded just now, it is not to be wondered at if you occasionally lose sight of the fact that you are-as I told you before-in the throes of the second birth, by which we mean that you are breaking away from the last influences of the habits, methods and limitations of the physical, in order to enable you to enter upon the illimitable and incorruptible inheritance of the spiritual, and while you are naturally fixing your attention on the outward aspects of what is taking place, we, as watchful experts assisting at the birth, are continually ascertaining what progress you are making, that we may accomplish your deliverance as quickly as possible. This last incident, as I say, proclaims that we have taken another step in the desired direction, and if it will interest you, I shall be pleased to give you an idea as to the nature and significance of it."

"I shall be more than interested," I replied with eager anticipation that his explanation might possibly lift a corner of the veil and afford me a glimpse into the beyond.

"Let me begin by asking you to remember that in his incarnate state, the intelligence of man is confined to a knowledge of only three dimensions in space; length, breadth and height. Within the circumscribed limitations, the whole citadel of science has laid its foundations, and, however trained or cultured the scientist may be, he knows nothing that lies beyond the gamut of his five senses, while as to the Why? and How? of the senses themselves, he is as ignorant as the child unborn. Of the nature and source of all life and being, which lie behind the veil of phenomena, man in the physical knows nothing, and one of the greatest and most profound problems he has yet to solve is-himself. If, therefore, the casket which is said to contain the gem defies all attempts to open it, what value is to be attached to the opinions, speculations, declarations and scientific conclusions of the self-constituted authorities who claim competence to value the jewel itself?

"Here arises the enquiry of those who watch the contention among the various schools of the wise men, 'Is it certain that such an inestimable treasure as an immortal soul exists, or does man simply perish as the beast?' It is in this atmosphere where agnosticism reaches a luxuriant harvest, assisted by the cold and indifferent formalism of equally illogical Churches, and the stream of humanity is swept across our frontiers-even as you have come-to be overwhelmed by the revelations of the love and justice of God which they should and might have known and practised in the flesh.

"In following these blind guides who find both their centre and circumference bounded by the physical, mankind has erred, strayed and ultimately lost itself in the wilderness of sin and rebellion. Now the harvest of the world's ingathering is at hand, and we-the reapers of the Kingdom-are commissioned to return to awaken the sleeping earth with the declaration that, 'It is written' that 'God created man in His own image, in the image of God created He him.' That image of the Creator does not consist of flesh and blood, and bone and sinew, or else the beasts of the field might be gods, and they who fashioned their image in gold, and silver, and brass, and wood, then worshipped them, might be right after all, and the centre and circumference of the philosopher would be established in the circle of which the gods and men alternately create each other.

"The attributes of Deity are-omnipotence, omniscience and omnipresence, and these are the hallmarks of the sonship which are reposed in the human family, each to be made manifest in due time and season. These attributes of God correspond in their number and order of unfoldment to the threefold nature of man-body, soul and spirit. Of the first, 'It is written' that when he created man 'God blessed them, and God said unto them, Be fruitful and multiply, and replenish the earth, and subdue it; and have dominion over the fish of the sea, and over the fowl of the air, and over everything that moveth upon the earth' (Gen. i, 28). Such is the record of the bequeathing of what we may call the first, or physical, attribute of God to man-omnipotence in the terrestrial-and though man has proved to be unfaithful in his disobedience, God has been unswerving on His part, so that the man who wholeheartedly seeks to return to his first estate, may still find that nothing shall be impossible unto him.

"That the earth is not consistently and harmoniously working under this rule lends no force to the hypothesis of its non-existence. It must never be lost sight of that the body is not the man, but the vehicle through which the man expresses himself, and that the period of incarnation is but the infancy stage of existence during which-for the testing and proving of one's fidelity-the exercise of a free will is granted, the responsibility for the use of which rests upon the individual. The result has been that-misled by a lust of the senses-man has trampled the traditional 'If' under his feet and has incurred the penalty; 'Because...thou hast eaten of the tree of which I commanded thee, saying, Thou shalt not eat of it; cursed is the ground for thy sake; in sorrow shalt thou eat of it all the days of thy life...In the sweat of thy face shalt thou eat bread, till thou return to the ground.' Consistent with that, the ascent towards dominion has been toilsome, sorrowful and in an agony of disaster, contention and bloodshed, but God has been true to His dowry, and man has achieved wonders in the hazards he has made, the advantage falling without respect of persons alike upon the evil and the good. But the measure of conquest that has been so wearisomely acquired has been illegally attained. The process that was ordained was that of obediently following, that humanity might grow into the knowledge and likeness of God, as the infant traverses childhood and youth to manhood, that he may be carefully established at every stage for the position he has to hold. The course pursued was, at the instigation of the enemy of souls, to defy obedience, seize upon the inheritance at a bound, and at once become as gods. The plot failed. No thief can break through and purloin the gifts of God. Because their hands have not succeeded in grasping the coveted sceptre, because they cannot lay their sacrilegious hands upon the King and so depose Him; because they are unable to arraign and compel Him to come to terms, the scientist and the philosopher have agreed to say in their hearts, 'We can find no God.' Hence, 'Vanity of vanities-all is vanity.'

"Such is the conclusion of the whole matter as it presents itself to the wisdom of the Magi, who sit beneath and feed upon the fruit of 'the tree of knowledge,' in disobedience of the Divine command, and heed not that which is written in the law. We, however, will be satisfied with taking note of the result, then return to pursue our original enquiry.

"The second attribute of Deity which becomes accessible to man by virtue of his creation in the image of God is Omniscience. In its relation to the other attributes, it occupies a corresponding position to that of the soul in man, which is neither physical nor spiritual, but is an externalization of the body and the tenement of the spirit. Or, to make use of another, perhaps better recognized figure, it is as the twilight which overlaps and interblends the night with morning; or again, to use another of the Biblical similes, it is the Wilderness of Wandering, between Egypt and the Promised Land; or yet again, the state of convalescence between sickness and health-a purely Psychic quality. In the expanse of its outreach it embraces, in its approach to the physical, the lowest form of clairvoyance which scarcely transcends the normal vision and thence upwards until it includes 'the pure in heart [who] see God.' To those still incarnate, this priceless guerdon throws open the doors of possible entry into the halls of communion during the time of emancipation, which the soul enjoys in the hours of sleep. But here again the authority of science, philosophy and religion has stepped into, to denounce such a superstition as 'seeing the invisible,' lest the dicta of the Magi should be imperilled. Upon this ground the battle for supremacy between the flesh and the spirit is being stoutly waged with, at present, variable effect, but the ultimate result is certain, since 'that which is born of the flesh is flesh, and that which is born of the spirit is spirit'-the one transient, the other eternal.

"Approaching the third attribute of God, in whose image we are created-Omnipresence- we enter upon the domain of the spiritual, where 'old things pass away and all things become new.' The true light has come; the last lingering shades of the twilight have given place to the glory of the morning; the lusts of the flesh and the pride of the eyes has been overcome and left behind; the psychic stains of sin which disfigured and marred the soul have been removed by purification; the homeward bound pilgrim has reached the Court of the Voices and has heard the verdict of acceptation; thence moving forward towards the gate of the kingdom he is brought to an unexpected halt on the edge of an impassable gulf! Has there been a mistake? No. That yawning chasm is the allegorical Jordan which divides the physical from the spiritual. It is provided that there shall not pass through the gate on the other side 'anything that defileth' and in preparation for the soul's admission, the traces of its contact with the sin-contaminated earth have been gradually and scrupulously removed, one by one, in its progress through the psychic spheres, until, at length, the last trace of the earth's impurity eradicated, the soul ascends to enter its spiritual abode. This breaking away from the last filament of physical thraldom is the true second birth so absolutely essential to admission to the kingdom-the liberty wherewith Christ makes His people free. That freedom is liberty indeed. It bestows the faculty of the third great attribute of God-the power of Omnipresence, in the exercise of which we are able to operate in the fourth dimension."

"The fourth dimension! What is that?"

"The realm of the unlimited spiritual," he replied.

"When Omra brought you to the edge of the gulf, and invited you to cross, you stepped back."

"Was that to be wondered at?" I enquired.

"No! It was a perfectly natural action. It was fear-an earth stain-that held you back. Omra understood the indication and drew you aside until the process that was working in you should be accomplished."

"How long will that be? Have you any idea?"

"Yes, the evidence is too tangible to admit of the slightest doubt. You have already attained to it."

"Are you sure?" I enquired with doubtful expectancy.

"Absolutely certain," he answered with a reassuring smile. "The evidence of it was given to me in the way by which you accompanied me here."

"How? I am altogether at a loss to understand."

"Of course you are," and Rael could not refrain from laughing outright at my bewilderment. "That is what made you enquire what had happened."

"Won't you explain it?"

"Certainly. Hitherto, when you have paid a visit beyond your own condition-say to Myhanene's home-you have needed assistance to enable you to reach your destination."

"Yes," I assented.

"And, however rapid your flight has been, you have always been aware of the fact that you were travelling."

"Yes."

"But in this instance I simply asked you if we should come hither, touching your shoulder, and we were here."

"Yes, but how?"

"By virtue of your having broken away from the last contact with the earth's limiting influences, by which you enter upon the spiritual inheritance of the third attribute of God-that of Omnipresence, which imparts the germ of ubiquity up to the measure of purity to which your soul has acquired strength to ascend. For I would not have you to understand that any of these attributes can yet be enjoyed in their perfection. Like all the other divine bestowments, they are each planted within us in their due season, and then the cultivation thereof proceeds according to the care and attention we bestow upon them. We bear the outline of the image of God in our creation, the design is filled in and the finishing details added as we choose to devote ourselves to the endeavour, in our ascent from stage to stage in the hierarchy of heaven, until we see Him as He is. In the step you are now about to take, you will pass the limitations of time and distance, both of which will henceforth be inappreciable to you. A thousand years will be to you as a day, and a day as a thousand years, as regards your capacity for the accomplishment and experience of whatever you may be engaged in. Ideas of the past and future will begin to fade away from your recognition as you grow acclimatized to your new condition of this fourth or spiritual dimension, since you will unfold the power of actually being there, first in the past and then in the future of the one eternal Now. For this reason this fourth dimension or estate can only be expressed by the term 'Thereth.' Some have ventured to express it as 'througheth,' but such is misleading, because such a term implies a recognition of passing, which does not necessarily exist, because the act of transition may be accomplished on the wings of thought, as in our transit here, a process which admits of no recognition-we desire, and it is done."

"It is almost incredible, wonderful. But shall I now be really able to cross that awful void?"

"Yes, but it will no longer produce its first awe-inspiring sensation. I should not be surprised to see you pass over without the consciousness of the fact. But before we return, I am desirous that you should notice what a different aspect this scene assumes to what you found it to be at your first visit."

* * *

CHAPTER 17

A FEARFUL AWAKENING

I have been glancing at the record I made of my standing on that Mount of God in the company of Eusemos, and comparing the different aspect it assumed on the occasion of my visit in the company of Rael. And yet the scene itself was practically the same; the remarkable change that had been wrought was entirely in the condition of the beholder. Aforetime my strong desire was to move backward in the direction of the mists, which Helen told me, was due to the attraction of the body; now, I was anxious to move in a contrary way, and cross the rubicon into the spiritual. Then, I viewed the varied roads of what I called the prismatic landscape artistically, indicating the way to some vague condition or destination; now, every individual tint in that symphonic harmony throbbed with life, inspiration and revelation. Then, I wondered at the seeming lack of law, order and organization which I observed in relation to new arrivals; now, I saw not only the wisdom, but also the loving-kindness that was manifested in the arrangement.

In drawing my attention to this, my conductor brought home to me some consciousness of the progress I had made under the direction of Myhanene's ministry, and, in reviewing this first scene of this discarnate life, I was enabled to revive the memory of my first impressions which were only superficial, and also to read the deeper lessons which had since been opened to my spiritual vision.

"What a commentary on the value of retrospection," I said to my companion, after leisurely surveying and comparing the many details of the scene.

"Yes, there is a way of looking back by which we may add to our zest to press forward, and in this review, you may find a most emphatic example of it. Calling the stronger, clearer vision you now have acquired to your aid, you are able to penetrate the depths of certain mysteries in this scene which were insoluble to you before; and in coming back again, with a yet increased insight, you will be able to look yet deeper and deeper still. Thus are all the works and ways of God ever throbbing with new and deeper revelation to him who boldly dives into the depths."

"If that is so, then does not every step, scene and place we pass on the pilgrimage become instinct with a similar attraction to that you speak of in relation to the Court of the Voices?"

"In a sense-yes! But every spot possesses its own peculiar charm. The surpassing attraction of the Court and its precincts is, that it is to every soul who has passed it what the Mount of Olives is to the Master Himself-the spot from which He ascended into the glory after He had shaken off the last of the shackles of the flesh. It is there that mortality is finally swallowed up in victory."

"Now I begin to realize something of its stupendous significance," I answered, amazed that I had so far failed fully to appreciate the fact before. "Oh Myhanene, how wonderfully apt is your familiar aphorism-'Great issues turn on diamond points.'"

"Might we not ask whether there is such a comparison as great and small in the light of the Kingdom?" enquired Rael, and then-"But what have we here?"

As he spoke, with a slight gesture of his hand, he drew my attention to two who were approaching from the busy scene in the valley below us. The one was at once identified as one of the ministering attendants engaged as Eusemos, who so kindly came to my assistance; the other-I needed not to be told-was a new arrival who, by his manner and bearing, was suffering under the sense of some injustice which he strenuously resisted. He was still some distance from us when he curtly addressed himself to Rael:

"Am I correctly informed that you are one in authority here?"

"If I can be of any service, it will be a pleasure to render it," replied my companion.

"I am looking for someone who can correct a most serious grievance, or to direct me to where I can get it corrected."

"May I enquire as to the nature of your trouble?"

"Will you tell me whether you have authority to deal with it? I wish to reach someone in a responsible position."

If the irate questioner had not been so blinded by his passion, surely the look of pitiful compassion with which Rael regarded him would have softened his acerbity.

"We are all not only responsible for, but also pleased to render whatever service may come in our way," he replied.

"But is your service authoritative?"

"Won't you tell me your need?" he enquired with kindly persuasion, "then, if I am not in a position to assist you, I can readily bring you to someone who will instantly do so."

"Is it necessary for me to state my grievance? Look at me," and he spread his arms in most dramatic disgust.

"Look at my filthy condition. Does it not declare itself?"

"Poor soul! Yes, it all too sorrowfully declares itself. Who are you?"

"I am not asking for commiseration, young man," he replied with haughty scorn. "What I am seeking for is the respect and attention due to my position."

"And I ask again: Who are you?"

"I am the Dean..."

Rael interrupted him. "You mean, you were the Dean."

"I am still the Dean, until I have rendered an account of my stewardship," he insisted.

"But have you not been removed from that office by an act of God?"

"By an act of God I rest from my labours, but that is only to enter into my reward. But is this vile parody of attire the only reward I am considered to be worthy of?"

Rael did not hasten to reply, but looked upon his disconsolate appellant with a tender, brotherly commiseration I shall never forget. It was such a look as, I think, must have rested on the face of Christ as he uttered that heart-breaking lamentation over Jerusalem from the brow of Olivet. When he spoke, it was to ask another question in return, like a groan of helplessness from the cavern of regret.

"Is not the reward commensurate with your expectations?"

The tone of the enquiry surprised-seemed to disarm the pugnacity of the suppliant, who was at a loss for a reply; then in a chastened mood made answer:

"I had not built so much on personal expectations as on the promises."

"What promises?" The searching query was put in the same spirit of tender consideration. "And did you always plead them as a miserable offender, with a truly penitent heart, or was it merely a part of a general verbal confession without any reference to a true repentance and anxiety for remission?"

The old rebellious spirit lifted its head again as Rael pressed his enquiry.

"What authority have you for this cross-examination?"

"The authority of an elder brother who, having been appealed to is most sympathetically desirous to clear up a painful misunderstanding," he replied.

"But I fail to see the relevancy of your question."

"Do you not? I think I can readily enable you to do so. I am with yourself grieved to find you attired in these filthy garments, and on your appeal to me, am anxious to show you that no mistake or injustice has been done in this respect."

"But I insist that it is monstrous; and I demand to see someone who has authority to act in the matter."

"You will see no one who will be more able or willing to assist you than myself, if you will allow me to do so."

"Will you, then, see that I am supplied with decent clothing? Then, I will be prepared to listen to what more you have to say."

As I heard this peremptory demand I recalled the well-worn saying, "You would try the patience of an angel," an operation I was witnessing in a very literal sense. But Rael seemed to grow more calm, self-collected, and, if possible, more pitifully patient as demand increased.

"Have you not been here long enough to discover that the

clothing you wear, miserable as it is, is a part of yourself-woven, provided and adjusted to yourself, and that no one but yourself has power to change or remove it?" he replied with great persuasiveness.

The declaration was met with an incredulous and disdainful ejaculation, and in a rashly irate determination to discredit it, a violent effort was made to cast the loathsome clothing aside. The effort proved to be of more effect than any argument. In the condition of the sufferer-attempting to discard the base that he might don the noble-it was like tearing himself asunder, and with a cry of agony he ceased to torture himself, turning his crestfallen face to Rael in mute appeal for an explanation.

"My poor, unfortunate brother," Rael began, "for however sad your condition now is you are still a member of the family in which I am more happily circumstanced. I wish you would try to grasp this and remember that I shall always he ready to help or advise you whenever you may need my assistance. You may scarcely be able to accept this as freely and fully as I offer it, because it is difficult for you to understand such an offer being made, on so short an acquaintance, without it being a cover to some ulterior motive. You will not be here long before you discover that these sinister undercurrents of pretence and deception cannot be concealed amongst us. We are each and all known and read of all men. Had you known this, you would have understood me differently from the beginning-you would have understood why you are wearing the garments you are so anxious to get rid of-you would have felt the force of my enquiry when I asked you whether you had been in the habit of pleading the promises with a truly penitent heart, or as a verbal confession without a thought of true repentance. I needed not to ask-I could read it all too plainly in your vesture. I wanted to bring to your own remembrance your usual confession so perfunctorily made when you said, 'we are all as an unclean thing, and all our righteousness are as filthy rags,' but you would not hear me."

"Do you forget our sacraments-are they of no avail? If not -then what is true or effectual?"

"When any gift or creature of God is legitimately, faithfully and reverently used, it becomes a sacrament-outward and visible sign of an inward spiritual grace, but the most sacred sign, symbol or ceremony which heaven can devise, sacrilegiously employed, or lightly misrepresented, becomes riot only of non-effect but an active agent in turning the truth of God into a lie, and an instrument in turning the flock of Christ out of the way into the by-paths of folly and countless sins. The one sacrament God has instituted for observance on earth is that of Love, shining from heaven as the Pole-star to guide humanity homeward; then to be reflected from man to man, each individual commanded to communicate the sacred flame to his brother's torch for the enlightenment of the whole world; and finally, the earth having been baptized with the glory of the Divine Splendour, shall return its bounteous harvest to fill the garner of the Father's house with a race of children who were begotten, nourished, trained and perfected in the image of the Love from which they sprang.

"But this simple, natural and all-sufficient sacrament of God did not commend itself to the minds of the wise men in the University of Babel, who for the aggrandizement of their cult have invented a group of fictitious and counterfeit sacraments -ecclesiastical, ritualistic and theological-through the labyrinthian mystery of which even the greatest authorities fail to discover a clear and definite path. The system brought upon them the denunciation of the Christ, 'Woe unto you scribes and Pharisees, hypocrites! for ye shut up the kingdom of heaven against men; for ye neither go in yourselves, neither suffer ye them that are entering to go in.' This specious fallacy of a theology built on the philosophy of men, instead of the revelation of God, has not only survived the anathema of Christ, but it has since branched out into a multitude of contending schools until confusion has become more confounded, and the name of the Prince of Peace is used as the battle-cry for inhuman slaughter.

"So successfully have the Magi reproduced the specious

allegorical tragedy of Eden in the hypnotic temple of Babel, where the tares have been so ingeniously sown among the wheat, that it has become a vain task to separate them before the scythe of Death makes the task a sad but easy one. Then comes the rude awakening as the hand of Truth arouses the sleeper to 'Arise and see!' This is the startling revelation under the staggering influence of which you have appealed to me. And now"-here Rael's voice took a deeper and if possible more tender tone than ever-"what is it possible for me to say, for me to do to help you? Why were you so blind and deaf? Why did you so deceive yourself as not to know that the Master was speaking equally to yourself as to those to whom you spake when you read His words, Woe unto you, scribes and Pharisees, hypocrites! For ye are like unto whited sepulchres, which indeed appear beautiful outward, but are within full of dead men's bones, and of all uncleanness'? Now your house is left unto you, not only desolate, but grievously dilapidated. You all too lightly took upon yourself to occupy a sacredly responsible position you did not understand-to discharge a spiritual duty to which you were not called-to declare the counsels of God which had not been revealed to you-to direct the souls of men in a way of which you yourself were ignorant-to declare a way of salvation the first principles of which you were a stranger to, and now you must needs reap the harvest of your audacity-now you have to pay the penalty of your incompetence to the last farthing of the just demand that is made upon you. And there is no escape."

As Rael delivered himself with calm and sympathetic consideration, the haughty spirit of the cleric gradually gave place to a rising sense of serious apprehension, and as Rael concluded, with a very chastened mien, the enquiry was made:

"But though I may be all the offender you point out, am I not also something of a victim? I am not the originator of the system you declaim, but accepted and embraced it at the value my forefathers had placed upon it-am I not entitled to any mitigating consideration for this?"

"Yes, my hitherto misguided brother, you are entitled to and will receive consideration now that you have fallen into the hands of God-not the God you have been authorized to set before your fellow-men as the central figure in a man-made system of theology, but the God who was made manifest in the life, the teaching and the works of His anointed, who 'will have all men to be saved and come to a knowledge of the truth,' the power of whose irresistible love you will no longer be able to escape, when, once, like the wretched prodigal, you awake and come to yourself.

"Let us sit down for a moment while I tell you something of the loving-kindness of the Father with whom you have now to do," and the four of us threw ourselves on the crest of the slope while Rael poured out his soul in a setting of the gospel that was old and yet entrancingly new by the way in which it was declared.

"The epitome of every life the world has known-ever can know"- he began-"is to be found in connection with the records of the life of Jesus; the commentary and details, so far as are essential, are set forth in the other parts of scripture. The law and the prophets are not doctrinal, philosophical and scientific codes, placed in the hands of priests for the government of the people; they are allegories given to children that the older may teach the younger the simple love-stories the Father has written to excite and stimulate the love of His beloved ones. But as the variety of time, place, circumstance, position, mental ability and inherited gilt will be combined in producing an innumerable diversity of personality, while frequently large groups will be more closely held together by one or another of distinctive traits, so interblended as to retain the union of the whole family, the stories are not told in consecutive chapters and complete volumes, but the allegories are set, like jewels in the histories of men, families or nations, that the child playing at 'hide-and-seek' may search and find, and, learning to piece each lesson in accordance with its own conception of its Father's image, may present its own idea of its unseen Father's portrait in the life it builds.

"Perhaps it will be of some service if I place before you your own story in accordance with this arrangement, as I see it portrayed in the scriptures-as I should present it if I were preaching the gospel from the point of view where we are now beholding. The Christ outline of it I should find in the beautiful story displaying the ministry of the Good Samaritan. You occupy the place of the victim who, attracted by some unspecified advantages offered by Jericho, and oblivious of the royal curse which had been anciently pronounced upon the city (Josh. vi, 26), not being superstitious, turned his back upon the city of the great King, walked in the way of sinners, and fell a victim to robbers who beat and stripped him.

"The terse description, 'leaving him half dead,' together with the rest of the allegory, shows the eloquent masterstroke of the speaker in revealing so much in the silences for those whose spiritual ears and eyes are open-the avenues down which God makes His significant revelations. How could the position in which I find you be more graphically described than in the words, 'leaving him half dead'? Stripped of all the accessories of your proudly boasted profession, even to the body you adorned with the insignia that vaunted your exalted office, so that even a casual glance of the priest and Levite passing by do not recognize your dignity, surely no more brief and non-committal phrase could be employed to express the situation?

"And yet it is but the half of death that you have endured-the way from Jerusalem to Jericho is the way of death, but the city of the allegory was destroyed, so that whosoever could escape the robbers who infest the road and reach the site would find no city there-the eternal King hath declared that 'Death is swallowed up in victory'-when now you reach the uttermost of the extremity of wandering, you reach the extremity of all but the eternal, and the sweep of the circumference takes an upward turn. You cannot suffocate in the filth of the swine-trough, since there is an everlasting arm even underneath the mire to lift up the head until the vilest prodigal awakes with the latent determination to escape.

"I am not saying that you have to meet this limit-far be that from me. You are now in the realm of law and justice, not administered as in the earthly court, but in accordance with the inviolable righteousness of God. You will be neither dragged nor escorted to any place for which you have prepared yourself, but when we leave you, our brother Eldare may save you much trouble-perhaps also sorrow-by pointing out the way in which your own place lies, then you will be left to find it for yourself, and when you select it, no one will attempt to dispute your choice.

"But though you will be free from outward restraint in selecting your first abode, it is quite certain to me where your choice will fall."

"Will you be kind enough to tell me?" he entreated in a still more chastened spirit. "Will it be with other clerics, since you say we each go to our own place?"

Rael met the half-expectant gaze with which the entreaty was made with a look of pitiful commiseration, and did not hasten to reply. Then with a marked deliberation he said:

"There are no clerics here. Such distinctions, with all such like accessories of Vanity Fair lie yonder," pointing away to the great banks of mists. "All the pomps and vanities of the seductive revelries of the flesh lie buried with the body. These cannot rise again. For you that Fair is over; its attractive drama is ended; the plaudits of the entertained have ceased; the curtain has fallen; the robes in which you elected to strut the stage have been doffed, and I have before me not the popular hero of the footlights, but the miserable actor who is seeking for a shelter where he can lay his head-for some friend who will break and give him the bread for which he is starving. How gladly would I give you to eat, but in your infatuation for your art, you have so weakened your constitution that to give you solid food would only be to increase your suffering. You need the most skilled and careful treatment to secure your recovery. It will be painful to begin with-due to your neglect to take precaution in the past. You aspired to fame, and won it, but in your victory you lost your soul's health; now you have to fight a sterner battle to recover it. But you need not despair. However drastic your treatment may have to be, let this help you to bear it-it cannot end fatally. Nor will you be left to bear it unattended. You may have to pass through a Babylonian furnace on your way, but fear not; the fire is only an agent for purification to carry away and get rid of the filth; it cannot destroy life, and though in the pains of the ordeal, you may not be conscious of the fact there will be with you, in the midst of the furnace, one like unto the Son of Man, to watch and deliver you when the purifying effect is secured. It may be that the crucible may be necessary to remove the dross that is poisoning your life; if so, the refiner will be in constant attendance, and when, at length, he can clearly see his own image reflected in your depths, he will bring you forth back to the spot on which we are standing now.

"When, in the providence of God, you are able to do this, you will be altogether another man-your eyes will be opened, your understanding enlarged, and taking a review of your whole career, you will be filled with wonder and surprise at the tender loving-kindness of the Father which has been made manifest to you. I would that I could save you from all that lies between now and then in the pain of the purifying process, but the seed has been sown and the harvest must be reaped, but in the reaping you will find the blessing that maketh rich, and when we meet again, you will tell me that the gain has been far in excess of the cost."

With this we left him.

It may be that I am wrong in my estimates of the comparison, but as I look back upon this incident, I cannot recall an experience that filled me with a greater yearning to do something to alleviate its consequences than the case we were then leaving behind us. Several times did I turn my head and cast a look of melancholy desire upon that suffering soul.

At length, my sympathy grew too strong for resistance, and I entreated Rael, "Is it not possible for us to do something in some way to help him?"

"Nothing more," he replied laconically, but there was a volume of eloquent meaning in the sympathetic shake of the head by which it was accompanied.

"It seems to me to be almost criminal to leave him alone just as he is," I responded.

"His case is not exactly as it seems to your inexperienced eyes," he replied. "For us to attempt to do more at present, will not only be ill-advised, but detrimental. Eldare is far more competent to render the aid he needs than either you or I, and much as either of us would be glad to assist him, after what has been accomplished, we must be content to leave him until such time as further treatment will be helpful rather than otherwise."

"Pardon the presumption of my ignorance, Rael," I pleaded in my importunity, "but if we remained at hand, could we not the more readily assist him when he really needed it?"

There was more of commendation than reproof in the look he gave me as he asked:

"And would you suggest our neglect of other legitimate duties while we waited until he should appeal for assistance, then to discover that others had been appointed who were better qualified for the purpose than ourselves?"

"Ah, my friend, forgive me, I am admonished indeed. In my ignorance I knew not what I asked, but in my sympathy with suffering, I wanted to stretch out a hand to help."

"There is nothing to repent of or be forgiven in anything you have done, my brother," he replied, his face brightening into a beam of commendation. "So far as I am permitted to read it, this whole incident has had for one of its purposes the presentation of this test to you; to ascertain whether at the instant when you might put your newly found power of 'thereth' into operation, you would be willing, at the call of duty, to waive your personal gratification in order to perform a doubtful ministry. Your response has been the equivalent of having successfully rendered the service for which you pleaded, and the reward of it will be yours."

"Oh Rael," I cried, almost trembling with gratitude at the protecting power which had been afforded to me in the trial, "what manner of men we ought to be as we move to and fro among these interblended opportunities of Providence!"

"Now you are approaching that attitude of soul that it is necessary to attain on earth in order to prevent such catastrophes as the one we have just encountered."

"Should I be wrong," I carefully ventured to enquire, "if I asked the nature of the sin to which his downfall was due?"

"No I could read his record as in an open book from the motley character of his apparel, and you will presently be equally able to do the same, but it is neither necessary nor advisable to practise too close a scrutiny. We are not judges, but rather ministers. It is no part of our work to examine and discover whether 'the last farthing' of the penalty has been paid, but rather to try to anticipate the redemption by imparting what strength we may to leave the bondage at the earliest available instant. But of the general aspects and symptoms of a case, it is well for those who are brought into contact with it to be familiar in order to become the more efficient in its treatment. In those main features this case is a very common one; it is one of spiritual petrifaction arising from a mechanical and insincere formalism without any approach to real spiritual life to control it."

"Is not much of that due first of all to taints we receive from our parents, then as children from observation, and finally from the spiritual teachers who claim authority to teach us?"

"We recognize that perhaps more clearly than you may have inclined to admit. That is why I have said, 'we are not judges.' At the same time, I can refer to yourself in support of my claim that a man has power, if he chooses to use it, in most cases, to break away from these restrictive influences and worship God in the beauty of holiness, in spite of any and every spider's web, whether of science, philosophy or theology, which any organization or combination may seek to throw around him. The standard of judgment by which a soul is judged on his arrival here is not perfection-no man is perfect, or can be so until he is lost in his union with God-but by that approach towards perfection which he, personally, had been able to attain. An exemplary instance of that was given by the Master Himself in the case of the woman who had broken the box of costly ointment over his head. He expressed no opinion in respect to the act in itself, whether it was discreet or otherwise-that He left as it may or may not have been-but of the motive which had prompted it He said, 'She hath done what she could.' Such is the standard of the judgment here delivered, not by the verdict of any individual, but by the revelation of the life which has passed through the searching ordeal. God demands to know how the balance of our stewardship stands concerning the soul He has entrusted to our care. We have to meet Him with the reward of our trading with our fellow-men in our hands; if we have been slothful or buried our talents in the earth, there is no admission to His presence until we have corrected our folly- unless we wish to be condemned. But having discovered this fact on arrival here, it is demanded that we set about correcting our error at once that we may all be found ready to present ourselves in the day when He shall make up His jewels."

* * *

CHAPTER 18

CROSSING THE BRIDGE

We were back in that entrancing shrubbery from which Omra had previously spirited me away. In suggesting our return, Rael humorously challenged me to observe and discover something of the process by which the transit was accomplished.

"I will..." I was about to say, "I will do my best to do so," but I had scarcely begun to speak before it was a fait accompli, and Rael, highly amused at my discomfiture, was asking:

"Had you not better report at once, before the memory of the details evades you?"

Omra joined us as Rael was speaking, and was not one whit behind the speaker in his enjoyment of the pleasantry.

"We might have made our return in a far more leisurely way," Rael proceeded to explain, "only the repetition of the former plan threw the door of opportunity open to my pointing to a matter that will sometime be valuable to you in your ministry."

"If you can do that, I will readily forgive you the advantage you have taken," I replied.

"That is generous of you, Aphraar; at the same time you must allow me to think that it was too bad of Rael to make capital out of your embarrassment," Omra facetiously observed.

"If that capital had been for the common weal," Rael replied with the same quiet badinage, "I rather imagine that even the sedate Omra, had he been there and seen the face of Aphraar, as he cried, 'What has happened?' would have ventured to encore the experiment, in the hope of seeing a repetition of the amazement."

"But surely an encore is always shorn of the initial surprise? However, proceed with the lesson you are anxious to reach."

"Yes, after the music of the Smile, let us seat ourselves again at the feet of Duty. In doing so, I wish to carry you back to what I have said in relation to the fourth dimension, because, though it is actually beyond the comprehension of man in the physical state, there is one illustration of it that may be used to great advantage occasionally in your ministry."

"If so, by all means point it out to me," I implored him, for, in all things, I would be that which Paul admonished Timothy to be, 'a workman that needeth not to be ashamed, rightly dividing the word of truth.'"

"My reference is to the subject of Prayer..."

"A most important subject," interjected Omra, "one upon which I have already said something to Aphraar-take your own way, Rael."

"It is a question upon which there can be no ground of difference between us, so without any reference to what you may have said, I will proceed. Nor shall I concern myself with offering a definition of Prayer, nor generally with attempting a reply to the question, 'Does God answer prayer?' I want more particularly to direct your attention to a specious pseudo-philosophic objection to prayer which exercises considerable influence on many minds on account of its semblance of a logical basis. The argument may be variously framed according to the speaker and the particular need of the moment; I will state it in my own way; 'The idea that prayer can become available in contributing to the arrest, change or obviating contemporary affairs is not only fallacious, but absolutely impossible. Let us look at a very necessary premise we need to lay down as a basis upon which to work; How far has the petition to travel from the petitioner before it reaches the ear of God? And next; at what rate is the petition despatched upon its errand? We will suppose, for the argument's sake, that the throne of God is located in one of the nearest fixed stars to earth-Sirius-and that the prayer travels at the inconceivable speed of light-186,000 miles per second. It will require more than eight years for the petition to reach its destination. Under such circumstances, how is it possible for prayer to avail in influencing passing events? It is only necessary to state the case to refute it with derision.'

"So it seems. But things are not exactly what they seem to be. 'Who is this that darkeneth counsel by words without knowledge? Hast thou not known-hast thou not heard' that God 'taketh the wise in their own craftiness?' The argument just advanced is from the lips of a philosopher whose knowledge is circumscribed by the limitations of three dimensions known to the physical, while prayer is a spiritual faculty and operates in a region which is neither visible, tangible nor comprehended in the physical. The speed at which light traverses space in comparison to that of prayer is scarcely that of the ancient footman to the modern wireless telegraph. While light is preparing to fashion its first rippling wave, prayer, on the wings of desire, is at its destination, and waits, in eager haste, to bring its answer back. The broken-hearted penitent cries, 'God, be merciful,' and turning homeward, while yet the philanthropic Pharisee continues his self-laudatory harangue, finds the answer to his prayer already attests his justification. 'Go ye and learn what that meaneth'-the spirit knows neither time nor distance when once it standeth in the light of God."

"Ah! Ah!" cried Omra, "you have just finished your discourse in time, for here comes Myhanene with our sister Zisvené."

"Who is Zisvené?" I asked. "I have not met with her before."

"Have you not?" was Omra's astonished reply. "She should be particularly interesting to you."

"Indeed! In what way?"

"I think Myhanene would tell us that she is actually the first-fruits of your ministry to earth."

"My ministry to earth! How come she's here, then? Surely you are mistaken," I exclaimed.

"You will find that I am not mistaken, but Zisvené's is a most exceptional case, I can assure you. She was an earnest and most indefatigable searcher after truth. Not being able to satisfy herself on theological husks and superficially accepted dogmas, through various vicissitudes, she pressed forward assured that the living bread for which her soul hungered was to be found somewhere.

She heard your voice as she wandered in the wilderness. It appealed to her. She followed. Your evangel of the possibilities of the sleep-life charmed her. She prayed for guidance, and in response found her way across the frontier, and now she spends almost the whole of her sleep-life in mission work with us. But you must hear the story as she will tell it to you."

"Omra-you amaze me. It seems to be a thing incredible!"

"Is it not almost time that you abandoned speaking of the incredible?" he enquired with his encouraging smile.

"The whole book of Revelation, which you have but just begun to read, is written to record those things Paul spoke of when he said; 'Eye hath not seen, nor ear heard, neither have entered into the heart, the things which God hath prepared for them that love Him.' You may depend upon it that in the womb of the infinite there are revelations gestating, the birth of which will strike the archangels dumb with astonishment. Cease, then, to speak of the incredible. Be prepared at each step to penetrate further into the Evermore, and as your eyes open to each successive vision, worship with reverence and with awe. But, here is Zisvené now."

So it was that Omra opened yet another door in heaven through which I might gain a still different glimpse into the expanse of infinity. I had no opportunity then to enter into the contemplation of the vision, but as I glanced at it, there flashed through my mind the overpowering conviction of the Psalmist; "Such knowledge is too wonderful for me. It is high, I cannot attain to it." Then our friends were upon us-Zisvené stepping forward with greeting as of an old and well-tried friend.

"We need no introduction, Aphraar; your books have already made you well known to me, and with my whole soul I want to thank you for what an untold blessing they have been to me."

She turned to walk with me as she spoke-Myhanene joined Omra and Rael, who had fallen behind-and so we continued our walk.

"Why should you thank me?" I replied as soon as I could recover from the surprise her warmth of greeting occasioned.

"Should not all the thanksgiving be laid at His feet who made such a ministry possible? Is not the honour of being permitted to take part in such a most glorious mission, not only a recompense, but a super-abounding joy, that will not permit the thought of labour in connection with it? Think of the transcending honour of it! Called to be a fellow-worker with God in the salvation of-if so be just a simple soul-one soul, which is so intrinsically valuable to Him that the whole inanimate creation is but an air-bubble in comparison. Again-and more than that-to have the knowledge that I have succeeded in it-and for Him! Think of it! Do you think I have any need of thanks? Ought I not rather with broken-hearted joy to pour out my thanksgiving to Him, through you, for the inestimable honour He has bestowed upon me?"

"I can understand all you say, as well as something of what you feel. The water of a new life which I have been able to drink has been inexpressibly sweet, reviving, life-giving, and I am unspeakably grateful to the source and Giver of the stream from which I have been permitted to drink; still, I cannot be unmindful of the channel by which it has been carried to me. Are you fond of music?"

"Most passionately," I replied.

"Have you never listened to some great master playing on that King of instruments-the violin-until in the embrace of the soul of music you have been carried away into an elysium of harmony-all, within, without, around, blending into an ocean of melody, and there has been nothing existent but music, in which your soul has found its ideal of heaven in your rapturous dream?"

"Have I not! Oh, how many times have I lent myself to the blissful enchantment!"

"And when the dream was over-when you woke to find yourself on earth again-did you never give a thought to the beauty of the instrument through which the soul of the violinist had so wonderfully influenced you?"

"I don't think it ever occurred to me to separate the one from the other; they were so inter-blended in my mind that to have done so would have been to have wrecked the dream; or that is how I now imagine it would have been."

"Just so, my dear Aphraar, would it be with me if I tried to dissociate you from the Great Father, in the priceless blessing I have received through your ministry. I have, at length, been able to reach you-a boon many times craved for when pouring out my soul to Him in the sanctuary of prayer-and shall I now be forgetful of the debt I owe? Shall I not send afresh to Him through the channel He has ordained to use to bestow His blessing, another acknowledgment of my gratitude and love?"

"Yes, certainly, we should in all things give God the glory; but after that, there is another to whom whatever is left of recognition is due before I can lay the slightest claim to consideration."

"And who may that be?" she asked alertly.

"Myhanene! If it had not been for the brotherly assistance he gave me, you would never have heard of me.

"I believe he has been of much assistance to you. It was just what one would expect from his generous soul. Searching around earth's lumber-rooms to see what neglected treasures of the Master were laying there in forgetfulness, he came across, and set himself to reinstate you-he determined to bring the lost favourite back to the heart that was yearning for the restitution of the loved one. That is like Myhanene, and he will receive a due recognition for the discovery; but Myhanene would be the last to take credit for more than that, nor will I forget him in that respect. But after we have given to Myhanene his full deed of recognition for all he has done, you still remain the instrument the Master has chosen to employ in recalling me from my wandering, and wooing my soul into His embrace; why then should you refuse to allow me to tender to you the gratitude I feel?"

Why need I further contend the point when I saw how firmly she was resolved to carry out her purpose? I did not desire even the slightest recognition. When I reviewed my experiences, the vast amount of care and attention that had been bestowed upon me, the exceptional privileges that had been granted me, and then compared them with the meagre and altogether unworthy record I had made-not wilfully, but under the exigencies of my infirmities-I blushed to think of accepting any sort of congratulation. But Zisvené was looking upon my work from another and very different point of view. She was looking with other eyes, hearing with other ears, basing her conclusions upon evidence I could not understand, any more than she could comprehend the shortcoming I was so sensitively conscious of. When the difference in the points of view was recognized and allowed for, was not her conclusion equally well founded with my own? There was no point of principle involved in my yielding to her desire-perhaps my refusal to do so might throw some obstacle in her path, and at such a thought my resistance collapsed.

As I thus reflected, the silence lengthened, during which I caught her eloquent blue-grey eyes stealing furtive but confident glances at my irresolution, until at length, with an attempt at gravity she could ill conceal, she asked:

"Has the defeat been so absolutely crushing as to leave you quite speechless?"

"It is not any sense of defeat, but rather the knowledge of how, personally, I come of being worthy of your commendation that silences me."

"Well, that is a point we need not begin to argue just now; but will you allow me to be generous and suggest a possible way of taking your revenge?"

"Are you attempting to lay another trap for my unwary feet?"

"Now, look me in the face and tell me if you think I could really do such a thing?"

"Your presence here is sufficient evidence that you would not do so viciously, but there is a gleam of playfulness in your tell-tale eyes which bids me-Beware. Still, I would like to hear your suggestion."

"I was wondering whether, if we had the opportunity of crossing lances in my waking state, you might not be able to recover yourself. I should be very pleased to test it, if you could prevail upon your Recorder to pay me a visit."

"That must be reserved for after consideration. Arrangements in that direction are for Myhanene to decide. In the meantime, I should be pleased to speak with you of your sleep-life experiences. Perhaps you might be able to assist me in an endeavour I am hoping to undertake."

"If at any time there is anything I am able to do in return for the obligation I am under to yourself, you have only to name it. But you must remember that I am only here by favour..."

"Are we not all on an equality in that respect?"

"In a measure that is so. But my own case is most peculiarly -I believe almost uniquely so; therefore you must not expect too much of me. This much I will readily promise you, that, if I am able to assist you in any way, you may always be sure that the service will afford me more pleasure than I can express. Now let me call your attention to the view around us."

Zisvené had held my interest so closely by her conversation that I had ceased to notice anything but the absorbing fascination of her personality and discourse. When, at length, she did recall me to notice our surroundings, I gave a shout of involuntary surprise-almost dismay-to find myself brought to a stand in the very centre of that awesome bridge, with the Yawning gulf sinking into the bosom of the unfathomable blackness beneath our feet.

I gasped as I looked and realized what a step I had unconsciously taken; but my confidence did not forsake me, for I was not left to encounter the ordeal unattended, except by Zisvené. Around me were gathered, not only Omra, Rael and Myhanene, but Walloo-Malie, Avita, Rhamya, with the rest of the friends I had left in the Court of the Voices, and a great company of others, among whom I recognized many I had known in the lower life, together with others to whom I had been well known in the ministry of guidance and protection.

What a gathering! How could I entertain a fear as to the safety of the structure on which we rested? My eyes wandered over that crowd of faces upon each of which I read an unspoken note of welcome in that sacred, silent anthem, too sweet, too musical for sound, and my soul surged with a joy inexpressible, except in the breathing of "Peace-be still." With one instinctive impulse, every head was bowed to receive the mystic benediction, after which Walloo-Malie spoke to me.

"In that sublimest allegory of a wandering soul and its return to the Father's house, as told by the Master to those who hung upon His teaching, He gives to verbal expression a very meagre place. Words, at their best, are but crude suggestions of intangible ideals, which people the inner shrine of the soul. If we would understand their real worth, poetry and beauty, we must be able to gain admission to the shrine and by inter-blending with the soul wherein they were conceived, sink into and lose ourselves in the spirit where they dwell-know them as they really are. This is a boon-a power which only God possesses. Hence in His parable, the Master only introduces speech to give an order, they make no attempt to express the Father's feelings, 'Bring forth the best robe, and put it on him, and put a ring on his hand, and shoes on his feet; and bring hither the fatted calf, and kill it, and let us eat, and be merry; for this, my son, was dead, and is alive again; he was lost, and is found.'

"Following that august example, there are really only two words that need to be spoken as we stand here on the boundaries of two worlds-the physical and the spiritual. To You, in the providence of God, the time has come for the glorious-the eternal daybreak, in which every shadow must flee away, and you, consequently, must say Farewell to the yesterday which is passing away in this new birth; to us, who are here as a reply to your oft-repeated enquiry:

Will anyone there, at the beautiful gate,
Be waiting and watching for me?

is granted the great privilege of speaking that second word; 'Welcome.'

"It is a familiar word-one you often have heard before;

sometimes with a deep, clear, sweet vibrant intonation that sounded like Home; at others, with a brazen, harsh and hollow flippancy, that aroused shadows of suspicion in your mind, and your ears were quick to catch the whispered echo-Beware. I have been asked to speak our word of Welcome to you as you step across our threshold, and as I do so, with the baton of my tongue calling the waiting orchestra of heaven to prompt attention, we sound the keynote of an anthem of peace and goodwill that shall reverberate through your soul, in ever-increasing music till God shall cease to be.

"You cannot understand it? No! We do not expect you to do so before your eyes have beheld the glory. You do not yet understand the sounds you hear in the word with which we greet you. This is but your natal hour. You are not yet across the threshold of your new birth. How can you comprehend? But your eyes can see-God has breathed into your soul the breath of a holier life, and in that act, has tuned your life to vibrate in harmony with that which is to be. Let your opening eyes look into our faces; let the first sounds that fall upon your ears be melodious with tones that fall with soothing cadences, and woo the sacred confidence of the newly-born love within you. We have no elder brethren here who harbour resentment against the return of the lost one; no cold shoulders; no askant looks; no veiled innuendoes; no drawing aside of robes; no autocracy; no sycophants or goody-goodies; the shadows of these have all passed away even from where we now are standing, and their substances fear to essay the passage of the bridge. Therefore, 'Come in, thou blessed of the Lord,' we bid thee 'Welcome home!'"

* * *

CHAPTER 19

IN THE GARDEN AT THE GATE

It would require not only one, but a series of volumes to record all that took place in that memorable gathering on the Bridge. Old friendships renewed and new ones established; sweet and bitter memories of struggles, conquests and defeats in the past recalled; tracing the development of the stream of hopes and fears until we saw the wondrous expansion in the ocean of a Divine love and purpose; review of the varied paths by which pilgrim feet had been led through many vicissitudes to the rendezvous we had reached; the comparison of experiences encountered between recent arrivals and the pioneers who had toiled homeward across the unbroken stretches of the earlier centuries-these, and a thousand-and-one engrossing themes of interest, might be enumerated and discussed to helpful purpose, each of which would serve to throw its special ray of useful light on the path of some who are following after us.

Nor is it that I would shun the task of compiling the record, but I have to remember the limitations by which those who come after me are circumscribed-a bondage from which now I am happily set free-therefore I must content myself with scattering fragments, not volumes, to mark the path I am taking, in the hope that-in the future gatherings in the Father's house, in which we all shall take part-all the details of earth's chequered pilgrimage will be filled in and comprehended in an illumination of Divinest love and mercy.

While all this was going on, I had several times lost sight of Zisvené. I was not disturbed as I noticed it-I knew that I could reach her again by the help of Myhanene-but I wished, without unnecessary delay, to speak with her relating to her experiences in the sleep-life, having a hope that she might assist me in a project I had in mind.

Presently someone laid a sympathetic hand upon my shoulder,

and, turning, I saw her behind me.

"Don't you feel as if it were almost impossible to tear yourself away?" she enquired.

"Indeed, I do," I returned, emphatically.

"Yours is not an isolated experience. I am told it is so with every soul that is brought into the influence of these surroundings. To me it is very much like an enchanted land, and yet we must move, for in the garden before us the banquet of your welcome is awaiting us."

When Zisvené thus made her presence known to me, I must have been for some time absorbingly interested in the unfolding of a most trivial matter I had quite forgotten until it was mentioned to me by the stranger who told me the astounding sequel. I would like to tell the story, but marvellous as it turned out to be, it is one of the omissions I am compelled to make. It must suffice to say that I became so engrossed in the narration as to be oblivious of the fact that our friends had been gradually withdrawing in the direction indicated, until Myhanene and some half-dozen of his particular companions were all that were left to await me.

I shall not court disaster by attempting an impossible description of the expanse of garden which lay before me, outlined by the crescent-shaped open colonnade of what, on nearer inspection, appeared a kind of pinkish alabaster, over which crept the diaphanous screen of a magnificent floral creeper. In the centre of the arc rose the delicately artistic and regal towers supporting a bridge of aerial beauty corresponding to the architectural theme of the colonnade, and beneath the bridge swung the opalescent gates, the gem and crown of the matchless scene.

Within the vast area thus defined, lay a kaleidoscopic picture of angel-land defying the most perfect dream of idealization to reproduce. And here, attuned to perfect harmony of minutest detail in form, colour, perfume and sound, were dainty stands of angel food, or fountains of sweet refreshment played, that while we moved about in the shadowless communion we might take, eat, drink and thus live in the actual paradise of God.

Our little group was leisurely approaching the foot of the bridge, while my eyes wandered hither and thither in contemplation of the restful and inspiring scene. Presently Myhanene's arm stole across my shoulder in his familiar fraternal embrace, and he asked:

"Do you remember the record of Jacob's home-coming, Aphraar?"

"To which particular homecoming do you refer?" I enquired.

"The time when he wrestled with the angel by the side of the Jabbok," he answered.

"Who could possibly forget that? And that reminds me Myhanene, I have often wondered who that angel was. Do you think it was the Saviour, as some have supposed it to be?" I eagerly questioned, hoping to have one of my old uncertainties set at rest.

"Perhaps Walloo-Malie might be able to say more about that than myself," he replied. "He has been here much longer than I have. But it is not so much who the angel was, as something he did that interests me just now."

"What? The shrinking of the sinew on Jacob's thigh?"

"No, nor that even. What else did he do?" And he turned on me that peculiar tip-tilt of his playful eyes which all who know him love to see upon the face of Myhanene.

"I am afraid I shall not be of much service to you in your enquiry," I answered. "Perhaps my memory is at fault, which may be pardonable under the circumstances, and I never was an adept at thought-reading. Won't you tell me what he did?"

There was another gleam of amusement flashed upon me.

"Did he not ask the patriarch his name?"

"Certainly he did-however could I have been so stupid as to forget it? But why should he do so when he knew it already?"

"To give emphasis to that which was to follow," he replied. "Scriptural names were not often bestowed or assumed apart from expressing some characteristic reference to their possessor, and when a man changed either his position or his character, it was not unusual for him to also change his name. Jacob had passed a crisis in his career during that night of wrestling. His contest with an angel had made another man of him. Henceforth the name Jacob-supplanter- would be a misnomer, and he must cross the river into the homeland under the new name, Israel, 'for as a prince hast thou power with God and with men, and hast prevailed,' Aphraar,"-and as Myhanene spoke the name in his tenderest, most fervent tone, he came to a halt; another step and bridge would be left behind.

"You, too, have now passed the one great crisis in your career; just one more step and you will stand upon the homeland-the homeland from which the Master speaking to His beloved John has promised to bestow on all who overcome a new name on their arrival at the self-same place. This is a necessary part of the welcome we rejoice to give you. Aphraar-the seeker-is no longer applicable, for your quest has been rewarded. Now, as Astroel-a star of God-we bid you enter into the rest that remaineth," and as he spoke, drew me forward and I set my feet upon the Fatherland. "Go forward, from strength to strength, from glory to glory, until your feet shall tread the sacred streets of the City of our God."

Such was my reception and entrance into the Garden of the Gate.

I had a desire, as I moved among that concourse of people - where everyone sought an opportunity to speak, if only a single word of recognition, congratulation, welcome or commendation-to assure myself as to whether anywhere or at any time, from my first meeting with Helen to my arrival here, I had once felt conscious of being a stranger. In the sense of not being familiar with my surroundings, I had naturally felt it, but as being out of place, or an intruder, the idea had never crossed my mind before, so far as I was able to remember, and such a sensation is one not likely to be forgotten. And as I searched my memory, two or three words that fell from the lips of Walloo-Malie recurred to me;

"The shadows flee away."

"Yes," I continued, "I begin to realize what that means, even the least indication of strangeness and mere acquaintance is banished from this abode of love.

There is a soul of welcome, of rest, of desire to remain, in the atmosphere, which caresses and woos me to remain-that appeal to me as a part of myself I have never known or discovered until now. Is it some memory of an elusive dream that has come back? Have I returned to the suburbs of that City of Compensation to which Cushna introduced me long ago?"

I withdrew myself, and walked in a quiet part of the colonnade while I meditated; then my mind wandered back into the old life, and I saw myself stealing away from the family circle that I might be alone in my longing for something I did not understand-a vague something I could not touch. I was living over again the scene I sketched in The Life Elysian-reading again the magazine I had taken up from the library table; I re-read again the poem that had so stirred me; again I lingered over the final stanza:

> *How I pray while my heart-strings are breaking,*
> *How I count all the days as they come!*
> *I watch in my sleep for my Mother,*
> *In my dreams I sigh for her Home;*
> *Two words, oh, how sweet! Earth, earth! Let me go!*
> *In their music is heaven-all the heaven I can know!*

That key opened the door to a vision of the mystery that had led me to seek isolation and reflect. When Myhanene drew me to take that step from the bridge he said, "One step and you will stand upon the Homeland," but the words had no particular significance to me as I heard them, since I had never known what the blissful sacredness of the Home-life was. The veil had been lifted at last! As Myhanene spoke those words, I had felt the mystic thrill there is in a brother's-a sister's hand; my ears had been opened to respond to the music of the word Home; my eyes had caught the true expression of a fraternal smile- above, beneath, around, a flood of revelation was breaking upon me, sweeter, holier, and more ravishing than any I had hitherto gazed upon!

Oh Jacob! In the heavenly glory of this new daybreak, I can read a deeper meaning in your wrestling than ever I had dreamed of before! No wonder that you would not let the Angel go! Had I held him, and in the daybreak caught one ray of the glory that now I see, I would have continued to hold him-even though a thousand sinews had shrank-until the sun had risen into the full glory of the heavens and my whole soul was flooded with the heavenly light.

At length-even so long after the chapter of my physical life had been closed-my ears had been permitted to hear the full volume of the music, my eyes had beheld the radiance of the glory, my mind had been able to conceive the ideal, my soul had expanded wide enough to embrace and appropriate something of what God has wrapped up for mankind in that resonant monotone-Home. It is the keynote to the grand triumphant anthem-Heaven.

In the enjoyment of my meditation I had wandered into the companionship of solitude. Such solitude is only to be found in such Alpine heights of Heaven, where the soul finds meat to eat which cannot be found in the valley below. Lonely? No! One is always at the very heart of life-the metropolis of being-when he is with God! Alone in the midst of a multitude of revelations, while the seals were breaking. Who would not, like John, revel in such loneliness? Who would be impatient to be away?

Walloo-Malie, Rael, Omra, Myhanene and Zisvené were not with me. I had been called apart for awhile by Another-an even sweeter Voice; and, for the time, I had forgotten the existence of all others. Dracine was the first of my known friends to meet me on re-entering the garden from my temporary seclusion.

"Come, Astroel, and tell me," was her cheery greeting, "do you not find it good to be here?"

"Good? My dear sister; I feel as if I should like to meet Myhanene now."

"Do you wish to scold him?" she enquired archly.

"Now-do you think it likely that I should?"

"I simply asked the question," she replied, modestly.

"Far from that, but I would like to ask him if we were not now beyond the limit of his favourite asseveration that, 'It is better on before'?"

My companion laughed with a genuine ripple of girlish merriment.

"I can tell you how he would answer you," she said.

"Tell me-then, when I have seen him, I will tell you whether you answered me correctly."

"Well," she began with a very solemn tone, "he will place himself in front of you, so," suiting the action to the word; "take hold of you so," gripping my robe with either hand on each side of my breast; "look you straight in the eye with his calmly steady gaze; slowly shake his head and say, 'No, my brother, because there are no limits to that asseveration. It is one of the infinities.'" And when she had so delivered herself, she blithely enquired, "Now, don't you think I make a fairly good proxy for the wise young ruler?"

"Excellent, in tone and manner," I answered, "but I am not quite so sure about the substance."

"Of course-that you have to discover," she responded airily.

"I wonder whether I could find Zisvené." I next hazarded.

"That is doubtful," she said. "You see, Zisvené is a bird of frequent passage to and fro-only present with us while the body sleeps. She is a rara avis in that respect, in fact, so far as I know, she is unique. Yes; it is as I thought-she has been recalled."

"It is respecting those sleep experiences I wish to speak with her. I have heard something about it, but there is much more I want to know."

"I am not surprised to hear you say so. It is not only a most interesting subject, but one of the most important in many respects, from what I know of it. Zisvené, of course, will be able to tell you of her personal experiences, but if you want to understand its purpose, working, scope and possibilities, I should recommend you to consult, say, Cushna, Myhanene or Rhamya."

"Both Cushna and Myhanene have already given me a good

introduction to the subject and I am anxious to watch it in the working, in the hope that a practical observation will enable me to understand its theory better. In addition to this I am most deeply interested in one particular case I would like to secure assistance for, as a thanksgiving memorial of my arrival here."

"Under those circumstances," she replied, "I would see Myhanene at once-or, it may even better serve your purpose to see Walloo-Malie, who I see is yet with us," having evidently caught sight of the latter as she was speaking.

"Ah!" I exclaimed, delighted at the idea, "Walloo-Malie knows the case I speak of, and it would be a capital plan to get his assistance."

And at once we sought my illustrious friend.

* * *

CHAPTER 20

INSIGNIFICANT OMNIPOTENCE

nsignificant omnipotence! What an outrageously preposterous qualification to combine with such a potentiality! Is it? Perhaps so. But I am inclined to think a little calm reflection will correct the error of the first impression. Let me ask the question, "Where would the great circumference be without the almost invisible speck from which the sweep is struck? Or where would be the Alps or the Himalayas if the electron had not been?" I think you will agree with me not only that they would not, but absolutely they could not, be. Hence what majestic potentialities may be stored up for us in the undiscovered archives of the Invisible!

But even when we step across the rubicon into the orbit of the visible, how meagre do we find our powers of observation to be. I am not forgetful of the advantage I hold in this respect over my readers; I am rather desirous, of accentuating the point, because I wish to mark the boundary beyond which these limitations are not found, and drop a word of intimation as to the faculties which supersede. Take the organ of vision, for instance; the unaided eye is incapable of noting the ripple in the waves of light, and yet its waves roll on as ceaselessly as the waves of the sea. That this failure is due to the inconceivable rate at which the light waves roll, only confirms the limitation I mention. But if we turn our eyes in another direction, and try to watch the changes that creep over our most intimate friend from youth to age, again we fail to catch the change of individual steps, hour by hour, and recognize it only by comparing stage with stage, because in this phase, the process is too slow.

The germ of the consciousness of such a reflection was impressed upon me with the spontaneity with which Dracine and myself discovered the whereabouts of Walloo-Malie, but the full development of it came afterwards. For the moment I was about to be plunged into a maelstrom of revelation of which I should like to sketch some vague indication, but I almost fear to make the attempt because of the numerous limitations by which I am surrounded.

I am like a prisoner looking through the bars of my cell across an untrodden land beyond which freedom lies. I break my bars and gain my freedom, then long to shout the news to those who follow, that they may also find their way to the liberty I have won. I have neither path, compass, chart, nor sun to guide me-only my longing to render a needed service to my fellow pilgrims. If I do my best-and fail to make myself as clearly understood as I would like to be, forgive me. Others will come after me, and they may leave a clearly marked path by which the desired end may afterwards be attained.

Having seen Walloo-Malie in the distance, Dracine and I appeared to project ourselves to him. It was not a similar transition to that I experienced with Rael, but an outreach of our invisible selves of which he was instantly aware, and though no words were spoken nor recognition made, we knew that he understood our purpose and that he would come to meet us; which assuredly he did, and at once took leave of the friend with whom he was in converse. At the same time we returned to ourselves and set out to meet him.

That trifling incident, which, for want of a better name, I have termed, outreaching, aroused at once my curiosity and interest, but, in the sequel, it proved to be vastly more important than I imagined. In fact, it was the insignificant omnipotence of my earlier reflection-the breaking of the seals and opening of the volume of the revelation of a life such as Paul speaks of when he says, "Eye hath not seen, nor ear heard, neither have entered the heart of man, the things which God hath prepared for them that love Him." (1 Cor. ii, 9)

We had scarcely moved to carry out our intention when I completely lost sight of my environment, and found myself following some invisible guide down a dimly lighted corridor, leading into a cave where I was carried into the blackness of its darkness and left alone in the awful silence. I had no fear; nor did I speak or make a sound, for memory came to support with the whisper, "The Lord saith that He would dwell in the thick darkness.' (1 Kings viii, 12) So I waited patiently until the light of guidance should come. It seemed to linger through a time of strenuous testing, in which I held my confidence without a thought of doubt or wavering-kept my trust inviolate even to the extent of wondering how I could maintain it. Then a voice, soft, musical and clear, broke upon my consciousness in a whisper from afar. Whether it spake from within or from without is one of the problems I shall perhaps never be able to solve. In the light of the whole experience, as I look back, it is even doubtful whether there was a within or without that could be differentiated. It came to me with the tranquilizing authority of the voice that had spoken to me in the Court. At its first utterance I comprehended light, and with all my eager soul I listened that I might not miss one word:

"Child of the Infinite, fresh from the Gardens of the Lord, we welcome thee into the cave of God's Mystery-the workshop of the Creator, whose hand has guided, directed, shielded; whose love has watched over, provided for and sheltered thee throughout the pilgrimage of the Shadowland, by the ministry of the mysteriously veiled angel-Faith. That ministry terminated as you stepped from the Bridge into the Garden, where Faith advanced you into the unveiled fellowship of Sight. The weariness, agony and cross-bearing of the night being ended, you have toiled through the morning twilight until the sun has risen, now, for the Sun of Righteousness arises over the horizon of the eternal day you are called to 'Come and see.' Henceforth you are to know even as you will be known; the seals of the Book of Life-which Faith is not permitted to read, being unable to understand-will now be broken, the veils of mystery will be removed, the enigmas solved; life's rough places will be made plain, its details explained, its philosophies interpreted, its limitations pointed out, its sorrows and

chastisements will be illuminated and the Divine procedure will be made clear, together with their harmonious combination which has been overruled to bring you hither.

"The doors of opportunity are now thrown wide open, and you are invited to enter, behold and see, and in seeing, so great will be the light that will be at your disposal that you will understand, comprehend and know. The plans, processes, schemes, designs, laws and purposes of creation will be laid bare to your study and investigation. The frustrating influences that have been at work will be equally open to your inspection and study, as well as every branch of enquiry which your soul may wish to probe. From the conception of creation to its perfected completion, you are at liberty to examine and become acquainted with; from the meanest lessons in its elementary schools; then on to higher standards, colleges, universities, workshops, laboratories, studies, libraries, museums; then the great multitude of master-minds who have passed before you, and the serried ranks of the Sons of God, who watched and sang the great anthem of welcome at Creation's Birth. Let this be your employ until, gazing on the handiwork of the Eternal Father, you reflect the glory He has impressed upon it, and feeding upon the wisdom by which your soul will be nourished, you shall be perfected in His sacred likeness and thus see Him as He is."

While the voice was speaking, a curious, indefinable consciousness crept over me that, in the darkness by which I was enveloped, silent, secret activities were beginning to work. As the voice ceased, the darkness lifted sufficiently for my keenly watching eyes to discover a movement as of the rolling of cumulous clouds shrinking from the advance of light. Gradually the morning broke, the veils of night withdrew, the doors of day were thrown open, and before me lay an overpowering and indescribable vista of-so far as I could see-infinite revelation. And in that sublimely majestic circle I stood as the insignificant centre.

Standing in that Workshop of the Infinite, with the accessories of creation and sustenation present in orderly readiness to carry out the Divine purpose with minute and faultless precision, I needed not to move to make what scrutiny my soul desired, nor did I want a guide to tell me of the use, the purpose, or the power of anything. Distance was not, for had I not the gift of outreach? With the darkness, ignorance had disappeared, and in the new light which shone over all to see was to know, to understand, to comprehend.

I lost myself in speechless awe and wonder in the glory-light of that ineffable vision. So vast, so numberless, so enthralling were the allurements, that centuries and millenniums seemed to slip past me as I revelled in the explorations and discoveries, nor had I scarce entered into the fullness of its rapture before a hand was laid upon me and with a shock of consternation, I was aroused to find that we had met Walloo-Malie.

The glance he gave me revealed that the situation was as clear to him as it was, in a sense, confusing to myself, and he instantly relieved me by the tactful remark:

"You wish to ask me for counsel and direction, Astroel; need I say how pleased I shall be to assist you?" Then he added as an afterthought, as if he suddenly noticed my perturbation; "But why this embarrassment? Have you met with an even greater surprise than that to which Rael introduced you?"

I tried to answer him, but found it to be impossible. He quietly took my hands in a close, fraternal fold, and gave me a look that sheltered and encompassed me as a fortress of refuge, and then went on:

"I know-I understand! The pearls of silence are always Wisdom's best adornment in such a crisis. Let me explain briefly what has taken place, and when you have regained your quietude so as to be able to comprehend more clearly what I have to say, I will help you to understand the episode more completely."

"Will you?" I enquired, eagerly grasping at his unexpectedly generous offer. Myhanene or Omra would certainly have come to my assistance in my dilemma, but that Walloo-Malie would do so was far beyond my venturing to hope.

"Will I?" Why of course I will. If the Master found it worth His while to speak with the captious Nicodemus, ought I to withhold my help from one of the Master's brethren? I think not. Therefore permit me to explain that this bewildering perplexity which you are experiencing is common to every soul who passes through the crisis you are now experiencing."

"Crisis?" I ejaculated apprehensively.

"Yes, for the experience you have just come through was the culminating point of the mystical birth, the supreme importance of which the Christ declared in the assertion, 'Except a man be born again, he cannot see the Kingdom of God.' (John iii, 3) In the mind of the carnal man, such a claim at once arouses the contemptuous enquiry, 'How can such a thing be-can a man enter the second time into his mother's womb, and be born?' for the carnal man cannot grasp the fact that 'that which is born of the flesh is flesh, and that which is born of the Spirit is spirit,' but it is so, and the latter fact is as clearly and definitely evidential as the former. Nicodemus himself is a witness to the truth of this, for though he was one of the masters in Israel, when he argued the question with the Christ, he asked, 'How can these things be?' His flesh-born eye and brain and mind were unable to understand what was meant. Until the breath of God has been breathed upon a man, quickening him into the potential image of his Creator, he is as blind to the existence of spirit as an elephant is blind to the reality of a microbe, an atom, or an electron.

"But you, my beloved Astroel, have felt this quickening breath, and under its energizing influence have been conducted from the fleshpots of a carnal Egypt, through the wilderness of wandering, into the Promised Land. In the period of your spiritual gestation-passing from death to life-you have traversed the ante-chambers of the soul's unrobing, where, one by one, the earth defects have been removed in the purification of your soul, until, at length, your feet reached the Court of the Voices, where you beheld the judgment of the balances. In that Court, a higher series of influences than you had known before began to actuate you. You wondered why no verdict was pronounced, and Omra needed to explain. When you reached the foot of the bridge and saw the awe-inspiring gulf beneath it, you shrank from attempting the crossing. Without seeking to persuade you to change your mind, Omra carried you away to the shrubbery, and showed you the vision of the earth lying embedded in its psychic environment, through which you had passed under the conduct of Myhanene and his friends. Then Rael, by that mysterious transit, carried you to the Mount, enabling you to realize what a change had taken place in your powers of observation and condition, during your progress through the Spheres. In all this, you little suspected that every detail of the programme had been designed, ordered, and was being carried out with carefully guarded precision in order to secure a definite purpose. You did not dream that you were being, at every move you made, freed from some earth-born limitation, or attached to some new spiritual expansion; that your hitherto blind eyes were being opened, your deaf ears unstopped, that powers were being aroused to activity, faculties and capacities were being awakened within you that had been so long hidden in the secret vaults of your dark ignorance, but were now to answer to the call of the Voice that would even awake the dead in its command to 'Come forth!'

"Step by step, first Omra, then Rael, led you down this path of preparation from the Court of the Voices, watching with keen and never wandering scrutiny each trivial change in your condition until your struggling soul swung in the balance of consummation, and it only needed the thistledown-weight of influence which Zisvené was able to cast into the scale to carry you into the centre of the Bridge, and your birth could be announced in the first heaven.

"There I was permitted to welcome you to our Father's house- your spiritual inheritance as a son of God, an immortal soul, from whom the last fibre of the earth's influence had at last fallen away. At the foot of the Bridge, as you stepped onto the homeland, Myhanene gave to you your new name of Astroel, and in the

Garden you ate and drank your first communion with the redeemed family into which you had been born, and in the bosom of which you woke to a recognition of the sweet music that ever rings in the Home of the Soul.

"It is in the strange contrast presented by the restful peace and harmony of your new surroundings with the double uncertainties and distractions of the past, where the confusion arises which has been perplexing you. You have not yet learned how to wield your newly acquired faculties with ease. Nor do we expect that you should do so. You have not been admitted to an irrational, but rather to a super-rational community. We understand that, for the instant at least, the natal breath has not qualified you to contend with the victorious athlete; the birth-struggle has not left you sitting in the philosopher's chair.

"Allowing for the necessary interval for the communion, the greetings and the natural reflection you would need. I have been awaiting your call in order to discharge this latter part of the duty entrusted to me. And having thus far indicated what the trend and purpose of events have been, let me now congratulate you on the initial effort you have made to employ your newly acquired faculty."

"Will you forgive me," I interrupted him to ask, "but I am scarcely sufficiently composed at present to clearly apprehend your reference."

"Perhaps not," he replied with an indulgently forbearing gleam suffusing not only his face but his whole personality; it was as if he had awaited the opportunity to cover my perturbation with a robe of repose, which he accomplished before he went on to say, "but if you will allow me to change my figure, I was reminding you that I did not expect the unfledged wing to carry you quite as far as the sun when you first expanded it. Let me also tell you-for it will assist you in what I have yet to say-I would like you to notice how accurately I am aware of all that has taken place, because I am apprised of it by the exercise of the power of which I am about to speak.

"The faculty to which I have specially referred-that by which I am informed and you have as yet failed to understand-is one that has already been mentioned to you under the name of 'Thereth.' It is a somewhat clumsy term, but for that very reason it is appropriate in its relationship to the physical- and I do not want you to forget that we are on the threshold of the two estates for the moment-because the physical laughs at the idea of a fourth dimensional space as a sort of unimaginable monstrosity. You will better understand and sympathize with this attitude of mind presently when you come to recognize how absolutely this power of 'Ubiquity'-a term I much prefer-is a spiritual function. In the physical condition it is the mysteriously hidden Cause that lies at the back of all phenomena; on the psychic plane it becomes visible as a prize to be reached when a definite goal is gained; but entering the spiritual, we are born again with the image of God, who is Spirit, and all things become ours as joint-heirs with Christ."

"And now...?" I enquired; but came to a sudden and awkward pause in the anxious enquiry I wished to make. I knew he had got more to say, and I was equally yearning to hear, but my tongue seemed paralysed and my petition had to be presented through my eyes. Still, it received a gracious answer. "Is it not an inviolable law of the kingdom into which I had just been admitted that 'everyone that asketh, receiveth'?"

"And now," he resumed, adopting the words of my own entreaty, "I will come back to what I was saying in reference to your attempt to use your newly acquired power and come with our sister Dracine when she wished to speak with me. When you are able, with calm introspection, to review this phase of your career, you will discover what a significant advance you had made since you entered the garden to enable you to make that outreach so naturally. But still there remained one other step-a step you had to take alone and unattended-before the supreme crisis was successfully complete. It has been negotiated now, and it is in explanation of this last, and by far your most astounding revelation, that I wish to say one word to you.

"The confusion, to which I aroused you as we met, was due to a gasp of astonishment at the instant failure to reconcile the two aspects of a most unique situation. As you came to meet me, your feet stepped across the boundary where the finite merges into the infinite. By a transit grander than you made with either Omra or Rael, you passed through the door of Omnipresence, and stood in the workshop of Creation, enveloped in the blackness of uncreated light, where God is. You poised in the birthplace of Creation, at the fountain-head of Cause, where Omniscience lay on the bosom of Omnipotence, and from the rapture of their love, Wisdom was conceived. The gleam from the eyes of Love broke the density of the darkness, until you saw the veils of Mystery gradually lifted and were enabled to behold, and beholding, saw; and seeing, comprehended. There was no need for anyone to interpret, describe or explain. In that light you saw light, and all mysteries were made clear. You stood in the store-realm in which the fibres from which Creation was woven were gathered, and in the fibre lay the germ of the process and the consummation of life and being. Limitations vanished, boundaries faded away, failures were not known, impossibilities could not exist.

"The whole family of Time-past, future, beginning, end, first, last, young and old-slept peacefully in the arms of the Eternal Now. And as with Time, so was it with Distance, Knowledge, Wisdom and every other faculty of the soul-you were there at the fount and source of it. Every rivulet of Intelligence had its rise in an apparently insignificant fount of hidden Omnipotence, which rose at your feet, and, in that radiant light, you watched each current perform its course and circle, until it came and emptied itself again into the source from which it sprang. In a word-In the Visions of God you were carried to the centre from which the circumference of all existence is struck, whether it be physical, psychic or spiritual, and in that great laboratory, in the true and shadowless light, which is there alone, under the microscope of the Spirit, you were permitted to direct your newly acquired power to an analysis of that central electron. What did your study reveal? The acorn holds in its embrace a thousand potential forests of oak trees, but in the far more insignificant atom, there you found enclosed, not a potential world, or a family system of worlds, but a whole universe of systems, converged into one tiny speck-and that invisible speck is-God.

"You need not wonder that ages and aeons seemed to roll past you in your study; that vision, viewed from the centre at which you stood, was prophetic of the Divine course of approach which lies before you as you travel from that centre to the circumference into all the beauty, majesty and glory of the image of God.

"Now perhaps you will not wonder at the confusion you experienced when, by the touch of my hand, I suddenly recalled you to the consciousness of these half-way surroundings."

* * *

CHAPTER 21

CLARICE

A s Walloo-Malie finished speaking, I made the discovery that Dracine had departed, but the exposition he had given me had been of such absorbing interest that I was lost to everything but the one great theme of his discourse. In his valued exposition I had again passed over every step I had taken since reaching the Court of the Voices, listening and watching, as he caught up every thread of detail, blending them together in orderly sequence, then throwing upon them the light of His clearer illumination that I might fully understand the nature, purpose and design of each and all. And the crowning charm of the service he rendered lay in the spirit of brotherly love in which he environed our communion.

As he finished, I became aware that we were walking in a path covered with a floral creeper which possessed a soothingly sweet perfume, and that Myhanene and Omra were on the point of meeting us.

"Well, Astroel," was the cheery greeting of Myhanene. "What do you think of the invisible fortifications by which we are protected from undesirable invasion?"

"That is a question not to be lightly or hastily answered," I replied cautiously. "For the moment, let me content myself by saying that I think Isaiah was quite justified in declaring of the habitation of the church of God that 'no weapon that is formed against thee shall prosper'."

"Well done, Astroel," was Walloo-Malie's prompt and generous commendation, expressed with a look of pleasurable animation that I was somewhat surprised to see in him. "Such discretion is most praiseworthy. It is never safe to deliver a judicial opinion respecting an incident revealed by a lightning-flash; wait until you have gained control of, and are able to meet the electric fluid; then, having investigated at your leisure, you will be able to speak with greater confidence."

"That was a professional habit I contracted in the physical, and I have not yet seen any reason to discard it," I replied, glad to find something of the old life that I could carry forward. "But changing the subject-if you will allow me to do so-may I ask your advice on a matter I had in mind when Dracine and I met you?"

"Certainly. Let me know in what I may be able to help you."

"I scarcely know how to put it," I began, with an uncertain diffidence; "but since you first mentioned the case of Clarice, I have wondered a great deal about her-where she is, how she is placed, and whether I can do anything to help her, should she need it. While hoping that I might be able to be of assistance to her, I heard of the work that Zisvené is doing in the sleep-life; presently I met her, and, if she might be permitted, I am sure she would be glad to join with me. Again, if I may, I would like to do something to express the boundless gratitude I feel to God for the great mercy I have received in the exercise of His super-abounding love, and I can think of nothing which so commends itself to me as an expression of what I feel, as trying to help poor Clarice. Do you think I might do so, and would it be permitted for Zisvené to go with me?"

We were still standing where Myhanene and Omra met us, and as I spoke, I read not only approval of my proposition, but the great pleasure it gave to Myhanene especially to hear me make it. Walloo-Malie gave me a calmly veiled look that searched me through and through, then deliberately enquired:

"Can you forgive her for what she did?"

"There is nothing on my part to forgive," I replied. "The loss of her dealt me a wound that would have been fatal had you not bound it up, but it did not kill my love for her-true love cannot die-is it not of God, eternal? Since I have met you and learned the wonderful story of your interposition on my own behalf, that love has been resurrected, strengthened, beautified, purified, and I feel as if I cannot go forward until she joins me. May I not get the best assistance that heaven can afford me, and do for her what so many have done for me?"

"Yes! In the strength of such a love you may do so, and you shall find it omnipotent to save; but as to whether Zisvené will be the best to go with you, you had better consult Myhanene."

"So far as Zisvené is herself concerned, there will not be any difficulty, either on her part or my own," Myhanene at once assured us. "We must ascertain where Clarice is to be found."

With the faculties, and experience in the use of them, which each of my companions possessed, the information was received in less time than is required to write it. Clarice was in a very similar condition to that in which Cushna at first found Marie. Myhanene explained that Zisvené had already rendered good service to one, even in a lower condition, and he was confident that in her eagerness to lift up the fallen, she would be glad to assist me in my endeavour.

"Are you sure that all the circumstances are favourable to success?" Walloo-Malie enquired.

It was a veiled question, cautiously framed in order to avoid even a ripple of uneasiness on the surface of my ardent desire. I read its compassionate intent before I solved the deeper meaning of its depth. The one robbed the other of what might have been a sting of dread, and Walloo-Malie understood the thanks I enclosed him in a silent look.

Myhanene smiled in his optimistic confidence of the success of our proposed mission. It might be that we should find some initial difficulties, but Zisvené had already displayed something of a genius for surmounting them, and he had also noticed that she, being a sleep visitor, was occasionally able to exert a more persuasive influence over earth-bound souls, owing to being more physically sympathetic than he found to be the case with the usual ministrants. This unexpected development in her casual service had prompted him to watch her progress with interest, as possibly opening a new avenue in which the sleep-life might be more closely interblended with the spiritual.

Walloo-Malie became so impressed with Myhanene's enthusiasm that it was presently arranged that Cushna should accompany us on our visit, if Zisvené consented to go, and the result was to be ultimately reported to Walloo-Malie.

On Zisvené's next visit, the scheme was instantly confirmed, and under Cushna's guidance and control, the three of us found ourselves again on the Mount, en route to my first practical mission of mercy.

It is no part of my desire or purpose to dwell in detail over the sufferings of the frail unfortunates who, yielding to temptation, have sought the shelter and oblivion of the soul's dark cavern while they pay the penalty and endure the purgation of their sins. I have done that sufficiently already in describing the Harvest of Jealousy. Again we are engaged in reclamation. Let us hasten forward.

At the entrance of the cavern through the labyrinth of which we had to find our way in search of Clarice, Cushna and I experienced that change of dress which enables advanced ministers to meet the lower ones on more equal terms; as for Zisvené, her sleep-robe was already of neutral grey from which the sheen naturally disappeared as we went forward into the darkness, where we carried just sufficient light to find our way through the apparently interminable windings.

Cushna led the way, enabling us, by the light he shed, to follow in comparative safety, but even so, we shuddered at the thought of those who had not only to find their way, but more so for those who were compelled to dwell in the horrors of such a place. Whether we passed by any who hid from us as we went by, I cannot tell, but no one answered to Cushna's frequent call of 'Clarice,' nor, as we listened, did we hear the slightest sound of response.

Presently the rough passage opened into a cave of considerable proportions, at the entrance to which Cushna stopped, and we saw him raise his hand in an appeal for silence.

"She is here," he said calmly, after a careful survey.

"Where? Let me go to her," and I dropped Zisvené's hand to

hurry forward. But Cushna restrained me.

"You must be both cautious and patient, or she will get away," he said. "In a place like this, neither trust nor confidence is known. We have first to discover whether she is in a violent or submissive mood, and act accordingly."

But we had not long to wait before we heard a sharp, antagonistic challenge:

"Whose there? ...What do you want? ...Have I not suffered enough? ...I have not injured you! ...Why do you want to torment me further?"

The intense agony of the final appeal was terrible, but Cushna was adamant in his demand for silence until he was assured that her invective was finished. Then, after a brief silence, he whispered:

"Now-speak softly and calmly; put all the tenderness and sympathy you can concentrate into the word, and call her name."

"Clarice!" And all my yearning soul rushed out in the lingering utterance of that name as dear as life.

There was a silence as of death ...Then-was it a sob or a contemptuous, "You!" followed by another silence. Then, at a second sign from Cushna:

"Clarice!"

What would the answer be this time? Would it confirm the sob or the interjection? How can I record the intense eagerness with which I awaited the reply which did not come. Then, for the third time:

"Clarice! Do you not hear me?"

Silence again, and then a snarling sneer.

"Hear you? -Yes! And know you too and if you are not-" She had evidently slipped or fallen with a groan. Cushna firmly held me back when I would have rushed forward. When all was quiet again, I asked at his suggestion:

"Do you forget...?" She stopped me there with:

"Forget? Oh! Who will teach me how to forget, to remember?"

"That is one of the reasons for which we have sought and found you," Zisvené instantly replied, at Cushna's suggestion. "Won't you come to us, or let us come to you, and help you?"

"Who are you, and what do you want?"

"We are friends, and one is..."

"You lie," she hissed. "No friends can ever come here. This is the pest-house of fiends. Go! Your company would only add to my tortures."

"Clarice, do you forget Don Fred?" I asked, and as I spoke Cushna led Zisvené towards where she was hiding in the darkness.

"Don Fred? Pshaw! Did I not say you had come to increase my torture? Is not hell's rack sharp enough without you coming to give its wheels another turn?"

While Clarice was thus speaking, Zisvené, guided by Cushna, had approached and reached her. It was Zisvené who answered the enquiry.

"I would give it another-a backward turn, if you will allow me," she said with calm, sisterly sympathy. "Surely you have now been sufficiently torn and mangled? Surely you have paid in full the penalty of the errors you have committed, and the hour of your redemption has come?" As she spoke, she gradually drew nearer and nearer, trying to encircle the poor sufferer with an embracing arm, an effort which was at first repulsed, then sullenly permitted as Zisvené continued. "You have not been forgotten in your loneliness and desolation, but have been watched over in love, and..."

"Stop!" shrieked Clarice, as she savagely tore herself away. "Never mention that accursed word again in my hearing. Do tigers love as they tear the quivering flesh from the bones of their helpless victims? Love, forsooth-then in pity's name show me what hate is like!"

"I understand all you mean by tigers and victims, my sister," Zisvené replied soothingly as she cautiously moved forward. "But because some ghouls prey upon..."

"Stand back! Stand back!" Clarice cried in wild alarm. "For

when the fires of this memory blaze up, I am aflame with fury. Don't let me reach you, for every tortured nerve of my body cries out for revenge!"

"I think we had better leave her," suggested Cushna.

"Not just yet, Daddie," Zisvené pleaded. "I am sure she will be persuaded presently."

"I hope she may, but I fear it," he replied, acceding to her entreaty.

Again Zisvené addressed herself to the distressed one.

"Clarice, will you listen to me for a moment and try to calm yourself while..."

"Calm myself?" she ironically interjected. "Could you stand calm in the path of an avalanche? Could you keep cool in the embrace of a furnace?"

"I am afraid not," Zisvené admitted; "but let me beg of you to hear what I wish to say to you, even though you refuse what Fred wants to tell you."

"I know all he has to tell me," she answered with stinging scorn. "He is a man, and would retrieve himself by talking again of love. Bah!"-and she broke into an outburst of hysterical laughter. "He!-who loved me so faithfully that, when I left him, could throw himself at once into the arms of a-"

"Stop!" I cried, for even for Cushna's sake I could not longer keep my silence. "Don't perjure your soul by making groundless accusations, Clarice. My love for you has never wavered or been trifled with, but is as pure and sacred now as when I first laid it at your feet. When the blow of your departure fell upon me, I lost my faith in women, as you have come to repudiate it in men. Through the years I wearily waited, watched, hoped and prayed for your return, and, could I have found you-no matter how or where-I would have taken you back to my heart and sheltered and defended you against the world. But I have only just heard of you from the lips of one who saved me from taking my life at the thought of losing you. What he made known to me revived my lingering hope; I appealed to him for help to enable me to find and save you. We have come for that-for that alone; for I love you so that I cannot enter heaven and leave you here, now that I have found you."

Whether it was the sting of her false accusation, or whether it was the impassioned yearning of my soul to secure her liberty, I know not-perhaps may never know-but as I began to speak, something arrested, then stifled her hysterical frenzy, and with a strange, almost ominous silence, she listened until, in the intensity of my feelings, I found myself at a loss for words and suddenly ceased. Then came a brief, problematical and trying silence, before she answered in a voice as quiet and calm as it had hitherto been furious, but with a keen and bitter sarcasm.

"It was the act of a genius to make a lawyer of you. How Lucifer must envy your magical power to make black appear white-your poetic skill in the manipulation of a lie. It is my misfortune that I have met you before, and am acquainted with your art, or you might impose upon me and catch my feet in the net your lying tongue so gracefully spreads. Go! Leave me! I had better bear my present torture than let you lead me into something worse." And the shudder with which she accompanied her decision swept over us like an icy blast.

Again Zisvené stepped into the breach with the suggestion:

"But you have not met me before. Won't you allow me to try to help you?"

"Our not having met before may or may not be my misfortune," came her prompt and snappish reply. "Strangers must be content to be judged by the company they keep. Your company may be your misfortune on this occasion, and I want none of it."

But Zisvené was persuasively, affectionately insistent. "Are you quite sure that you are not mistaken as to what Fred's conduct has been in relation to you? Is it not possible that you may be doing him an injustice and, at the same time, yourself a terrible wrong, by cherishing these feelings against him? When you knew him, valued being in his company, and hoped to marry him, did you know him to be the man you now imagine him to be? Would you have endangered your own good name by associating with him, had you thought that others saw him as you now charge him with having been?" As she spoke, Zisvené drew nearer, touched, then took her hand, then a sympathetic arm crept round the unresisting waist as the speaker proceeded with an ever-increasing tenderness in her voice; "I am asking you, not for myself, dear, nor for Fred, but for your own sake, to consider what I suggest. You knew him intimately; I did not-do not. I am equally a stranger to both of you; but I am a woman, with a woman's heart, a woman's sympathy for those who are suffering, and a woman's desire to help a sister who has met with misfortune."

Zisvené's soothing appeal at once touched and commended itself to the almost expiring or neglected sense of justice in the sufferer. The storm of resentment and guilty humiliation at being discovered in such a condition was arrested, and a brief period of doubtful uncertainty trembled in the balance, as Zisvené continued. When she acknowledged to being a stranger to both equally, Clarice gave a perceptible start, and as the speaker ceased, she anxiously enquired:

"Are you really as much a stranger to him as to me?"

"Yes, almost equally so. I have known of him, but we have only met once before he mentioned you to me and said how anxious he was to find and help you. Then I asked to be allowed to join with him. Are you curious to know why? I will tell you." Zisvené had by now adopted an almost maternal tone and attitude towards the half-distrustful, half-hopeful unfortunate. "You will know me better presently; then you will discover how terribly I suffer at the sight or thought of even an animal in pain. I love them so that the sight of a bearing rein on a horse, the use of a whip, a heavy load, or inconsiderate pace up a hill, will torment me for hours; and if I feel so for the dumb brute, is it strange that I feel even more so for children and my fellow sisters? So when Aph..." she stopped and corrected herself- "Fred spoke of his coming to find you, you can scarcely imagine how I wanted to come with him. I did not know you-knew nothing about you, save that you were an old friend of his, but I learned that you were in trouble; and I wanted to help you. That is how and why I am here. And now that I am here, won't you let me help you?"

"No, you do not know me," Clarice responded with almost despairing sorrowfulness. "If you did, you would not want to touch me. Let me tell you what I have been and done."

"That would make no difference, nor is it the least necessary for me to know. It is enough for me that you are in need of help and sympathy. You may be even worse than you would care to confess. If so, you stand the more in need of the Christ-like ministry that would say to you, 'neither do I condemn you; go, and sin no more.' I have come to you in that same spirit, to tell you that if you recognize that you have been wrong; there is no necessity for you to continue so. No one wishes for you to hide yourself here. Don't you remember how you used to hear, 'If we confess our sins, He is faithful and just to forgive us our sins, and to cleanse us from all unrighteousness'? These were little more than a form of words to us in the thoughtless days that are past, but they have a life and death meaning to us now. I have felt the import of them; you have learned the awful truth of not heeding them. But they are still true. You are wanting to tell me what you have been, and done; but why should you? He who reads the heart, in the wish to tell me, hears and knows your full confession, and has already sent us to lead you out of this vile darkness towards His marvellous light. Won't you come? Is this horrible place so much your ideal of happiness that you wish to remain? Have you lost all desire for the innocent and unsullied pleasures of life? Do you not wish for reunion with the friends of the past, before you fell into the hands of the tempter? Looking back from this place in which your sensitive soul is quivering in loathsome agony, does the glorious and vanished past possess no attraction for you? We want to lead you back. You may come. Won't you? You have been here, alone, too long. Will you not come back? Come! We know the way and will go with you."

As Zisvené thus tenderly and patiently pleaded with Clarice, while intently drinking in her persuasive arguments, I was carried away and was again beholding that wondrous miracle of the Magnetic Chorale, with eyes that were now open to behold its inner mystic meaning. While Clarice fell more and more under the spell of Zisvené's entreaties, I saw a halo of that life-giving sympathy beginning to tremble around the speaker, which I had first seen poured forth to fill that great temple of love to be used by the hand and will of Siamedes, to bathe and set at liberty the contorted forms of those who had been held in bondage.

In this case it was not an anthem that rolled in soul-stirring harmony as the miracle of love proceeded, but my quickened senses caught the solo effects of light, and sound, and perfume, as the sisterly sacrifice was laid upon the altar of affection. Oh, with what suppressed sighs of gratitude did I watch the progress of the ministry-the gradual snapping of the cords of resentment, the wonder excited by the tender and passionate pleading, the cautiously responsive yielding, the birth of confidence and hope, the first thrill of sympathetic response: then the fountain of feeling bursting forth, and Clarice fell in a paroxysm of repentance into the arms of her newly-found sister.

What she passed through in that awful spasm, neither of the three who watched could possibly conjecture. That can only be known to the sufferer and God. But, happily, it was of short duration, but it paid the balance of the penalty. Presently the storm began to subside; Cushna saw there was no need to continue his disguise, and the cave was at once softly illuminated by the natural light we possessed; the arms that clung so tenaciously to Zisvené's, relaxed; the storm-swept face was lifted and with wondrously perplexed eyes, Clarice looked upon the scene.

"Come, dear," Zisvené entreated. "Let us take you out of this horrible den."

"You cannot-there is no way out," she sobbed.

"Are you quite sure, dear? Come and let us try if we cannot find one."

"I didn't...mean that," she answered in a voice that was still broken by sobs. "There is a way...somewhere...but no one...is allowed to pass."

"Who or what is there to prevent us?"

"Is not the blackness, the innumerable windings, the many pitfalls"-she shuddered-"and tortures by the way enough to defy our escape?"

"Not when you have a light to guide you; and the light of love which now shines upon you will go with us all the way. Come, let us be going."

"I cannot-dare not; much as I long to get away. If you knew the agony of the torture I should incur, you would not ask me," and she shook as with an ague of dread at the thought of it.

"May she not come, Cushna?" asked Zisvené. "You have been on these missions many times. May she not come?

"That is why we have been sent to help her. Come, my sister, we will lead the way and guide you. There is nothing to hold and keep you, but your own refusal."

There was something in Cushna's tone and bearing that seemed to arouse a degree of confidence in her. She took a step forward in the process of awakening, passed her hand across her eyes, shivered slightly, then looked around in an endeavour to realize what was really taking place.

"Oh! My God-My God!" she groaned as she shook herself free from Zisvené's arm and stood resolutely still. "If only I could dare! But I am not able to run the risk-to bear the light."

"Let Zisvené and I lead and support you," I volunteered, "and the light will come so gradually that you will scarcely notice how gently the darkness will loose its hold. We will hold you up while your steps grow strong and certain. As we go, your confidence will return, the terrors of these caves will be overcome, the dread will be left behind, your loneliness will be past, and our dear friend, Cushna, will show us where you may rest in peaceful comfort, beyond the reach of this hell of torture."

As I spoke, Zisvené and I took hold of her on either side; Cushna going on before, and so we moved slowly forward.

you."

"I have indeed," I answered her, "and the last has been the strangest and most wonderful of all."

Her whole being-not her face only-seemed to be suffused with a soft radiance of glory as she listened to my words.

"So it will always be-it must always be," she replied, as her eyes travelled into the familiar far away. "Always more and more, ever higher and higher, glory on glory, and yet we can never get beyond the threshold of the Evermore. Tell me what this new wonder has been?"

There is something so irresistibly charming in the calm confidence of Eilele-her outreach is so far, and her hold on the invisible is so firm, that whenever I am in her company, I seem at once to be carried into the very bosom of the inner heaven where God Himself is, and the atmosphere is that of the vast primeval Peace. She knows and leads me into the secret habitat of Confidence, across the azure skies of which no cloud of Doubt has yet been known to pass-the Rest that has not yet been broken or shaken-where Omnipotence is gentle and tender and the Wonderful is natural, naive and ingenuous. I can speak to her with more ease and freedom than I can to Myhanene, with the perfect assurance that, with her, I cannot possibly be misunderstood or doubtfully interpreted. So in reply to her invitation, I flung the floodgates of my soul wide open and poured out my pent-up feelings in the full story of my visit to Clarice and the success with which it had been crowned.

She listened with that calm, meditative abstraction I am getting to know so well, without asking a question or making a word of comment until I had finished. Then, without the least token of surprise or animation disturbing her attitude, she placidly replied:

"Yes! That is just how I should expect the Father to respond to your aspiration. 'He giveth to all men liberally and upbraideth not,' even though the petition be made on behalf of one in hell. Even there, the soul is still lying in the domain where 'all things are possible,' being yet within the boundary of the uttermost. In that paroxysm of penitential weeping, you saw one of the most glorious providences of God at work-if there is such a thing as one providence being greater than another-you saw where, in the Divine wisdom and justice, a single stab or spasm of remorse is capable of liquidating the penalty of certain great sins-where an instant of intensity is accepted as the equivalent to a period of duration. The just weight of suffering has been secured, and at the same time, the petition granted. Yet the law of God is perfect, because the prayer of faith had the effect of calling into operation a provision of providence that had been arranged to meet the contingency. 'The prayer of faith shall save the sick' (Jas. v, 17); hence you brought Clarice away with you."

"But Eilele!-think of the wonder of it!" I cried, marvelling at the placidity with which she spoke of it.

"God Himself is wonderful, why then should I be disturbed and surprised when I see the quality displayed? I might rather be moved to enquire if I did not see it; while, at the same time, I can feel the deepest sympathy for the-shall I say, consternation you experience at your first beholding the varied demonstrations? Your eyes are now being opened to understand what you were so surprised to hear me say when first we met-that you were then standing on the threshold of the vestibule of heaven, and just as you are now discovering how true my words were then, so you will yet come to recognize that now your eyes are only opening to the beginning of the revelations that eternity still holds in store."

"Yes, I am now, and only now, beginning to understand what you meant when you said:

> *Oh, the vision would o'erpower us*
> *If it suddenly were given,*
> *So we wait in preparation*
> *In the vestibule of heaven.*

"But if all that I have seen, heard and learned is only the, beginning, what will the fullness, the glory, the extent, and the knowledge of the ending be?"

"God! In all the perfection of the splendour which began to be revealed to us in Jesus Christ," she replied, as her face shone with the reflection of the vision on which her soul was gazing in the far away.

"But was not the Christ the 'fullness of the Godhead bodily'?" I enquired.

"Yes, bodily. Not the fullness of the perfect Godhead, but the measure of the fullness that could be manifested through the limited capacity of the earthly body. He was one with God, as a word is one with the speaker who gives expression to it, but as the speaker is greater than the word, so He said, 'My Father is greater than I.' What the extent of that greatness is, only eternity will reveal, and to arrive at the knowledge of it, we have to ascend from height to height, from holiness to holiness, from purification to purification, until by a sevenfold sanctification we are able to reflect His undimmed lustre, and can bear the brightness of seeing Him as He is."

"And is such a goal really attainable? The prospect you open up rises to such a height as to appear an impossibility for me ever to reach it."

She turned a benevolent smile upon me as she quietly replied.

"Just so impossible does it appear to the child that he can ever be as his father. If you had brought Clarice here, directly, from her dark abode, she would have said the same in relation to her ever reaching this point where we meet, but you would shatter her doubt by telling her how you yourself have actually made the journey, step by step, from where you have now left her; and by the same way you will lead and guide her, not only to where we stand, but onward still through and beyond the gate, up the celestial staircase where Myhanene pointed you towards Omra's home, to glory upon glory which you have not yet beheld. The heaven of God, like every other attainment, whether it be of body, soul or spirit-cannot be reached by a single and sudden bound, but by the patiently ordained process of 'line upon line.' As drops of water aggregating will fill the bed of an ocean, or atoms of matter will eventually build up a continent, so holy aspiration will enable us to reach the pinnacle of divine perfection to which we are called, and we have an eternity before us in which to reach the goal."

"Divine perfection?" I dubiously enquired, thinking she had made an unintentional slip. But Eilele met my somewhat anxious reminder with a ripple of real laughter.

"My dear Astroel," she replied, "if mortals arrogate the right to call themselves 'divines,' surely it is not presumptuous to apply the term to the highest rank in the hierarchy of heaven-the position held by the sons of God, to which dignity we are all called-which goal we must all ultimately reach by virtue of that call."

"When you open up to me such vistas of that which lies beyond us, it reminds me of what-was it not Paul who said, 'It doth not yet appear what we shall be"?

"No, it was the beloved John who said that-he who beheld the door opened in heaven allowing him to behold something of the glory of the kingdom into which you are now about to enter-a kingdom that was set up on earth, but the earth, by man's disobedience, has been temporarily placed under the dominion of sin. But, even on earth the kingdom shall be restored, for there shall be a 'new heaven and a new earth wherein dwelleth'-she paused as with uncertainty for a moment, and then added-rightness.' Yes, I like that better than righteousness under the circumstances. The meaning is the same, but the less familiar word gives it an emphasis we do not notice in the older form. One pauses over the innovation to enquire as to its correctness; 'Rightness'? Is it really so? A new heaven and earth, wherein dwelleth rightness. Curious idea; yet when you come to think of it, it is nothing more than a new setting of an old idea. Still, the abbreviation carries a suggestion which does not sit quite so comfortable as the word we are used to. Therein lies the value of the change; men have grown so familiar with the confession that 'all our righteousness are as filthy rags,' that it has emptied itself of all meaning in its mechanical automatism until the soul awakens with surprise to find that those 'filthy rags' of unrighteous indifference have become an impassable gulf yawning between itself and the kingdom.

"The crystal sea is a tideless sea; nor has it any current or favouring breeze that will carry listless, dreamy souls to the foot of the throne."

"It is always more than a pleasure to me to hear you talk," I took the opportunity of saying, as she paused for a moment in her reverie.

"Every sentence you utter suggests a new string of questions I would like to hear you answer; but may I just ask you this one? Do you think there will really be a new heaven and a new earth, or is it to be regarded as a metaphor only?"

"So far as it has been revealed unto me," she replied with cautious deliberation, "it partakes of both the literal and the metaphorical, something as the twilight is an interblending of light with darkness-it is of both, and yet is neither. In the olden life it was not an uncommon event for us to renovate and turn an old garment and, as we used to say 'make quite a new one' by the process. It is some such change as this that I anticipate when the dear Master shall re-establish His Kingdom upon the earth. And just as the time for the renovation and reconstruction of a garment rests with the determination of the owner, so does the time for the setting up of the Kingdom rest with the decision of God, since the 'earth is the Lord's and the fullness thereof, the world and they that dwell therein.' When the Chosen of the Lord went to establish the Kingdom by the preaching of rightness, His own received Him not-Rome mocked and crucified Him, and the nations cried, 'We will not have this man to reign over us.' He will not return in such simple guise the second time; the circumstances of His advent will be in accordance with the second Psalm, 'He that sitteth in the heavens shall laugh; the Lord shall have them (the kings of the earth) in derision...He shall break them with a rod of iron; He shall dash them in pieces like a potter's vessel.'

"It will then no longer be a question of free-will-He will subdue the nations and bring them into subjection unto His rule. 'Then [when he has accomplished this] shall the Son also himself be subject to Him that put all things under him, that God may be all in all.' With this the whole world will awaken to the discovery that the Sermon on the Mount is not an impossible idealism, but that it has become an actual living force in the new Kingdom, in which the golden rule will be seen in operation and the will of God will be done on earth as it is done in heaven. The various experiences you have met with here, Astroel, should help you to understand how feasible it is for this to be accomplished by Divine decree, and the result would be, practically, a new earth wherein dwelleth rightness."

"Yes, the advantages I have already derived from the viewpoint of this higher life are almost incalculable, but where the prospects are so vast-so infinite in every direction, I have not yet grown sufficiently confident to trust in the reliability of my novel power of vision, so I fall back upon maturer knowledge, and gather strength and encouragement as I hear you discourse on the wonderful revelations of God. Is it not better for me to do so?"

"Far better, my brother; if men would make sure of their ground, their feet would more seldom slip."

"Thank you, then may I ask you yet another question?"

"Yes; ten if you desire it."

"Having now obtained the key to your idea of a new earth-for which I desire to thank you-I should be glad to know why a new heaven should be considered necessary. Is not heaven itself the perfection of holiness?"

Eilele seemed to have anticipated the nature of my enquiry, and I had scarcely begun to formulate my request before I saw her pass into that realm of reverie where I so fervently wished for the power to follow her, and gaze upon the visions which her enraptured eyes beheld as her tongue gave a semi-conscious utterance to its interpretation of the inspiration.

"It would be an absolute impossibility," she began in her dreamy ndecision, "for one whose life had been spent in an Alpine valley to conceive any correct idea of what an American prairie looks like; or for the lad, whose conception of a lake has been modelled on the dimensions of a village pond, to imagine the outline of the Atlantic Ocean. Just so would the mortal, limited by the environment of the finite, fail to comprehend the true beauty and perfection of the Infinite. Few, indeed, are they who are privileged to have their ears so attuned as Isaiah, who was permitted to hear and record the music of the Voice that said, 'My thoughts are not your thoughts, neither are my ways your ways...For as the heavens are higher than the earth, so are my ways higher than your ways, and my thoughts than your thoughts.'

"He, being 'Lord is a great God, and a great King above all gods, perfect in all His works and ways'. It is in the glory light of this supreme perfection where our eyes are blinded as we try to look upon it, and we are lost in a greater splendour than that of the midday sun. 'As the heavens are higher than the earth,'"-and her eyes were lifted, climbing, climbing, higher and higher still, until her soul's flight wearied and she reluctantly shook her head as she added; "Who can attain to it? 'Perfect in all His ways.' And so, knowing the end from the beginning, when He created the earth He provided it with every requirement, to the minutest detail, that would be necessary to accomplish all His perfect purpose. In the strength of His omnipotence He might have commanded and a perfected earth would have sprung into orderly being at His word. But He was building a schoolroom for a race of sons who were to bear His own image-to be in His own likeness-'to come into the inheritance of His own perfection, into which they must needs be brought by the discipline of suffering.' (Heb. ii, 10)

"Why needs be?" I enquired.

"In order that they should be proved, tested, tried, purified, sanctified and be found worthy to occupy the high and holy position to which they would be called as sons of God. For this they had to be fitted by a course of subjection and obedience to parental authority. But while the prospective inheritance idemanded a purity without spot or wrinkle, taint or stain, as a qualification, God knew the weakness and frailty of the flesh in which the spiritual germ had first to strike its roots. Knew also and remembered that He had established this law by which the earth should bring forth its fruit, 'first the blade, then the ear, after that the full corn in the ear.' If such duration of time, and succession of seasons, were necessary for the production of the bread that should nourish the flesh, could love and wisdom demand that the soul should reach its divine standard at a single bound? Therefore, in the beginning, when God created the earth, equipped in all respects for the sustenance and requirements of the flesh, according to His own riches in glory, He also created a heaven annexed to earth (Gen. i, 1-8), equally provided as might be required, as nursery, schoolroom, hospital or convalescent wards, for all and every soul that stood in need of its varied ministries. You have in yourself experienced, with wonder and surprise, how beautifully and perfectly several of its departments are adapted to the particular necessities of the individual; you have also been permitted to see the unexpected outreach of love which assists in the reclamation and restoration of those who have erred and strayed; and at length you have discovered how absolutely impossible it is for any soul to cross that great divide while yet a taint of stain or sin contaminates it. Think of this, and then you will understand the need for the purification by suffering.

"When, however, the new earth comes into existence by the establishment of the kingdom, and righteousness covers the earth as the waters cover the sea, then the need for the lower heaven will be at an end, and the Paradise of God will again touch the earth. Oh, that we might see it now, that God might in very truth be all in all.

"But here comes our sister Dracine with the Gardener, and he is sure to want to show you some of the beauty spots that surround us."

* * *

CHAPTER 23

THE HERO OF BOZRAH

Who can imagine what the arresting, stupifying, paralysing effect would be if the world was to awake some morning with a clear understanding and comprehension of the declaration of Isaiah-"My thoughts are not your thoughts, neither are your ways my ways, saith the Lord"? What an inconceivable revolution would suddenly be experienced! The mad rush of egotism arrested; with what trembling anxiety would pride, arrogance and oppressive prosperity be deserted; what a concourse would be struggling at the fountain of hypocritical purity to wash head and hands and feet-the outside of the platter-in the hope that the all-seeing eye might not notice the plague-spot of the heart.

Well might the Master in the depth of His sorrow at the blindness of human perversity exclaim, "O fools, and slow of heart to believe all that the prophets have spoken." The messengers of God do not always travel with royal robes in golden chariots, so as to be seen and greeted by men. It is recorded of one that, footsore and weary, he walked and climbed the hills and trod the plains of his missionary sphere-that at noonday, in a fainting condition, he approached a well and craved a drink of water from a woman too vile for her neighbours to associate with-that he had not a place to lay his head at night- that he was a man despised and rejected of his fellow men, "a man of sorrows and acquainted with grief." If this is so, Isaiah was right. God's messengers, as the God they serve, seek to be known for what they are, not for what men judge them to be. Let all men be wise and careful whom they entertain.

Some such thought occurred to me as I saw Dracine approaching in company with a stranger. Had not Eilele spoken of him in an official capacity, I should not have regarded him with distinction, since he wore no dress or mark to denote it-no mayoral chain, no diplomatic insignia, no judge's robe or pleader's wig, no bishop's apron, dean's gaiters, doctor's stole, or clerical collar. As a minister in the household of God he wore the uniform of his King, and was known to be one of the disciples by the love he manifested to his fellow men. He was not singular in this respect-it is the household rule laid down by the Master, "By this shall all men know that ye are my disciples, if ye have love one to the other." Hence the change the recognition of this law would bring about.

But if I were about to make his acquaintance, I would be glad to know something of him.

"Did you say the Gardener?" I enquired.

"Yes. Why; does it surprise you?" she replied.

"I am not sure," I hesitated. "It does seem somewhat strange to think of gardening here."

Eilele's face glowed momentarily with an amused, compassionate smile.

"Perhaps so, but for some reason I can scarcely explain, I have habitually called him by that name since the special sphere of his ministry lies here, and I love to think of myself as being planted in the garden of the Lord, and in that way, retain a claim I like to feel I hold on Voormere."

"Thank you; that enables me to understand part of the difficulty," I answered reflectively; "but it does not satisfy me altogether. Perhaps I am still not altogether sufficiently clear to understand."

"Then let me try to help you. What is the particular point upon which you are not clear?"

"It is my failure to harmonize these-what I may call local appointments with the idea of the infinite opportunities I have recently been contemplating. Do you understand what I mean?"

"Perfectly. The confusion arises in regarding what is a voluntary ministry as a definite appointment. We each and all are now workers together with God, with an intense desire to find our own place and render Him our highest service. You answered to the same impulse when you wished to go to Clarice. That service has been in no wise hindered-it has rather assisted your passing through the gate, because your action was a Christ-like one and has already met with a certain reward, but the full measure of what you accomplished, only eternity will reveal. God oftentimes conceals infinite results in the mustard seeds of a trivial act. In this way Voormere finds his present services best rendered here, but presently will hear a higher call, and then he will promptly reply."

I could easily discern that she was pluming herself for another flight, but Dracine and Voormere were close at hand and she was compelled to restrain herself.

"Shall we be regarded as intruders?" Dracine enquired archly.

"The addition of Love and Wisdom could never be an intrusion," Eilele returned as she made room for Dracine beside her.

"As I am neither of the virtues you name, I will leave Voormere to wear the double crown," Dracine replied, taking the proffered seat.

"For myself, if I have but wisdom to love, and love enough to serve, I shall be well satisfied," Voormere adroitly replied.

"I have been trying to satisfy Astroel's desire to correlate and harmonize the different experiences through which he is passing," Eilele explained.

"My suggestion would be to defer any such attempt for the present. They will naturally fall into orderly sequence presently, but until you are able to understand the relation of part to part, how is it possible for you to build up the whole? Let me illustrate what I mean by supposing a case in your own former profession. In the absence of a legitimate claimant, a vast estate has been managed by a representative of the crown for three generations. One day a simple working man calls upon you and presents credentials which appear to establish such evidence as leads you to take up the case, and eventually you substantiate the claim. When you secure the decision, does that son of toil, whose past has been one long struggle to make both ends meet and live honestly in the sight of his fellows, immediately realize all that the decision of the court means to him-the peerage, extent of his acreage, the rent-roll, mineral rights, residences in town and country, foreign investments and accumulated capital at his bankers?"

"Thank you. I see it now. So far I have only been collecting evidence to make my claim, and when I reached the Court of the Voices, I substantiated it. It is no wonder that I have been confused."

"And even now," Voormere continued, "you have only a very limited and partial conception of the inheritance upon which you are entering. Has the thought ever occurred to you that though you have many times seen the gate, you have never caught a hint or glimpse of what lies beyond it?"

His mention of the fact struck me with an amazing force. Imagination may have filled in the background of the prospect, but calmly as I reviewed my vision I could recall no memory of anything that lay beyond the portal. It might have been oblivion.

"No-o! It never once occurred to me-but it is so."

"And if you will quietly continue your survey you will make another astonishing discovery. In the visions and reviews you have been granted since you passed through the Court of the Voices, the new light which has so far been granted has led you to feel that every veil of mystery had been removed and you were looking upon things without a cloud between; but I ask you again-from where we are standing now-to cast your mind back to any single feature, and you will now discover that though certain veils have been lifted, enabling you to see what had hitherto been hidden, there are still veils remaining to be withdrawn before your eyes can look away into the infinite. You may have had flashes, but you have not yet beheld the glory. The flash passes and dies away; the vision is the light eternal that never faileth or passes away. So far you see, know, understand and comprehend in parts, as you behold this garden; but when, by and by, you stand upon the tower above the gate, you will be able to see beyond the colonnade which now bounds your vision and trace, not only all the way by which you have travelled to and through the flesh, but also the psychic gestation which brought you to the second birth, that which you have now accomplished. Then, turning round, you will look away along the pathway of the shining light, in its ever exceeding glory, until you reach the aureole of the vision beautiful. You have not even seen that yet, therefore it is no wonder that your mind is confused. You are like the erstwhile penurious claimant only standing on the threshold of your inheritance. Let me ask your company that I may show you an instance in the garden of the value of standpoint in relation to knowledge. We will rejoin our sister presently."

As he finished speaking, without waiting for any reply, he turned and started to carry out his suggestion. We crossed the colonnade, passed through the creeper curtain draping the arches, and at once entered a more charming and beautiful shrubbery than that I had passed through with Omra across the gorge. With that tactful consideration I have so many times referred to, my companion made no attempt to engage me in conversation, seeing that I was already too engrossed with the indescribable floral attraction of the scene through which we were passing to pay even the slightest attention to anything he might have said. It was a symphony of colourable rapture in a variegated composition such as dreamland could not have suggested, and yet it was but the prelude to that which we presently beheld on entering a plain we reached through a narrow defile in a range of hills I had not hitherto observed.

In shape it was slightly rectangular rather than square, bounded on three sides by the chain of hills through which we had approached, and on the fourth by the abyss. In width it may have measured perhaps some half a mile, with a slightly added length, with a broad fringe of matchless sward running round its great central feature, towards which Voormere waved his hand and said:

"That is the illustration of which I spoke."

"What is it, and its meaning?" I enquired after quietly contemplating the most curious, compact and gorgeous mass of bloom it had ever been my good fortune to behold.

"It is an allegorical picture woven in the warp and weft of carpet-gardening for the purpose of dispelling such confusions as the one you have experienced. We have many of them occupying the borderland of heaven, written in the original language of your Scripture-eloquent with poetry, fragrant with inspiration, bright with revelation, melodious with love, and attractive with irresistible beauty, when once the soul has discovered the necessary point from which to study it in the true light. But failing to find that mystic spot for contemplation, the eye can see, and the mind trace nothing more than a riot of confused colour, void of any design, suggestion, harmony, balance, taste, or any other artistic feature."

"Then it is evident that we have not reached the necessary point of vantage yet," I ventured as my eyes wandered over the unattractive confusion.

"No! The approach has been especially designed to emphasize the contrast I have spoken of. Standing where we now are, and looking upon this great allegory for the first time, it arouses in your mind something of the same confusion as you have experienced in connection with your first contact with the new faculties and powers you are discovering in yourself, of which Eilele was speaking. To you, in both cases, the outlook is chaotic, but to myself, knowing the detail of each and every part, where you see confusion, I can recognize the necessary individual strokes and shadings of colour that contribute to the superb beauty of the picture as you will presently behold it. You could not take away or change the position of a single flower-out of place as some of them may appear to you here-without the effect being noticeable, and the perfection of the design interfered with. Such is the difference and great importance of a correct view-point, not only in pictures, but equally in all affairs of life, as I will now show you."

He turned, and we ascended one of the hills bounding the pass by which we had entered the enclosure.

There is only one Artist capable of sketching the perfect vision of the soul's ideal; only one Chemist who has discovered the secret of the attraction of the perfume to the rose; only one Poet who can correctly sing the song of rapture; only one Psychologist who has ever been able to analyse and declare the purity of love-only One. That One has taken from the essence of each and compounded for the Emmaus heartburn a balm-a feast at which the stricken soul may sit, and eat, and live for ever. Voormere was not that One, but somehow, somewhere, somewhen, the mantle of that One must have fallen upon, or touched the shoulders of Voormere, for never had I walked under the influence of such a sacred spell as I experienced in that never-to-be-forgotten ascent. Myhanene, Rhamya, Omra, and even Walloo-Malie failed to be remembered in comparison with the soul-stirring music with which Voormere held my every faculty enthralled. It was not the vision Elisha's servant saw around the Hill of Dothan that Voormere opened up to me; neither that the favoured three beheld on Tabor at the Transfiguration; nor yet again that of the seventy on the brow of Olivet, when the ascending Lord passed into the heavens; nor that of Paul in the third heaven; nor yet of John when the great revelation lay unrolled before him. To me it was more than any-more than all of these, even though they were all combined in one-so great I dare not attempt-cannot find words to begin to essay a description of it. That is one of the things necessity ordains shall remain until such time as you, my toil-worn reader, shall reach the same or kindred spot in your pilgrimage; then, should you be blessed with the companionship of Voormere or likeminded friend; you too will understand how my heart burned within me as I listened to his discourse, until he turned again and bade me sit down.

Then I beheld the picture from which my eyes had been diverted in all the transporting beauty of its perfection. I was so overcome by the influence of the vision, as my eyes fell upon it, that I gasped, but lacked the power of exclamation.

I was advisedly assisted to a seat before my companion's hand invited my attention from his discourse to the scene! Long and silently did I study its subject, composition, detail and voiceless eloquence. Now I understood what Voormere meant when, down below, he had said that not a single flower could be changed or taken away without noticeably disturbing some point of detail. How I now rejoiced for the blessing I had been granted of his restraining presence.

Oh, how inestimable are the considerate anticipations of heaven. Our converse by the way had wooed me into a contemplative mood, and, being seated, I was left alone to read the story of the allegory as it should be unfolded to my particular need. The importance of the viewpoint was at once made clear. Soon, as the question of the subject began to suggest itself, I heard a voice, as if from the Court across the abyss, speaking to me, and in the language of the silver-tongued Isaiah afforded all the explanation needed:

"Who is this that cometh from Edom, with dyed garments from Bozrah-this that is glorious in his apparel, travelling in the greatness of his strength?"

The answer came as if on the roll of a great organ hidden somewhere in the heart of the garden, the music breathing also a perfumed flame which added another ray of glory to the scene.

"I that speak in righteousness-mighty to save."

Again the enquiry came:

"Wherefore art thou red in thine apparel, and thy garments like him that treadeth in the wine vat?"

Then came the minor response of infinite tenderness from the soul of the organ, changing to the shout of attack as the hero felt his powers strengthening him to victory:

"I have trodden the wine press alone; and of the people there was none with me...and the year of my redeemed is come. I looked, and there was none to help; and I wondered that there was none to uphold; therefore mine own arm brought salvation unto me; and my fury, it upheld me."

How often had I lingered over that fascinatingly mystical, but unsatisfactory picture in Isaiah 63. It was always attractive in its form, but vague and disconnected in its substance-at least, so it appeared to me, in the olden days. From the view-point of my new position, however, all this uncertainty vanished, and the divine allegory lay unrolled before me in a form that could not be misapprehended. The royal Shepherd, having lost one of His hundred sheep, had cast aside His kingly robe, and ventured into the jaws of the abyss where the goatherd Edom had his haunt, determined to discover and reclaim His lost one. The toil, the pain, the agony and the danger He braved was clearly written in the picture before me. But victory was with Him in His quest. He had found the lost one, and placing it upon His brawny shoulders had bounded back from the abyss to the threshold of heaven with a triumphant song of gratitude and thanksgiving in which He called upon all His friends to join.

As I looked upon the carefully limned-marred features of the Shepherd, I knew Him, though I knew not that we had met before. His was the greater love in search of which I had left my mother and travelled far, and the discovery threw the portals of heaven wide open for my admission. Then the fountains of the great deep opened, and the flood thereof carried me away.

My soul overflowed. I fell upon my knees and bowed my head in adoration. I did not-could not weep. The stream of the new fountain had washed away all tears, which had been replaced by a perennial joy. Voormere had left me, and yet I was not alone! Another-and unseen hand reached out of the surrounding glory to lift me to my feet again. Another-a softer, sweeter, more authoritative voice spoke to me:

"Come up higher. Rejoice with me, for I have found that which was lost."

I looked, but could not see the speaker, and the whole scene had changed. Surrounded by a host of friends, known and unknown, I was standing within the gate that cannot be shut at all by day-and there is no night-here.

* * *

A BRIEF BIOGRAPHY OF ROBERT JAMES LEES

Robert James Lees was born in Leicestershire, England on August 12, 1849. He was better known as James and was a Spiritualist, a healer, a preacher, a philanthropist and a writer.

James believed that his psychic abilities were with him from the moment of his birth. He wrote very little about his childhood experiences, but he describes in Volume Two - "The Life Elysian" how, even as a very small child, he was aware of 'visitors from across the border'.

His first employment was with the Manchester Guardian and soon became involved in several London-based publications. He was a man who, having virtually no formal education, wrote fascinating works which continued to sell many years after his death. James wrote several books, which were dictated to him by friends from the spirit realm, of which the most well-known three-volume series being "Through the Mists", "The Life Elysian" and "The Gate of Heaven". "The Heretic" was written as his only autobiographical novel which was a record of his many years in London.

James was a loving and caring man. He, along with many other philanthropists of that time, worked hard to lift the less-fortunate of London's poorest areas towards self-respect and self-determination.

James' fame and prestige grew quickly in parts of Britain and he soon made his acquaintance with high-ranking philosophers, theologians and Prime Ministers. He claimed to have been present when Edison first experimented with recording sound and had the privilege of assisting the late Mr. W. E. Gladstone in the production of "The Impregnable Rock of Holy Scripture". He was also a close friend of the late Mr. W. T. Stead, the famous journalist who died in the Titanic disaster. However, many unsubstantiated claims have been made about James. For instance, it is claimed that he was involved in the arrest of Jack the Ripper, the Whitechapel Murderer of 1888. It is further claimed that he assisted in the arrest of the Irish Fenian terrorists. However, James spoke very little about his eventful life and until further research is made into these claims, they will remain a mystery.

James had sixteen children of which ten survived. His daughter, Evelyn Amy Florence (Eva Lees), was born on November 14, 1879 in Surrey, Kent, and always lived with her father. In her father's later years, she was his caregiver, housekeeper, counsellor and friend and continued to publish her father's books for many years after his death. She was also a devout spiritualist and was very active in the spiritualist circles of Leicester. She died in 1968 in Leicester.

Robert James Lees passed away in Leicester, England on January 11, 1931. He was 81 years old. He was cremated at Gilroes Cemetery and prior to the ceremony, a short spiritualist service was held in his study. His ashes were placed in Ilfracombe Cemetery, in the same grave as his late loving wife, Sarah.

Other Books in this series

Through the Mists - Volume One
or Leaves from the Autobiography of a Soul in Paradise
Author: Fredric Winterleigh
Recorder: Robert James Lees
This first book of a 3-volume series was recorded in 1898 and
dictated by the author from 'beyond' whom at one time resided in
London, England. All 21 inspiring chapters is chalk full of
information that is sure to grip the reader from start to finish. You
will walk with Fred as he experiences his first few years of a
most fascinating journey beyond the mists and learn the lessons
that his Spirit Teachers taught him by correcting his simple, but
false beliefs that he acquired here on earth, to an amazing reality
of truth as is known beyond. You will discover the true meaning
of life and death as has never been told before.

The Life Elysian - Volume Two
being more Leaves from the Autobiography of a Soul in Paradise
Author: Fredric Winterleigh
Recorder: Robert James Lees
This second volume was written in 1905 and has 25
comprehensive chapters that will capture the attention of the
neophyte to the adept. The experiences of Fred (now named
Aphraar) continue and embrace the period he spends in the
company of his beloved mother, but he soon discovers that his
journey does not end there. In attendance with advanced
Teachers, his spiritual urge for deeper knowledge leads him on a
journey to visit the lowest levels of deepest despair, as well as
advancing on to the most glorious heights of pristine beauty
where revelations are profound. The lessons are vast and are
sure to satisfy the reader from beginning to end.